'*It's All Greek to Me!* represents travel writing at its best. Mole's descriptions of the people and places he encounters do for Greece what Peter Mayle did for France in his bestselling *A Year in Provence* and Frances Mayes for Italy in *Under the Tuscan Sun*.'   www.greece.com

'Anecdotes come thick and fast... Mole's affable style suits the subject, and his self-deprecatory tone is a bonus.'   *The Good Book Guide*

'John Mole writes with clarity, honesty and humour... whether you are new to the country or share Mole's passion for all things Greek, this book offers an entertaining glimpse of life in rural Greece.'

Saga

'A wonderful book about Greece, the Greek people and transitional island life with hilariously recounted misadventures. Mole is a brilliant comic writer - and generous humorist as well, for he doesn't just sketch the various mad characters and situations he encounters, he lampoons himself first and foremost.'   *Greece in Print*

'Timeless, smashing stuff. The heady smell of herbs and ouzo wafting along with Mole's mission to find a piece of Greek paradise make this a hands-down winner.'   *Manchester Evening News*

'A love affair with Greece.'   *Daily Telegraph*

'Mole's realistic and amusing tales are a cut above the normal rose tinted glasses worn by so many writ

'His writing is delicious.'   *Living Abroad Magazine*

'John Mole's book is filled with stories about the real Greece and the real people, far away from tourist resorts and posh hotels.'

The Village

'The perfect fun and sunny read.'   *The Travel Bookseller*

About the author

John Mole has been at home in Greece for nearly thirty years. After graduating from Oxford with a degree in French and German and with an MBA from INSEAD, he spent 15 years criss-crossing Europe, the Middle East and Africa for an American bank. In the mid-1970s he was posted to Greece, which soon became central to his life. When he and his family were transferred they left behind a house on the island of Evia, to which they return every year.

John's fortieth birthday present to himself was to quit what V.S. Naipaul calls 'the humiliation of employment'. He prefers the term 'succession of occupations that seemed interesting at the time' to 'career'. For ten years after graduating he wrote reviews for the *TLS* while in the 1990s he tried his hand at various entrepreneurial ventures. An attempt to establish a chain of baked potato restaurants in Moscow came to an end after the Russian Mafia expressed an interest in participating. He enjoyed more success with importing Russian biotechnology.

John Mole's published work includes comic novels, travel memoirs and the bestselling guide to European cultures *Mind Your Manners*.

Also by John Mole

IT'S ALL GREEK TO ME!

Ruins, Retsina, a Mad Dog...

and an Englishman

~~~~~~~~~~~~~~~~~~~~~~~~~~~~~~~~

JOHN MOLE

NICHOLAS BREALEY
PUBLISHING

London · Boston

For Alexander, son of Greece

This revised edition first published by
Nicholas Brealey Publishing in 2016
An imprint of John Murray Press

An Hachette company

9

First published 2004

A CIP catalogue record for this title is available from the
British Library.

ISBN 978-1-85788-650-4
eISBN (UK) 978-1-85788-485-2
eISBN (US) 978-1-47364-474-8

Printed in the UK by Clays Ltd, St Ives plc.

John Murray Press policy is to use papers that are natural, renewable and
recyclable products and made from wood grown in sustainable forests.
The logging and manufacturing processes are expected to
conform to the environmental regulations of the country of origin.

Nicholas Brealey Publishing
John Murray Press
Carmelite House
50 Victoria Embankment
London EC4Y 0DZ
Tel: 020 3122 6000

Nicholas Brealey Publishing
Hachette Book Group
Market Place Center, 53 State St
Boston, MA 02109, USA
Tel: (617) 523 3801

www.nicholasbrealey.com
www.johnmole.com

Contents

Prologue

We fell in love with Greece decades ago. Like many love affairs it started with lunch – baby squid, suckling pig, fried aubergine, Greek salad and lemony, tart retsina – delicious things, exotic and full of sensual promise. So when I was offered a job based in Greece, we jumped at the chance.

That was more than twenty-five years ago. The currency was the drachma and somehow we lived without mobile phones and laptops and the internet. Greece was rebuilding after seven dark years of dictatorship and applying to join the European Union.

We lived in an olive grove on the outskirts of Athens. An ancient tree grew up through the middle of our balcony. From the kitchen sink we looked out on the mountains of Parnis, from the bathroom sink the mountains of Pendeli. Quinces and medlars grew outside the front door, bitter oranges for marmalade at the back. In season we gathered figs, apricots and grapes. We woke up to thrushes and fell asleep to nightingales. It was sunny most days of the year and wine was cheaper than water. It was a far cry from South London where we lived before.

'Oh Toad, I dread the thought of leaving here,' said Arfa once a week. The only consolation I could offer was *Ti na kanoume?* – what can we do? – an essential Greek phrase in the face of life's inevitabilities.

Arfa is not my wife's given name. It is short for 'just 'alf a glass', which is what she says when offered wine. The impression of moderation is undermined by having to fill her glass twice as often. My nickname, Toad, is short for Fat Slimy Toad, an endearment from our courtship. We have four children, Jack, Jim, Kate and Harry, who were then under ten years old.

Our transfer from Greece was imminent, probably to Frankfurt or Pittsburgh. We talked of staying on or at least owning a place we could come back to. Our dream was a little whitewashed house with a blue door and blue shutters on an unspoiled island in a picturesque village next to the beach with a taverna round the corner. So how did we end up with a tumbledown ruin on a hillside above a village called Horio, with no road, no water, no electricity, no roof, no floor, no doors, no windows and twenty years of goat dung?

The road to ruins

$\sim\!\sim\!\sim\!\sim$

Ajax led me round the corner of his butcher's shop into a muddy lane. He skipped from dry place to dry place to keep his shiny patent leather shoes clean, arms gracefully outstretched to retain his balance. I took as much care of my new desert boots. It was like an audition for *Singing in the Rain*. On both sides of the lane were houses in the New Aegean style – single-storey concrete cubes on stilts with rusty steel bars sticking out of the flat roofs so that new floors could be added when the owners had the money.

After fifty yards we left the houses and came to a new concrete road lined with pomegranates and cypresses. Many travellers have taken such a road thinking it must be the way out of town, not knowing that the best road in a village usually leads to the cemetery. With a perfunctory sign of the cross, Ajax hurried past the cemetery gates and carried on uphill along a narrow and winding mule track between blackberry and thorn bushes. He had the ruddy-faced look of slaughterers and his taut belly swelled over the belt of his jeans, but he was fitter than I was.

The dry stone walls and thorn hedges on either side of the path were so high that I couldn't see where we were going.

When I thought Ajax wasn't looking, I made little two-footed jumps to see over, like a child. The bright April sun broke through the clouds again, bees hummed and bright flies darted over shrinking pools of rainwater. Flowers burst out of every crack and cranny in the walls. Like a bucket of water thrown on an old tiled floor springing the colours back to life, the spring shower stirred up the heady smell of Greece. Wafts of mountain oregano and thyme and pine and cypress, spring flowers, damp grass and all the mineral, composting, meaty savour of freshly wetted earth over-powered even Ajax's cologne. At last we came to a small plateau with a cluster of old stone houses.

'There it is,' said Ajax.

I suppose he took my stunned silence for speechless admiration. It looked like a forgotten corner of a Balkan war zone. A couple of houses still had roofs. The rest were in various stages of collapse. A few were nothing but piles of stones and broken beams. A wall of one house remained, with a fireplace and windows and cupboards absurdly out of reach above where a floor used to be. Fig trees and thistles grew out of the masonry and goats browsed in the rubble. The only building left intact was a little whitewashed chapel twenty yards down the hill.

Ajax beckoned me to follow him to the house closest to the chapel. It was on two floors with rough stone walls a yard thick and a pitched roof of massive split stone slabs. Half the roof had fallen in and broken slabs littered the ground. An almond tree grew at the front, its top about level with the second-floor windowsills. The bottom floor, which had one small window, was for stabling animals and storing wine, oil and grain. The living quarters on the second floor were reached at the side by a broad stone staircase grown over by the grey, viny branches of a fig. In front of the steps an ancient olive, as round as it was tall, squatted in the middle of a yard enclosed by a wire fence threaded on rough stakes, the hoof-marked ground grazed bare and smothered in a thick layer of chocolaty dungballs.

'*Schön, nich'*?' Ajax asked.

I couldn't think what to say. Actually yes, I could: *If you think I'm going to buy that tumbledown goat shed you must be raving mad.* But I didn't say it. I was brought up not to say what I think. Instead, I used the classic English expression of disapproval.

'Very interesting,' I said.

'A beautiful house.'

'Why you not to live here you yourself?' My Greek was poor, but the meaning was clear. He looked at me as if I were crazy.

'My house is next to the shop. I have electricity. I have three bathrooms. But here it is so quiet, so peaceful. It is a most beautiful place.'

I wasn't convinced. We all know that location, location, location are the three most important things in real estate, but walls and a roof come pretty high up the list too. Ajax uprooted a stake, threw back the wire netting so we could tiptoe across the goat dung to the door on the ground floor. I stooped under the massive olive-wood lintel and gagged on the smell of old goat and fermenting straw that buzzed and rustled like a living thing. Breathing through my mouth, I came out and followed Ajax up the outside staircase, struggling through the fig branches that grew over it. I have never liked fig leaves, they rasp like cats' tongues. Ajax pushed open a rotting door and with an estate agent's flourish stood to one side.

'Careful. Don't fall through the floor.'

There was not much floor to fall through, only a few stumps of joists with a goat-stinking pit below. We stood on the stone threshold like trapezists waiting to jump. It was a long, rectangular room with a crumbling fireplace at one end and two windows at the other. What was left of the roof sagged like a waterlogged awning on fractured beams, held together by a ceiling of smoke-blackened reeds. In some places the plaster had fallen away from the rough stone walls, in others it was fresh and white, washed by rain flooding down the walls.

'Look. What do you think?'

'Very nice,' I replied in English, which was a waste of irony. Ajax dug down into his own English vocabulary.

'Very naice. *Spessial.*'

'It's special all right.'

'Here it is quiet and cool. Down in the village there is traffic and television and noise.'

'And roofs and floors and windows.'

'It's old. You foreigners like old things.'

He smoothed his handsome black moustaches. My Greek was not up to explaining that it is not old things we like but things that pretend to be old, that the English sense of tradition is nostalgia for an imagined past and not the discomfort and inconvenience of the real thing.

'The simple life. *Spessial*. Nine people lived in that room. Po-po-po.'

I struggled for my Greek. 'Why not to live here still?'

'Bah. We are European now.'

The place was a ruin. It would need months of work. There was no mains water, no electricity, no telephone. Where would I plug in the typewriter? The simple life was all very well, but I preferred other people to live it for me and write books about it. Even so, I didn't know the right words to tell Ajax to get stuffed. To avoid standing tongue-tied, I stepped into the room on a stump of a joist, holding on to the door frame.

I could now see through the front windows. The weathered frames swung open. The glass was shattered and the shutters hung loose. But framed by these imperfect windows was a perfect landscape. The ruins of the old houses and the concrete of the new Horio had disappeared, masked by trees and a fold in the hillside. The rain shower had clarified the air and a golden evening sun lit the scene.

In the foreground were almond blossom and the little chapel set against the shimmering green of olive trees and budding mulberries. Down the hill was a stone cottage with a terracotta roof and a wisp of smoke drifting from the chimney. A knotted vine covered the terrace and a cow grazed in a field at the back. In the middle distance was a round plain chequered with fields and orchards. In the centre sat a conical hill topped with a square stone tower.

Around it browsed a flock of sheep. Beyond were green and grey and purple mountains and in their cleavages the sea.

The landscape looked empty and pregnant at the same time. I was drawn into it like a tiny human figure in paintings of classical landscapes, overwhelmed by the grandeur of their setting but at the same time necessary to give it scale and narrative. Teetering over the gloom and goat stink, I felt light headed. I ached for that idyllic world. I longed to get closer to the windows to prove that the vision was true, but the gulf was too wide.

I was born and brought up in Birmingham. My earliest memories are a daisy lawn in front of a Yardley semi on the Coventry Road, cream double-decker buses, scraping Jack Frost patterns off the inside of bedroom windows to see smoking chimneypots, the old Birmingham Bull Ring. Later on the fussy gardens, closes and cul-de-sacs of Solihull, with escapes to the flat green fields and hedges and towpaths of Warwickshire, with little houses of old red brick. Like Odysseus making his legendary way home to Ithaca from Troy, the goal of my life's journey should have been Acocks Green.

Nevertheless, inside me was a Birmingham-shaped hole in the place of home. How it was filled by a view out of a Greek window I still can't explain. Perhaps it was the visions of Arcadia in Birmingham Art Gallery, where my Dad took me when we went into town. Who knows?

Half an hour later, by the chapel, watched by the goats, I surrendered to my fate with a token struggle and deteriorating Greek.

'So, Mr John, what do you say?' Ajax switched from the polite plural to the familiar singular. We were friends. We were accomplices. 'The house is yours. I know foreigners in Düsseldorf who would give their back teeth for a little house on a Greek island. It is their dream. Whitewashed walls, red tiles, blue shutters, an olive tree, a vine around door, a geranium on the steps, mountains in the distance, the dark blue sea. Smell the mountain oregano and the pine.'

'Walls not white. Roof *kaputt*. Shutters broken.'

'That's nothing. A month's work and you can move in.'

He reached up and put an arm round my shoulder. I was surprised at myself for not recoiling at the touch as I would in England. Although I was taller than him, I felt embraced by a bigger man.

'Soon I go back to England.'

'Take a piece of Greece with you, here in your heart.' His free hand slapped the wallet pocket of my Marks and Spencer's linen jacket. 'And leave a piece of yourself here in Greece. You're a foreigner, you know things. I am a simple man, but I know you will not be sorry.'

'I have no money. How can I buy?'

'Who cares about money? You are my friend.'

You are my friend. Nobody had said that to me since I left primary school.

'Vairy chip. Vairy chip.'

'I said I have little money.'

'How much do you have?'

'Not enough.'

'How much?'

'Two hundred thousand.'

'OK. I accept your offer. You strike a hard bargain, Johnny.'

'How to know the price is good? The house. Too cheap. Too dear.' I struggled for haggling words, but the few I knew had evaporated along with my common sense. Ajax lapsed into injured pride, his brown eyes reproachful, the corners of his mouth turned down and his arms outstretched with open palms.

'My friend, you can't buy a used car for that much. Ask anybody. Ask if Ajax ever cheated anybody.' This time he thumped his breast where his own wallet would be.

'Wait...' My brain was scooped out and my tongue cut off. Nothing was left except emptiness and light. His arm was around my shoulders again.

'You will not regret this. We will be neighbours. We will be compatriots. We will be friends.'

'*Eff-harry-stow*,' is all I managed to say. 'Thank you.'

Family matters

~~~~~~~~~

At that time we lived in Kifissia, a suburb of Athens. Until recently it had been a sleepy summer resort for upper-class Athenians escaping the heat of the city in the breezes and pines of the foothills of Mount Pendeli. A Roman tomb in the main street set the tone for this Kifissia, funereal mansions and mausoleum hotels haunted in the daytime by ancient ladies in twinsets and gentlemen in barathea suits.

Another Kifissia came alive at night. All through the year people came up by car or the little metro, the *elektriko*, to indulge in the Greek national pastime, eating. After a perfunctory stroll to get the digestion going, they descended on some of the best tavernas you could find anywhere in Athens. At midnight or so they could then take another little stroll to Varsos, whose yoghurt and milk puddings were famous all over Attica. Food went fork in hand with conversation, which was not always social. Politicians, bankers and businessmen were often to be seen stitching up deals or each other over the tsatsiki.

When we got there in the mid-1970s the old mansions were being pulled down and their gardens ploughed up to make way for apartments. Development was fuelled by the invasion of expatriates like us, whose business was in the Middle East and would have based themselves in Beirut if that tragic city had not been self-destructing.

Greeks and foreigners lived in parallel universes separated by language and custom. Greeks started work at seven, foreigners at nine. Greeks finished at three and came home for lunch. Foreigners finished at six and came home for dinner. Greeks went to bed for the afternoon and got up for coffee when the foreigners were having drinks. Greeks went out to dinner when the foreigners were coming out of the taverna to go home to bed. The American Club was for those who preferred to have dinner at six and brunch on a Sunday and avoid the stress of dealing with Greeks and their language. The rest of the expatriate community was Balkanised around its various national schools. Ours was St Catherine's British Embassy School, a model primary and a corner of Greece that was forever England.

The idea of buying a place in Greece had not come completely out of the blue. A few months previously we had held a family celebration on the balcony.

'Do you know why we're having this?' asked Arfa, as a champagne cork blasted off into an olive tree.

'Because you're alkyholocs,' said Jack, our eldest. He had started spoilsport lessons at school doing projects on smoking and drinking and sex.

'Noo,' said Arfa, dipping her fingers into a limpid pool of spilt bubbly and licking them.

'It's your wedding adversary,' said Jim, our second son.

'*Anniversary*. Right. Daddy and I have been happily married for ten years.'

Four little faces stared at us, bright blue eyes, hair bleached blonde by year-round sun.

'You're not happily married,' said Kate, our daughter. 'When Daddy's here you're always arguing. You threw a pot of paint at him this morning.'

More froth billowed out of the glass. Arfa and I were locked eye to eye, not knowing whether to gasp or guffaw. Banter was so much part of our conversation that we never thought how it looked to the children.

'That's not arguing, Kate. That's discussing. And it was only poster paint. Anyway, ten years is a long time to live together.'

'Daddy doesn't live with us. He lives up there,' said Harry, the youngest. He pointed up to the cobalt blue sky. Froth overflowed the second glass. Last week we'd had a conversation about hamsters and grandpas living in the sky with Jesus. Did he think I was dead too?

'He means in an aeroplane,' explained Arfa. 'Every time a plane goes over they say that's where you live.'

'Sweethearts, Daddy and Mummy love each other very much and we all live together,' I said, trying to sound convincing. 'Here, let's drink to that.'

I poured froth into four plastic cups and topped up the two glasses and we clinked to wedded bliss, not very satisfactorily, as plastic does not clink well. All in all it was a muted celebration.

Coddled in moonlight, jasmine and sentiment, after the children had gone to bed, slumped in canvas chairs, feet on the balcony rails, we gazed blearily at the olive trees and discussed our future without a trace of bicker or banter.

'That's it,' I said, 'I'm finished. I'm not going to be a stranger to my family. We'll make a proper home.'

'How will we live?'

'I'll write. Grow potatoes. Anything. I'm only doing this for the money. I'll take a sabbatical, see how it goes.'

'OK. I'll start lawyering again.'

'You'll be out of practice.'

'After dealing with four children and a Greek cleaning lady, judges will be a pushover.'

'We might have to go back to London for a bit. Until we've got things sorted out.'

'I don't want to leave Greece. This is where we've been happiest.'

'We'll always have a home here. I promise.'

So we decided that, as soon as we were transferred from Athens, I would take a sabbatical from my job travelling round the Middle East and we would buy a house in Greece that would always be our home, wherever we were living at the time.

We went about looking for a house carefully and systematically. We had lively family discussions, in which we tried to reconcile the children's vision with their parents'. On one side was a luxury villa with cable TV and a swimming pool and English-speaking children to play with; on the other a picturesque, whitewashed village house with blue shutters by the sea and near to the taverna. We made lists of islands and mainland villages, pored over maps and ferry schedules, planned weekend trips. The first pleasure of this house would be looking for it.

*B*efore I met Ajax the butcher we had been a few times to Evia, the island where Horio is located. It is less than three hours' drive from Athens. It is a thinnish island just over 100 miles long, the second biggest in Greece after Crete. A spine of mountains runs along its length. On the eastern side of the mountain backbone is the swell of the open Aegean. The coast is rugged, with steep cliffs and few safe harbours. On the other side is the Gulf of Evia, separating it from the Attica mainland. There are lots of little bays and anchorages and the water, sheltered on both sides, is generally calm. Unless you knew otherwise, you could be excused for thinking that Evia is part of the mainland. The swing bridge across the Gulf of Evia at Halkida, the capital of the island halfway down the coast, is only 40 yards long.

In classical times Evia was spelled Euboea, which means 'good for cows'. You may come across people who are called Negroponte, which was the name of the island when the Venetians and then the Turks ruled it from about 1200 to around 1830. It is obvious if you have a smattering of Italian that this means black bridge, as I informed the family on our first visit.

'It's not,' corrected Arfa, 'it's an Italianised corruption of Evripos, the channel that goes under the bridge.'

'Wrong again, Dad,' sang the chorus.

'Thank you, darling. Would you like to carry on?'

'No, darling, you're doing beautifully.'

You should know that between us 'darling' is more a provocation than an endearment.

'The Evripos channel has been a wonder of the world for thousands of years,' I continued, as we leaned over the railing of the swing bridge.

'Why?' asked Jack, the eldest, unimpressed.

'It's got trolls,' said Jim for little Harry's benefit, who had nightmares about Billy Goat Gruff.

'The water flows one way and then the other. It changes once an hour sometimes.'

'Why?' asked Jack.

'Nobody knows. There are no tides in the Mediterranean. It's a mystery. Who knows who Aristotle was?'

'He's the caretaker at my nursery,' replied Harry, quickly, pleased to have got the answer in first for a change.

'He was also a famous philosopher. He was probably the most influential philosopher and scientist in Europe until the eighteenth century. And he was the private tutor of Alexander the Great.'

As one of his given names was Alexander, Harry saw a second precious opportunity for glory, but as he opened his mouth his elder sister closed it again.

'Shuddup. You're Alexander the Titch.'

'Some people say that Aristotle died here in Halkida. He

was so depressed by not being able to solve the mystery of the Evripos that he jumped in here and drowned.'

'Why?' asked Jack.

'Don't you get frustrated when you can't solve problems at school?'

'Nah. Just go on to the next,' replied Jim.

'So why do you think the current changes?' asked Arfa.

'Oh Maam, just tell us. They do this at school. If you thought we knew you wouldn't ask us,' complained Jack.

'Don't you tell us, Dad. We don't want an enslapedia,' added Jim.

'I don't know why it changes. Nobody does. Even to this day,' I said.

'See, they gave up and moved on to the next,' said Jim.

'Evripos means fast current in Ancient Greek,' added Arfa.

'Fat lot they knew,' said Kate and tossed an empty Smarties tube into the historic waters to bob aimlessly on the spot. After a lecture on littering, which was the word then for environmental awareness, we resumed our study of the mysterious waters.

'It must be about to change,' I said.

'It's not,' countered Jack.

'It'll change. Just watch.'

'How long do we have to watch?' asked Kate.

'It's too hot,' they all said.

And so the process of broadening minds went on. If it sounds unrealistic, indeed it is. It would be much too tedious to include the sighs, groans, repetitions and interjections of *stop it...* *(s)he's annoying me... do that again and you'll be sent back to the car... you don't know where it's been... wipe that off right now... (s)he pinched/hit/slapped/poked/kicked/pushed/bit/scratched me... I'm hot/tired/thirsty/hungry/bored/busting... take that out of your nose/mouth/ear/bottom* and so on that enliven conversation in young families.

The children were right, of course. It was too hot to wait for the enigmatic waters to turn, so we sat in the shade of a café terrace for ice creams and lemonade and toilets. Nevertheless, amid the slurping and kerfuffle and mopping and mess involved in these things, there was no escape from mind broadening.

'You know Odysseus and Achilles,' I said.

'Yeah. We saw the cartoon.' (There followed a simulated sword fight with sound effects and threats of 'If you drop that ice cream I'm not buying you another'.)

'According to Homer, over there is where the Greeks launched a thousand ships and set sail for Troy. It used to be called Aulis.' I waved my cornet in the general direction of Halkida's cement plant, the oil refinery and the dry dock, and they screwed their eyes up against the sun. 'Who knows the names of any of the other Greeks?'

'Helen,' ventured Kate.

'She was a *girl*,' complained Jim.

'She was the most beautiful woman in the world,' Jack added.

'Like you, Mum,' said little Harry.

'Creep,' said the chorus.

'She ran away to Troy with a handsome Trojan called Paris...'

'We've been to Paris,' piped up Harry.

'...and her husband Menelaus started a war to get her back. It lasted ten years.'

'Why didn't they get a divorce? That's what Stephanie's mother did,' said Kate.

'What about other people?'

'Aggy Nemanemanon,' said Harry.

'Right. Agamemnon. He was king of Mycenae and the leader of all the Greeks.'

'And Hector,' said Jim.

'He was killed by Achilles,' said Jim, which was the signal for the great battle on the plains of Troy to be enacted once again.

Done

~~~~~~

Back in Horio, Ajax and I concluded the deal in Yannis's café. This was an excellent example of New Aegean architecture, a grey concrete hangar painted lime green, inside and out, as far up as a man can reach with a brush and the rest left bare. The side that opened onto the square was glass with metal-frame windows and sliding doors.

Inside smelt of coffee and tobacco, resin and sharp cheese. One wall was lined with shelves loaded with groceries. Within easy reach were the cans, bottles and packets in daily demand. The further up the wall, the more exceptional were the goods on offer. Right at the top and out of reach mouldered the unsuccessful speculations of two decades, flyblown and caked in dust, for which there had never been nor was likely to be a requirement: tiny bottles of medicinal olive oil, humane mouse traps, windscreen de-icer, melon ball scoops. On the opposite side were a counter and a refrigerated cabinet for cheese and salami.

On the wall facing the door was a floor-to-ceiling panoramic photograph of a Swiss mountain glade with white cows and a chalet in the distance, a glimpse of a perfect world far from the heat and humdrum of Greece. Even people who live in places the rest of us daydream about have daydreams of their own. Hanging on the Alpine idyll were various official notices, a shelf with a bakelite wireless, a grainy sepia wedding photograph of a man and woman with solemn, frightened faces. High on the wall in the corner over the door to the toilets, a colour television was mounted; a score of children craned to watch *Knight Rider*. The middle of the room was filled with metal tables and wooden chairs, where unshaven men in caps sat hunched over *tavli* – backgammon – or cards, slamming down the pieces and slapping down the cards like gauntlets, while a few sat reading the paper.

Ajax led me like one of his doomed lambs to an empty table and told me to sit down. He looked around the room and smoothed his handsome black moustaches. He did this by joining the thumb and middle finger of his right hand under his nose and springing them apart across his top lip. It looked vaguely insulting, like flicking snot. He went over to two men in tweed caps drinking ouzo. He muttered to them and they stood up and shambled over. One was bald with a genial smile and a thick grey moustache like a yard brush. The other was thin and pale and worried looking.

'This is Spiros, our carpenter. This is Dimitris, the builder. My friend Mr John is English. He's a good man. I'm giving him our house up the hill.'

'Why? Does he have animals?' asked Spiros.

Ajax scowled at him and then winked at me as if we shared a secret. We all sat down and Ajax rubbed his hands like someone expecting a good meal. Under their watchful eyes I took the two hundred thousand drachmas out of my wallet. This was nearly five thousand pounds or eight thousand dollars in today's money. Technically it wasn't mine, belonging to a client I had been visiting, but I reckoned I was good for it as soon as I got home. I shuffled it quickly and covered it with my hand as I slid it over. Where I come from money isn't to be talked about or flaunted in front of strangers. But Ajax snatched up the wad and counted it out loud, ceremonially, slapping the notes down on the table while the witnesses mouthed the amounts. It was all so public and embarrassing.

Yannis and his customers gathered round and two small boys pushed their way to the front. When Ajax finished he looked at them, stood up and stuffed my money deep into his shirt pocket. He reached across the table and shook my hand, gripping my shoulder tight with the meaty fingers of the left.

'*Danke schön. Und kalo risiko.*' The witnesses shook my hand too.

'*Kalo risiko.*'

'*Kalo risiko.*'

Greek has a formula for every event – weddings, christenings, buying a new dress, having a haircut, talking about children, going away, coming back, leaving a house, leaving home. *Kalo risiko* is for a new house. *Kalo* means good. *Risiko* means fate, but sounds ominously like danger.

'What about the papers?' asked a tall, handsome man with iron-grey hair who had been reading a newspaper.

'Papers? What papers?' Ajax smoothed his handsome black moustaches.

'The contract.'

'What contract?'

'The sales contract.'

'That's for pig-brained lawyers. We'll go to the notary in Aliveri tomorrow or the day after.'

'And if something happens? You've got his money. What has he got?'

This is the bare bones of what they said, although they went on for much longer. In a classical Greek play by Sophocles or Euripides, *Oedipus Rex* for example, the main characters don't so much talk to each other as make speeches to the audience. A chorus comments on the action and interrupts with its own ideas. It seems so artificial and unrealistic until you see an argument in a Greek café. They posture and declaim and gesture to the audience and bystanders chip in and repeat everything as if they were on stage in an ancient amphitheatre.

At first I didn't understand what they were talking about, although I pretended to, nodding and smiling in the wrong places, while I tried to puzzle it out like a dialogue on my *Greek-in-a-Week* cassette. The main problem was that the word for a contract sounded like symbol. Symbol? What could be symbolic about buying a house?

Yannis went to his till and brought back his spectacles, a ballpoint pen and the blue exercise book in which he kept his accounts. He sat down at the table, tore a clean page out of the middle of the book and, with contributions and criticisms from the others, crafted a single sentence out of a score of subordinate clauses, recording the sale in perpetuity, for consideration given, of a property in the old Horio to John, father's name Henry, employee, of England...

Ajax signed first, with a flourishing signature that filled half the page like a sultan's firman, ornamented with loops and curlicues. There was hardly any room for my crabbed little squiggle. He folded the paper and ostentatiously presented it to me as if it had been his idea in the first place. I put it in the pocket where my money had been. He said that he had urgent phone calls to make, shook my hand, called me friend and waved goodnight to everyone except my champion, who went back to his newspaper with studied indifference, erect and dignified.

I didn't know what to do now. My new neighbours milled around my table talking in low voices, obviously about me. I thought I should mark the occasion. I took a deep breath, clapped my hands and put on a cheerful expression.

'So, let's all have a drink. Yannis, a bottle of ouzo please.'

'How about a bottle of whisky?' asked Spiros the carpenter. 'That's what you foreigners drink, isn't it?'

'Swat the bloody Greeks drink when they get arfa chence,' added a short, foxy-faced man in mangled Australian. 'Gidday mate. Howa youse? The name's Alekos.'

He gripped my hand and pumped it up and down, a cobber's reunion. I was surprised by the wave of fellow feeling at hearing English, however distorted, after hours of unremitting struggle with Greek, so I did what Poms do in such circumstances: I recoiled. When we are abroad we take a holiday from social attitudes. We treat foreign peasants and workers and shopkeepers with the genial familiarity we would never use at home. But meet anyone with claims on Englishness and the portcullis of snobbery comes down again.

'Hello,' I ventured.

'Twenty yeers in Melbourne, mate. Grate city. Better than this ocker dump.'

'Really?'

'Yep. Twenty yeers. Ended up with two supermarkets and an apartment block.'

'Very interesting.'

'Grate loife. People are more honest than these sly bastards too.'

'Thank you very much. I've just bought a house from one of them.'

'Don' say I dint warnya.'

Spiros came up with half a dozen glasses and one of the implausible brands of firewater that you only find outside Britain with a name like Highland Crotch. It was still five times the price of ouzo. I knew they were taking advantage of a gullible foreigner, but what could I do? He poured for himself and the other two witnesses and for Aussie Alekos and me and we all clinked glasses.

'Our health,' we chorused and swigged the whisky down in one gulp. Three other men came over with empty glasses.

I watched with irritation as a second expensive bottle was fetched and passed round from table to table. News spread and men came in from outside to drink the health of the foreigner who had paid good money for a goat shed. Women in yellow scarves stared through the plate glass, tossed their heads and walked on. Children ran up to me, giggled and ran away again. I felt my face getting more and more flushed with drink and self-consciousness as I fended off the same remarks over and over.

'What did you buy up there for?'

'There's no electricity.'

'There's no water.'

'There's no road.'

'It's full of snakes.'

'Aren't you be afraid to be alone up there?'

'Aren't you afraid of the cemetery?'

'You paid *how much*? For a heap of stones?'

'Why didn't you buy mine? It's a proper cement house down here with a kitchen and a bathroom.'

In my faltering Greek, sustained more by cheap whisky than competence, I explained that it was a beautiful place and a beautiful house and that where I came from people liked to restore old things rather than buy new ones. But the principle of gentrification was lost on my listeners. In the end I shrugged off their questions with a vacuous smile and spent the rest of the evening swapping reminiscences about Melbourne with Aussie Alekos and Liverpool with Yannis, who had been a merchant seaman, even though I had been to neither city.

Meanwhile I caught the taste of the whisky and drank lots of toasts and got Yannis to open a new case of Highland Crotch. I drank through the buzz of befuddlement into perfect clarity and out again into the blissful confusion of true intoxication. The dreadful 'What have I done?' nagged less and less and finally evaporated by the time the last of my new neighbours staggered home and left me sprawling on five taverna chairs, one for my bottom and one for each limb, drifting in and out of what the sober observer takes for sleep but is in fact a whirling maelstrom of light and colour and rushing noises. I was conscious of Yannis tiptoeing gently round me, probably assuming that I was indulging in the British national pastime and would soon get to the next stage of looking for a fight or windows to smash unless I was allowed to sleep it off. The only other customer by then was an old lady watching *Ben Hur*.

I awoke with a start when Yannis turned the television off. It was about midnight. The part of my brain responsible for foreign languages had also closed down for the night. I managed to ask for the bill by scrawling in the air. Yannis slowly arched his head back and tutted. It had already been paid for. Since that night I have often tried to treat my Greek friends to coffees or drinks or meals in the taverna, but have never succeeded. The bill is always settled before I ask for it.

Next morning I found myself stiff and cold on the back seat of the mini. My head was pounding and I felt bloated and sick. An acrid taste started at the back of my nose and flowered into a pungent smell that filled the car. Goats with yellow scarves and black moustaches lurked in the dream space just beyond my blurred vision. I scrabbled at the door. There were no colours in the world yet, only shades of grey. I clambered out, bent double, willing my stomach to overcome the waves of nausea starting at my trembling knees, welling into my belly and burning their way into my oesophagus. I forced myself upright. Cramp in my back and legs was absorbed by the sensation of a cleaver burying itself in my skull down to my eyeballs. With a moan I slumped on the car. My forehead splattered into something wet on the roof and I hoped it was dew.

I stood like this, body locked upright, arms dangling, head in a puddle of unidentified moisture, until the various painful and miserable sensations found some sort of equilibrium. Among the symptoms was a terrible thirst. Moving slowly, head up and knees bent, I groped for a half-empty bottle of water, which had been rolling around behind the front seat since the end of last summer. I poured the dregs into my mouth and down my chin and over my shirt front.

'What have I done?'

The inescapable answer was that I had spent our money on a ruin on a Greek island because of the view from the window. I had also drunk too much cheap whisky. No wonder I moaned. Hard on the heels of the moan came another voice, familiar but not mine, an English voice, stern and full of moral fibre.

'Pull yourself together,' it said – which, as best I could, I did.

Breathing as deep as I dared, I set off to inspect our property, along the concrete road to the cemetery and up the mule track. On limp sausage legs it was slow going and punctuated by interludes of unpleasantness. My desert boots were soaked and I couldn't stop shivering.

By the time I reached the ruins the dawn had ripened into reds and golds. A fine mist blurred the plain and the tops of the mountains were wreathed in cloud. The corrugated cement roofs of the village below glistened with dew and pools of water lay bronze on unfinished flat roofs. Birdsong filled the echoing cavities of my throbbing head.

The only other sound was from the shuffling, chomping goats shut up for the night in the ruins of houses. They browsed in the rubble, penned in by fences of brush and thorn and wire, hard and knotted horns twisted back towards stubby tails. They softened the ground with acrid yellow urine and pounded in their shitballs with cloven hoofs. Bulbous dugs and swollen vulvas swung under matted hair. A bitter, rotting smell hung around them in the damp air. They stared at me with evil eyes as I stumbled past.

I trudged up to the house, our house now, and picked my way through the squalor of the yard. I climbed the stone staircase, struggling over the sprawling fig, and untied the rusty wire that held shut the door into the main room. I pushed too hard. It fell off its hinges and crashed into the void below. Holding my breath against the stink of goat, I stepped gingerly in, fearing the worst, that the vision of yesterday was an illusion.

It was still there, a glimpse of a perfect Greece, waiting for the figures to be painted in.

I sat down on the cold stone at the top of my stairs in defiance of haemorrhoids and in a turmoil of nausea and apprehension. The sun came up and burned away the mist and cloud. By eight o'clock there were signs of life down in the village, buckets clanking, pigs squealing, sheep bleating, chickens squawking. Vans with grainy loudspeakers broadcast news of fresh mullet and fat sea bass with potatoes and onions to go with them. A man with a *bouzouki* banged on about love. The church bell urgently announced the start of the morning service: bong-bong-bong/bong-bong-bong/bong-bong/bong-bong/bong-bong-bong.

I knew what I had done. But what was I to do now? I had minimal Greek, minimal building skills, minimal funds. It was madness to rebuild an old stone house with no electricity, no water and no road. My options were one, to go back on the deal and try to get my money back from Ajax, or two, to run away and pretend it had never happened, or three, to make the best of it and spend the rest of the year doing up the house. The first was the most unrealistic, as I could never imagine Ajax giving me my money back. The English voice, stern and full of moral fibre, would not hear of running away. So that left the third option, to make the best of it. But first I had to face the ordeal of breaking the news to my family.

I stumbled down the path, chilled to the bone and exhausted to the marrow, and headed for the car. As I drove out of the village, Ajax and Dimitris the builder, yesterday's worried-looking witness, were measuring the front of the butcher's shop with a tape and writing the numbers down on a pad. I felt too embarrassed to stop and say good morning.

I waited until the next village to phone home. When my beloved asked where I had been all night and why I hadn't phoned, I pretended I couldn't hear, said 'Hello?' several times and hung up. Lines were often bad from the islands.

Panic

~~~~~~~~

When I got back to Athens I was in the doghouse for staying out all night without phoning home. It was a less serious offence than it would be today, now that we have mobile phones and digital exchanges. In those days an island village usually had only one phone, normally in the café, and the chances of getting through to Athens first time, or indeed any time, were slim. As I had been to drop off some papers and collect a bank draft at a shipowner's house in Kimi on the island of Evia, it was assumed that I had been detained for an evening's entertainment.

This doghouse was a luxury kennel compared with my lodgings when I announced that I'd bought a ruined house on the way back home. Actually 'announced' is not the right word. 'Nervously let slip' would be more accurate. I prefer not to elaborate on the various stages of our dealings over the next few days – disbelief, anger, recrimination, the raking up of old sores, bitter silence and so on – but I can say that they gave lasting strength to our relationship, like a thick scar is stronger than the skin around it.

When the initial storm died down, I had to convince the

children that they were not going to spend the rest of their lives in a hovel, that they would not have to scratch for their dinner in the weeds on the mountainside and that they would not have to learn Greek – despite our efforts they reflected the resistance of the British community to grasping the language. The bribe was that we could have a television as soon as we had electricity. Until now the condition had been that we would have the box when all the children could read. As we kept adding to the brood, the elder ones were getting restive. The main issue with their mother was convincing her that this was not a unilateral decision but that through some psychic bond underlying our relationship we had taken it together. So it was a tricky few days before the weekend, when I could take the family to Horio and show them the paradise I had found for them.

The general mood in the camper could best be described as sullen and was not improved by the walk up the mule path from the cemetery, where we parked. Little legs that could racket round the house and garden all day suddenly became tired and tender bodies that fried happily in the noonday sun by a paddling pool became insufferably hot. The children whinged and moaned and Arfa scowled.

However, all this was nothing beside the general dismay when they beheld their new island home. I viewed it through their eyes, as I had seen it when Ajax the butcher first brought me up. I relied on the opportunities for mischief afforded by the countryside to bring the children round. As for Arfa, my best hope was that she would be as enchanted by the view out of the window as I was.

'Before you run away,' I begged, 'please look out of the window.'

Blinking back tears, Arfa scrabbled up the stairs through the fig tree and teetered on the joists, breathing through her mouth. I held my breath too.

'Toad, it's wonderful,' she said at last. 'It's like a painting.'

'It's more than a painting. It's real. Imagine waking up to this every morning. It's the Greece we always dreamed of. There are gods down there and nymphs and satyrs and shepherds dancing.' I am embarrassed to report these words and even more embarrassed to recollect that I meant them.

'But there's so much work.'

'Not really. A roof, a bit of carpentry round the windows, a wooden floor. We don't want anything fancy.'

'Like electricity, you mean.'

'If you have electricity you have televisions and dishwashers and ironing boards and things that wink and bleep. With electric lights you can't see the stars. For once we'll live the simple life. Like people have lived since the days of Homer.'

'I'm not having an outside toilet.'

'All right. We'll have an inside toilet.'

'A proper one. Not a hole in the ground.'

'All right. A proper sit-down with a flush.'

'Can you do it? I can't help. I've got enough to do.'

'A piece of *baklava*. I promise. I'll make us our own little

Arcadia.' I gave her a passionate hug.

Jim was standing on the steps behind us. 'Wow!' he said, 'Wowee!' He ran off to the others, who were testing different ways of flicking goat droppings at each other.

'What's the matter with him?' I puzzled. Arfa shrugged. We soon found out. The four of them rushed up, skipping and whooping.

'Is it true Dad?... Is it?... Is it?'

'Is what true?'

'We're going to have our own Arcadia?'

'Sort of. Just a small one.' There was more general whooping and cavorting.

'Can we have the thing with silver balls that goes round and round?'

'Yeah, I won fifty pee on that.'

'And the rifles where you shoot ducks...'

'Can we have foopball with men on skewers?'

And so they rhapsodised. Like the thing you roll coins into, where a pusher shoves them into a heap on the edge of a shelf and if they fall down you win, it took a long time for the penny to drop.

'I think they mean the amusement arcade Granny and Grandpa took them to last summer,' clarified Arfa and left the rest to me. I took a deep breath.

'Sweethearts...'

I had to watch four excited, happy faces pass through the stages of disappointment from puzzlement to gloom as I explained that the Arcadia I meant was not a fun house but a wild and beautiful place in the mountains of southern

Greece and the setting for poems about shepherds written by the Roman poet Virgil. These days Arcadia meant any beautiful place unpolluted by modernity where people led simple lives at one with nature and made their own fun dancing round the maypole. I did my best, but fun house it wasn't.

We spent the rest of the morning exploring the hillside and gradually the mood improved. There was something for everyone. We discovered more glorious views, gathered armfuls of wild flowers, petted donkeys, climbed trees, threw stones, chased frogs and generally convinced ourselves that Dad might get a reprieve after all.

We came across a cave and Arfa told the children about Pan, god of the shepherds, who has horns and a tail and goat legs and invented pipes made out of seven reeds tied together. He has caves all over Greece. I took the risk of bringing up a ticklish subject again by saying that his ugliness made the other gods laugh so much that he ran away to Arcadia, where he chased the nymphs and played his pan pipes and went to parties with equally ugly little forest gods called satyrs. He causes the irrational terror that mortals sometimes feel in lonely, desolate places, which is where our word panic comes from.

At lunchtime we swept goat droppings from the bottom steps of our new house and, with stern warnings against collecting them for ammunition, necklace beads or ersatz Maltesers, sat down to eat our picnic. We had scarcely started to tuck in when from under the stone that Arfa was sitting on emerged the head of a snake, with bright eyes and a flickery tongue, followed by the rest of its sinuous black body. Even making allowances for exaggeration, it was a good eight feet long and as thick as a man's forearm. I don't mean my weedy forearm, but one belonging to a proper working man. It didn't slither or wind or snake but poured vertically up the wall to the window above us, where it disappeared inside.

We were frozen to the spot, cheese and tomato sandwiches fixed in whatever situation the moment took us. Arfa's teeth were chomped down on hers. The only thing that moved was a trickle of juice from the corner of her mouth. The boys were the first to speak.

'Cor.'

'Cor.'

'It's a bore contractor,' said Jim.

'Nah. Cobra. Deadly poisonous,' said Jack.

'Nah. Chokes you to death and swallows you whole,' said Jim.

'Even someone as fat as Dad?' asked Kate.

'It goes for girls first. Straight up their bottoms and eats them from the inside.'

It was time to intervene before the wide eyes and trembling lower lip of their sister, not to mention their mother, turned to panic.

'That's absolute rubbish. Unless you're a frog or a mouse, the big black ones are totally harmless. They're very shy. They run away as soon as they sense a human being. In

~~~~~

ancient Greece it was very lucky to have a snake living in your house. You put out milk for them. Bit like a cat really. It's the little thin green ones you have to watch out for, but they live up in the hills, not down here…'

By this time I was shouting, because Arfa was already halfway down the path to the cemetery with a child under each arm.

'Wait. I'll get the money back. I promise…'

When I caught her up at the camper I knew it was useless saying anything. I had seen that grim, distant expression before.

'Beach?' I suggested with forced cheerfulness.

'Will there be jellyfish?' said Harry.

'Yeah, poisonous ones,' said Jack.

'Nah, giant squid,' said Jim.

'Will there be giant man-eating octopuses?' said Harry.

'Only sea snakes,' said Jim.

'There's sharks in the Mediretanean. It's true,' said Jack.

'They like girls best,' said Jim.

We weren't going anywhere. Down in the village it looked as though there had been an explosion in Ajax's shop. There was a ragged hole where the front should have been. A flatbed truck with its own hydraulic crane blocked the road. A queue of cars and pick-ups and tractors had built up on either side. Those stuck at the back klaxoned a medley of raucous tunes until their drivers gave up and came to watch. On the truck was a large wooden crate about two metres high, five metres wide and ten metres long, which four men were dismantling with crowbars. A crowd had gathered to give advice and criticism. Among them was my cobber Alekos.

'Gidday, maite. See where he spent yer money? He needed the last instalment for his German freezer. Youse turned up at the roite toime.'

Ruddy-faced Ajax stood in front of his half-demolished shop in shirt-sleeves, with his hands on his hips and his belly swelling importantly over his belt. His beautiful wife Eleni stood next to him, her dark hair loosely pinned up for work. She hugged a knee-length cardigan to herself, not for warmth but as if she were trying to pull something more impenetrable around her.

The wooden packing case was now a heap of planks in the middle of the road, leaving a shiny steel box on the truck. One side bristled with pipes and wires. Two men fitted straps around it, while a third stood at the controls of the crane behind the cab and the fourth set out the supports on the side of the truck. With advice and encouragement from the crowd, the crane took the strain. The straps creaked as they lifted the shiny box into the air. The operator shouted and pulled his levers, the crane turned on its axis and the box swung slowly over the shop.

The crowd was suddenly silent, as if a coffin was being unloaded from a hearse. Eleni watched it come towards her and Ajax shoved her out of the way. An old Cassandra in black muttered her opinion to everyone and no one.

'It's as big as his whole shop. He'll drive the other butchers out of business. That thing can take all the meat the villages can produce in six months. His father built that shop. What would he say? They all come back from abroad with big ideas. See where it gets him... it'll bring him no good.'

Snakes or no snakes, there was no chance of getting my money back. It was already spent. By the time we got out of the village it was too late to go to the beach. We drove home in silence, the children hushing each other as they could sense their parents' black mood. Finally Kate dared to voice the question on all their lips.

'Daddy, why didn't you buy somewhere nice?'

'It will be nice. I promise.'

All Greek to me

hose were more leisured times than now. Even ambitious young professionals were expected to go home in the evening, take weekends off and use their full holiday entitlement without blighting their 'careers'. If you were not ambitious you could take country reassignment leave, sick leave, public holidays, study leave, unpaid leave and any other time off you could wheedle without having to resign, which is what I did. It gave me a long summer to do up the house and decide what I was going to do with my future. The rest of the family were to stay in Athens until the end of the school summer term and come out to Evia at the weekends.

At first I felt awkward and embarrassed with our new neighbours. The standoffishness of my race was made worse by the suspicion that they were laughing at me for buying a ruined goat shed. It was tempting to take refuge in feelings of British superiority, although I disliked myself for it and hoped it didn't show. My primitive Greek made my English reserve even more tongue-tied. Some people in the village had a few words of English or German, acquired when they had been sailors or *Gastarbeiter*. The shape of my head being more Teutonic than Anglo-Saxon, their usual conversational gambit was '*Deuts*?'

Greek is a wonderfully rich and expressive language, which makes it one of the harder of the European tongues to learn. The active vocabulary is much bigger than other European languages. The constructions and the different endings are not easy to master, especially if you are an English speaker. Reading the paper was a particular challenge. The first barrier was the Greek alphabet. As well as letters we only come across in maths and American fraternities, the sound values of some familiar letters are different. I still have to think twice when I come across ΝΤΕΙΒΙΝΤ ΜΠΕΚΑΜ or ΡΟΜΠΕΡΤ ΡΕΝΤΦΟΡΝΤ.*

You might think from the conversations so far that my Greek was pretty good. This is writer's licence. If I recorded them accurately you would have as much trouble understanding what I said as other people did. And what they said to me I could only guess at half the time. For the first few months I went round in a linguistic fog. Often I only realised what someone had said minutes or even days or weeks afterwards. So the dialogue is not exactly made up but more approximate than it should be in a work of non-fiction.

As an example of what it was like, take my attempts to find somewhere to stay in the village until I made the house habitable.

'Ask Ajax,' said Yannis in the café, 'he owes you a favour. You took that place off his hands for good money to spend on his cold room.'

Heartened by this I went into the butcher's shop, where Ajax's wife Eleni was engrossed in dealing with a cow's head on the white marble counter. Behind her were the shiny steel doors of the new cold room, bought with my money.

'Good day. How are we? Are you well? Is your family well?' she recited.

'Good day. Well, thank you. I am looking for a tomato,' I replied.

She stared at me. Her eyes were green and wide, almond shaped and upside down like those on a vase painting or the prow of a trireme. She shook her head, but in Greece this doesn't mean a refusal. It meant she didn't understand. Tossing her head back with a disdainful 'tut' would have meant 'no'.

'Tomato,' I repeated, stabbing my forefinger into my chest. 'I want a tomato.'

Eleni shrugged her shoulders, raised her pretty eyebrows and put down her cleaver. She symbolically gathered together the contents of her shop and arrayed them on the counter before me. There were pieces of dead animal in various stages of dismemberment, but I failed to see what they had to do with lodgings. I spoke louder and slower, as though I were dealing with a half-wit.

'I – want – a – TOMATO...'

She replied eloquently but too fast. Although I picked out a few words like vegetable and winter and greengrocer, for the underlying argument she had lost me. She pouted like a starlet when she spoke, which I found distracting but

'I didn't know which flustered me more, that or her extraordinary eyes or her bloody-minded foreigner's way of refusing to be helpful. I tried pidgin.

'Tell – I – where – find – tomato.'

She shrugged again and said nothing. It was very irritating. Clearly, she was being deliberately unhelpful. Why? Did she have something against the British? She wore jeans and a white, loose-fitting T-shirt speckled with blood. It had baggy armholes and I could see her bra, which was embroidered with pink roses. She caught me staring and I pretended I was really looking at the icon on the shiny metal door behind her. Appropriately, it was a saint holding a lamb in his arms. Probably about to slit its throat and flog it off by the kilo. Eleni turned to a rack of knives on the wall beside the counter and picked out a cleaver.

I wasn't going to be put off. One of the first lessons of life in Greece is that everything is difficult and nothing is impossible. If only I had appreciated the subtle difference in pronunciation between *domata*, meaning a tomato, and *domatio*, meaning a room I might have had an easier time, but the embarrassment of that discovery lay in the future and I persisted in my efforts to find a cheap, clean, quiet tomato. I pillowed my head on folded hands.

'Here. Me. Bed.'

I hoped that is what I said. The word for bed is dangerously close to the word for necktie. But in any case, she was concentrating all her attention on the business with the massive cow's head that lay on the counter between us. It was dehorned and skinned. Blood trickled from its nostrils and the yellow tongue lolled wantonly from the corner of its mouth. Its lidless eyes stared back at me as if it were alive in a different world, more knowing and more terrible.

With the thumb of her left hand Eleni explored the top of the skull like a phrenologist. Her long fingernails were carefully manicured and painted a delicate pink and I imagined them stroking Ajax's scalp. She raised the cleaver and with a sharp thwack split open the cow's skull. She put the cleaver down on the counter, forced her slender fingers inside the crack in the bone and pulled it creaking apart. I wished I was somewhere else, but I made myself watch her scoop out the pinky-yellow brains in her bare hands with a slurpy sucking sound. She dumped them with a splat on a pile of plastic paper and wrapped them up. I felt sick.

'Why did you come here?' she asked as she turned to the knife rack for a short, curved blade.

'I need a tom...'

'No, I mean here. The village. Why do you want to live here?'

I had prepared several monologues for such questions. They were beacons of clarity in the rest of my Greek, although they got me into trouble because people assumed I was more fluent than I really was. Trying not to sound like an estate agent, I enumerated the various attractions and advantages of the area.

'Bah,' was Eleni's response.

With the curved knife she cut out the succulent cheeks and wrapped them in paper printed with pictures of laughing cows and sheep and pigs, little icons of happier times.

She prized open the jaw, cut out the tongue deep inside at the root and laid it on the marble like a giant yellow slug.

'Foreigners don't come here.'

'An English lord came here 200 years ago. He visited the Turkish pasha of Aliveri in his seraglio down by Lake Dystos.'

'Turks,' she hissed as she picked up the cleaver and drew the flat side slowly across her throat, leaving a smudge of bright red blood on her neck. I was shocked and it must have shown, because she laughed.

A girl of about ten came into the shop. Her hair had been hacked short with the help of a basin and her dark blue cotton dress and sandals were too big for her. She gabbled something to Eleni, too fast for me to understand, and held open a green plastic bag. Eleni leaned over the counter and dropped in the two halves of the skull, followed by the other bits and pieces. Money clanked on the marble like a cracked bell and the girl left, lugging the heavy bag on her right hip. A baleful eye looked out through the transparent green plastic. Eleni wiped the cleaver and the curved knife on a bloodstained muslin rag and put them back in the rack on the wall.

'Foreigners come here looking for buzzards,' she said.

Or it might have been gypsum. Or gypsies. Were we talking ornithology, geology or anthropology? They were equally likely. *Speak-Greek-in-a-Week-with-Accompanying-Cassette* was no help.

Ajax saved us from further cross purposes. He charged in from the back room like a bullock released from a pen.

He was not his normal friendly self. His dark eyes were blazing and his black, curly hair flopped over his ruddy forehead. He stabbed a finger at the counter and snatched up a muslin cloth.

'This place is filthy,' he snarled.

A string of ripe expletives followed that I did not understand but desperately tried to memorise. Eleni was obviously used to such displays of temper. She nodded in my direction and spoke very quickly with her hand over her mouth like a girl in a playground sharing secrets. Annoyance turned to puzzlement.

'Johnny, good day. How are we? Are you well? Is your family well? What do you want?'

'A tomato. Sleep. *Zimmer. Schlafen.*'

'This is a butcher's, not a hotel,' he replied. He said something to Eleni and she stifled her giggles in her hand.

'I want a tomato to live. I fix house.'

Ajax shrugged his shoulders and spread his hands, still holding the muslin cloth, as if he was about to give me a wipe down.

'There's no hotel. *Kein Hotel.* What can we do? Why don't you try Aliveri? Or Limanaki? Kyria Sofia has rooms.'

'It is too far. I want to stay here..'

'But you will be very comfortable. There are beautiful hotels, not expensive. *Spessial.* Vairy chip.'

'I have no money for hotels, Ajax. You have my money.'

'*Ach so.*'

'Have you a tomato in your house?'

Ajax frowned and flicked his moustaches. '*Tut mir leid*. I don't have any room, my friend. *Kein Zimmer*. Eleni is very busy with the babies and the shop and my mother and my sister-in-law are coming any day from Stuttgart. Why don't you ask at the café?'

'I ask yesterday. Yannis tell me ask you.'

'*Ach so.*'

'Haralambos has a big house,' said Eleni innocently, earning a sharp glance from Ajax.

Haralambos was the distinguished-looking man who had stood up to Ajax in the cafe.

'He lives on his own. Ask Haralambos. I hear he's a friend of yours.'

'Wait,' said Ajax, 'there's no need to ask Haralambos. Let's go and talk to Barba Mitsos. He has a big house and no family.'

He came round from behind the counter and took my arm and we left the shop in a cloud of aftershave and sweaty polyester. I looked back at Eleni, expecting a little smile or some other gesture of complicity, but she was busy wiping down the counter.

*I*n half an hour it was arranged. Barba Mitsos the melon farmer and his wife Elpida would rent me a room until my house was habitable. Barba is a rustic term of respect for old men, like gaffer used to be in English. Given the custom of naming first-born sons after their grandfather, it also helps to differentiate the generations.

Barba Mitsos was in his seventies. He was short and bandy-legged, with a bristly crew cut of white hair. His face was ruddy and veined and he had bright blue eyes that shifted from side to side as he spoke, wary of spies and predators. This mannerism made him look canny, although it was probably shyness.

The seasons were marked by his hats. At the beginning of winter he bought a new *trayaska*, a cloth cap, and in the summer a straw *republika*, a fedora. It was spring and we were still in cloth cap season. *Trayaska* is a Romanian word that dates from the first Balkan Games in Athens in the 1920s. The Romanian athletes wore caps. Their trainers wore fedoras. They had a double act when a Romanian won a medal. The athletes threw their caps in the air and shouted *trayaska*, which means 'long live…' The trainers threw their fedoras in the air and shouted *la Republika*. Since then *trayaska* has meant a cap in Greek and *republika* a fedora. In bad weather Barba Mitsos wore a montgomery, a duffel coat named after the field marshal on the same principle as cardigan and wellington. With his *zaketa*, *poukamiso*, *panteloni*, *kaltsa* and *bota*, he was entirely clothed in foreign loan words.

Elpida was short and bandy-legged like her husband, but plumper. She was always dressed in black except for the traditional yellow scarf of the island. She wore the scarf out of custom and to conceal her baldness, which nature had compensated for with a luxurious growth of hair on her chin. In church she officiated as candle snuffer. Her job was to pluck handfuls of slender caramel sticks from the front of the icons, blow out the flames and toss the candles into metal boxes underneath to make room for fresh ones. Her hands glistened with wax and the sleeves of her dresses were singed brown at the cuffs.

Their house was next to the church and had been one of the first to be built in the new Horio. It had bright green stucco walls and a pitched roof of Ellenit, large panels of corrugated asbestos cement painted red to look like tiles, until it washed off leaving blotchy pink stains on the grey. The small front garden was overgrown with fruit trees, lemons, peaches, apricots, walnuts, quinces. Breezeblock walls were topped with ten-litre margarine cans planted with herbs and flowers. The kitchen was at the back and opened onto a dirt yard with a goat pen and an olive tree hung with round cheeses left out to drip and dry.

In the best room at the front, where I was to live, was a sofa bed upholstered in pink Dralon to match the cushions on the purple leatherette armchairs and the flowers on the electric-blue curtains. A mottled brown flokati rug decorated the marble floor. On the white marble mantelpiece were souvenirs of coach tours to Yugoslavia and Bulgaria and photographs of children in Australia. In the corner of the room an electric lamp with a small red bulb burnt in front of an icon of a saint holding a lamb.

Elpida was not from Evia but from an island further east, near the Turkish coast. As a girl on her way to America with her parents, she had been snared like a migrating bird. The ship put into Aliveri with engine trouble. The church on the quayside was celebrating its patron saint and there was dancing in the afternoon. Elpida outshone the local girls with her beauty and her dancing and before the ship was repaired by engineers from Athens her parents had married her off to handsome Mitsos, a stonemason. They were glad to get rid of her without a dowry and to have one less mouth to feed in Chicago.

They need not have worried. The ship went down with all hands off the Canaries. Mitsos's family thought that he was mad to take a girl without a dowry. 'Her luck is good enough for me,' he said, when news of the shipwreck reached the island. She had dressed in black ever since because her parents had no graves and their souls still wandered.

'England?' she said. 'Po-po-po. How long does it take to get here from England?'

'About three and a half hours.'

'So long? Like here to Aliveri on a donkey.'

We discussed the relative advantages of the two modes of transport before passing on to the usual interrogation of how much I earned, what I paid in rent, if I was married, how many children I had and whether they were from the same woman.

As well as being a good dancer, Elpida was a good cook. For lunch on my first day we had meat balls, *keftethes*. They were not the usual tourist taverna offerings, lumps of clay swimming in sump oil. They were light and fragrant and melted like truffles in the mouth. With them was rice flavoured with goat's butter, fresh wild greens dug out of the hillside and dressed with lemon juice, creamy feta sprinkled with oil and dusted with rigani, crusty bread, wine from Mitsos's barrel…

I was not her only guest. Every day she loaded up a tray and put it to one side, covered with a cloth. When she had finished eating she took it over the street to the apartment of young Doctor Solomos, above his surgery. Newly qualified doctors have to spend a year or so in a village after graduation before they can specialize in a hospital or set up a practice in the city. I once suggested that the poor lad might like to join us for company instead of eating alone.

'In the kitchen?' exclaimed Elpida, shocked. 'But he is the doctor' – which established my own place in her social hierarchy.

Canny Barba Mitsos grew all their vegetables, kept enough sheep and goats for meat and milk and cheese and yoghurt, had enough chickens for eggs, picked his own olives for oil and made his own wine, with plenty left over to trade for what he didn't grow. His main source of income was growing melons in the drained bed of Lake Dystos. When I first went to stay with them he was busy scattering cantaloupe and watermelon seeds on the waterlogged ground. In June he sprayed them with insecticide. In July he cleaned out channels to irrigate them with lake water. In August dealers came up with trucks and loaded the fruit up.

'Melons like breasts,' he promised one day over our lunchtime ouzo. 'A gift from God and I deserve it.' He spat to avoid the evil eye, a dry spit as we were at table.

'Before the war those were the days for melons. They came from all over the island. They even came from

Athens. The men all dressed up in the old costumes and had a market at the side of the lake. The dealers didn't have trucks then, of course, they had mule carts. And there were peddlers and card players and gypsies with violins and clarinets. What a time we had. There was even a whore or two from Athens earning their holiday money. Summer was slack for them in those days because their clients spent August with their families. They say it's different now. With the fast boats and the good roads Father joins the family for weekends and says he has to work in Athens during the week. In fact he's having a good time with his girlfriends. And of course the girls stay in Athens for the tourists. What was I saying?'

'Rubbish as usual,' said Elpida, standing at the stove with her back to us.

We were having *keftethes* again. We had them three times a week. I had made the mistake that you learn to avoid with your mother of saying how much I liked the ones she had cooked the first day.

'The melon market,' I prompted.

'Ah yes. The whores rented tents from the gypsies. They had guards because we boys would try to cut the guy ropes. You should have seen the farmers drinking and gambling and strutting in front of the women in their old Albanian costumes with wads of money tucked behind their daggers in their belts.'

'What did their wives say?' I asked.

'Nothing. They knew what happened in the tents but what could they do?' He chuckled and shot one of his crafty glances at Elpida's broad rump. 'My uncle never went. He had been on the ships in Piraeus and when he retired he came back with a good-looking wife much younger than he was. Her name was Thekla. He told everybody she was from an old Constantinople family ruined by the Turks. She put on airs, I can tell you. You'd think she was the pasha's wife.

'My uncle got my father to sell his melons for him while he stayed at home with his wife, because he didn't want her to see the drunkenness and immorality that went on. The *papas* set him up as an example to the rest of us. You'd think they were Aghios Ioannes and the Virgin herself the way they carried on. They missed the melon fair two years running and then it came round again. Thekla was down in Aliveri when the ferry came in with the whores. They saw her on the promenade and fell on her like a long-lost relative. It was all round the island by nightfall. My uncle never recovered and he died a few months later. It turns out they weren't even married. She went back to Athens. Back to work with the girls, I suppose. What was I saying?'

'Rubbish as usual,' said Elpida from the stove.

'About the melon market.'

'Ah yes. Everyone had a good time. When it was all over the strangers went away with the melons and the money. All we had was a few trinkets for the women.'

'That wasn't much.'

'Bah. Those were good times. And we had seeds for next year.'

'What happens today?'

'The dealers come in their trucks and we pay the money into the mobile branch of the National Bank. It parks in the square on a Tuesday.'

'That's how it should be done,' said Elpida, plonking down the dish of *keftethes* in tomato sauce, along with its aura of garlic and tomato and mountain oregano. 'We aren't peasants any more. We are Europeans. We know things.'

We crossed ourselves and tucked in.

* If you are still wondering about ΝΤΕΙΒΙΝΤ ΜΠΕΚΑΜ or ΡΟΜΠΕΡΤ ΡΕΝΤΦΟΡΝΤ, try David Beckham and Robert Redford.

Labour of Herakles

~~~~~

Now I knew I wasn't going to get our money back, I launched myself on the task of rebuilding the house with an enthusiasm that took me by surprise. As anyone knows who has moved house, you don't feel you belong until you muck about with it, paint the walls, get a new kitchen. In this case muck was the right word. The first job was to clear out the goat dung.

Ever mindful of the opportunities for indoctrination, I pointed out round the family supper table in Athens that Herakles – or Hercules as he was known to the Romans – had a similar task. As one of his twelve labours he had to muck out the cowsheds of a king called Augeas in return for a tenth of the king's enormous herd. He diverted a river through them and did the job in a day. When Augeas went back on the deal, saying that it was the river that had done the work, Herakles killed him and installed Augeas's son in his place. In commemoration, Herakles founded the Olympic Games.

Having established my heroic credentials, we went through the other labours, most of which involved killing wild animals like lions and boars and dragons. One of the children asked why Herakles had to do the labours in the first place. We looked it up and discovered that it was because he had murdered his wife and children. They did the washing up and went to bed without argument that night.

Unfortunately, the only stream near the house in Horio came from the spring lower down the hill. There was no alternative to manual labour. I thought of hiring someone to do it, but I wanted to get stuck in myself, to feel the place was mine, to possess it.

I bought tools from Haralambos, the distinguished-looking man with iron-grey hair who had persuaded Ajax the butcher to give me a receipt. By trade a plumber, he owned a business that catered for every stage of house building, from piles of sand to doorbells that chimed *Für Elise*. His own house behind the yard was based on the design of a Texas ranch house, adapted to local taste by the addition of concrete stilts and a lean-to for the goats.

When I arrived he was reading the newspaper among the bathroom fittings. Even sitting on a bidet he looked distinguished. He wore a crisp, white shirt rolled to the elbows and was freshly shaven, even though it was the beginning of the week and not Friday, the customary shaving day. I admired his classic profile in a dozen bronze tints in a range of Italian bathroom cabinets. His Grecian nose was from a vase painting, a continuation of his forehead, long and straight with no indentation at the bridge. I warmed to him when he spoke to me in Greek and not German.

'My friend! Welcome! We are compatriots now.'

'Thank you. And thank you for the symbol.'

For a moment he looked puzzled and I wondered if he had forgotten his intervention in the café. But he had a mentally handicapped son and was therefore more skilful at dealing with foreigners than his fellow villagers were. He mentally adjusted a vowel or two.

'Ah, the contract. It is nothing. You have to do things right. A little cup of coffee?'

I turned down the invitation with the conventional 'I have drunk one, thank you' and escaped with a fork and a rake and a warning about snakes.

'Be careful. They are dangerous in spring. They live in the stone walls. There was a man in Rodi who fixed up an old house. He plastered over a nest. When he dug a hole in the plaster for an electric socket, a snake jumped out and bit him between the eyes.'

So I also bought rubber boots and thick gloves and relied on my Buddy Holly glasses for the rest. I plodded past the cemetery with the tools on my shoulder, feeling like an illustration from a mediaeval book of hours. It was a delicious spring day, warm sun and clear sky. The air was like wine, or rather gin and tonic with a zap of ice from the north and a zest of lemon from the south. I was apprehensive and excited as if I were setting out on a long journey. I still treasure the memory of those last moments, when delight and dreams remained unspoilt by the harsh reality of the weeks to come.

First, I dragged out the door that I had knocked down from the first floor. It was rotten but I salvaged the massive iron lock, although the key was missing. I set to work on several decades of manure. I found that by digging the rake in and pulling, I could roll up a layer of fermenting straw like a carpet and drag it out into the yard. Initially the warm and cloying smell was not unpleasant, like the sweetness of Turkish drains sniffed from a distance. It became worse as I dug down through the years. Although I breathed through my mouth, I gagged at every rakeful.

The character-building part of the project came sooner than I expected. My arms ached. Sweat poured down my body and filled my new rubber boots. Blisters sprouted on my hands inside the rough work gloves. It soon became obvious that goats were not the only denizens of the straw. If I stood quietly there were rustlings around me and the glimpse of a thin brown tail. On the first evening I left my work trousers hanging on a wooden peg in the wall. When I came back in the morning, all that was left was the leather belt, a few loops and a pile of metal buttons on the straw underneath. I woke up wild bees as big as walnuts and a nest of orange hornets. The air was filled with angry humming. Twice I ran away into the yard and up the hill, flagellating myself around the head and body with my discarded sweater like a demented Jesuit. I became more and more nervous as I dug deeper. What other creatures had made their homes in the manure?

With a grunt I dug the rake in and pulled back a swathe of matted straw. I looked down on a snake. Its black, whip-like body seemed to stretch from wall to wall. The grey scales around its mouth resembled the puckered skin of an old man. It had an eye like a glistening black pearl and a flickering tongue. It moved. I yelled. I swung the rake. A jarring shock like electricity ran up my arm. I heard the tines clang against the stone wall. I turned and fled.

I stumbled up the steep path, my heart thumping in my throat. My arm tingled as if it were still plugged in to the current. I wrenched it round with my other hand and plucked at the skin, trying to find the bite. The English voice, full of common sense, told me that this was a friendly, mouse-eating, milk-drinking, pussy-cat snake and that the pins and needles in my arm came from banging the rake against the wall. Eventually shame overcame fear and I tiptoed back to the house in squelchy boots, ready to run away again.

The snake lay on the straw, curled around the rake handle. Two tines pierced its head. It was about four feet long. Like a follower of Asclepius, the ancient god of medicine who has a snake curled round his staff, I carefully picked up the rake. I shook it at arm's length, spattering cold blood on the ground, until the snake slithered off and I could poke it under a bush.

After this I was more wary. I wriggled the rake in gently instead of whacking it down. About a decade down I found the missing key of the door. It still turned in the lock with a satisfying double chunk.

Fear of venomous creatures in the straw nurtured my feeling of being watched. When I glanced over my shoulder I saw only a flutter that might have been a bird or heard a rustle that might have been a goat, but once I was sure I saw a face peeping through a clump of buddleia. I had to tell myself not to be stupid, satyrs only existed to keep the children interested.

Around midday, on the second day of labouring at my dung, I looked round for the umpteenth time and found that I was indeed being watched by a man of about sixty, leaning on his stick in the middle of a flock of sheep. A khaki greatcoat was slung nonchalantly across his shoulders over a thick grey flannel suit of unredeemable shapelessness. A debonair red cotton scarf was tied round his neck in place of a collar for his striped blue shirt and his oxblood shoes were spotless. A grey cloth cap was perched at a rakish angle on his grizzled head and he sported a stylish brown-dyed moustache. He nodded to the house.

'Turkish,' he shouted. I leaned on my rake, reflecting his body language to facilitate bonding and grateful of the excuse to stop.

'Turkish,' I repeated in a low voice, hoping he would get the message that I was only foreign and not deaf.

'*Jawohl*. Turkish. House Turkish,' he boomed. 'Door very low.' His free hand patted the air about three feet off the ground.

'Turks little people,' I replied and nodded vigorously to humour him. Either he was retarded or he thought I was.

'Turks. On horses. Very big.' This time he patted the air about six feet off the ground. 'Get off horses no. Never. Greek door low. Turks in houses no come in. *Jawohl*.' He repeated this intelligence in a louder voice.

'Oh, I understand. The Turks always remain on horses so the Greeks made the doors low so the Turks could not ride into the house.' I said this softly in as fluent Greek as I could muster in order to get on syntactical terms.

'Bah. Turks,' he said and spat on the ground. Then something struck him. 'Greek? Speak Greek? Bravo.'

He made a loud brrrhing sound at a sheep that was clambering up my olive tree. His conversation was constantly heckled with brrrhs and shouts and whistles to stop his charges straying into a wheat field or climbing trees for their tender twigs. He stared me in the eye.

'*Deuts*?' he asked hopefully.

I raised my chin and tutted. '*Englesos*.'

But the breakthrough had been made and he spoke in whole sentences. 'I know the Germans. I was a soldier in the north. They are good fighters. They killed my two brothers. I walked back all the way. I have never been off the island since. When I got back home they had to cut the boots from off my feet. They were all one with the skin.'

He looked down fondly at his polished ox-blood shoes. I wanted to ask why he did not feel the same about the Germans who had killed his brothers as he did about Turks whom he had never met, but my Greek was not up to it. He brrrhed and shook his stick at a sheep that was chewing the sleeve of my sweater slung on the fence.

Ruddy-faced Ajax the butcher told me later that Barba Vasilis had killed an Italian in the war by hitting him on the forehead with a stone from twenty paces. The Italian had been coming at him with a bayonet.

In 1940 the dictator Metaxas refused to let Mussolini's army enter Greece. His defiance is commemorated every year with Oxi Day on 28 October – the *x* is pronounced like the *ch* in the Scottish loch.* *Oxi* means no. The story is that the Italian ambassador came to see Metaxas in the middle of the night of 28 October 1940 and gave him an ultimatum based on various pretexts about frontier violations with Albania. Metaxas waited for an hour or two and then gave his one-word reply. *OXI* was the massive newspaper headline the next day. Every Greek who read that headline must have tossed their head, raised their eyebrows and given a great inhaling tut of defiance, like a waiter in a taverna when you ask for something that isn't on the menu. To foreigners, even me after thirty years here, it looks contemptuous and bloody-minded, but in 1940 it was most appropriate. With great courage and resourcefulness the Greek army held the Italians in the mountains of the north for nine months, before Hitler lost patience and sent Germans to finish the job.

Barba Vasilis's biblical feat was not a fluke. Any Greek who keeps sheep is an excellent stone thrower. I often saw him hit a sheep on the head from twenty yards. When he was close enough he whacked their heads with his stick. They didn't seem to mind, although it's hard to know if sheep get a headache. From a distance they are soft and cuddly, but close to, underneath the woolly sweaters, they are hard and bony and a devil to catch hold of.

Stone throwing is also useful against the sheepdogs that guard the mountain flocks. Greek sheepdogs are not the

---

*What would we do without the loch? So many foreign words we wouldn't know how to pronounce.

eager-to-please collies of the Welsh borders but fierce creatures who will attack anything that comes near, especially wolves and hikers. Stones are the first line of defence and a stout walking stick the second. You don't see so much stone throwing among the young these days, however. Only the old people keep animals. Where's the boy who looks after the sheep? He's in school until he's sixteen and in the crammer learning maths and English in the holidays. He rides a motorbike not a mule and watches television instead of hunting cats and frogs and little birds with stones.

It took three back-breaking days to get down to the floor. Outside the house was a vast dung heap swarming with flies and villagers anxious to know what I was going to do with this treasure. There was too much to fertilise my own patch of land, which was already rich in droppings. Ajax had the most forceful claim. He insisted that he had sold the house and not the contents. It was his father's dung and his grandfather's dung. Spiros, the genial carpenter with the yard-brush moustache who had witnessed the deposit, kept doves and chickens in a ruined house opposite mine and stressed the duties of a neighbour. Aussie Alekos the taxi driver called on the bonds of patriotism – after twenty years in Melbourne he knew all the words to *God Save the Queen*. Dyspeptic Dimitris the builder had no claim at all, but made the most impassioned plea on behalf of his eight children whose imminent death from starvation and disease could only be averted by a few hundredweight of manure. He would collect it that very evening in his pick-up.

I faced a serious dilemma. In these early days it was vital to establish good relations with everyone in the village, but at the same time I had to make clear that I wasn't a pushover, a foreigner to be milked.

'What are you going to do with all that dung?' asked stylish Barba Vasilis, inspecting a long little fingernail.

'Why, you want it too?'

'Me? No thanks. But don't give it away.'

'What shall I do?'

'Sell it.'

'No. I don't want to sell it. It cost me nothing.'

Vasilis did not actually say 'Eh, crazy foreigners', but it was all in the shrug of the shoulders.

To tell the truth the thought had crossed my mind, but I shrank from the haggling.

'Give it back to God then. The priest wants to plant roses in front of the church.'

It was a great idea. I could get rid of the dung without favouritism and with credit. Even those who thought it a waste to decorate the church instead of growing vegetables couldn't say so out loud. The pious gesture would establish my public spirit and cost me nothing.

That evening I changed into a clean shirt and trousers as a sign of respect and lay in wait with an ouzo at one of the little metal tables outside Yannis's café. Every evening between six and seven Papas Konstantinos made his round of the village. He was in his seventies, with the long white beard, lined cheeks and large black eyes of a Byzantine saint. His hair was lumped into an untidy bun that never sat neatly on the nape of his neck but slipped round under one ear or the other. He stalked around the village with an air not of the shepherd tending his flock but the commandant showing the flag. As he passed, I downed my ouzo, took a deep breath and accosted him in the middle of the street. All eyes were on us.

'Good evening. I am the foreigner who bought a house on the hill.'

'I have seen you,' said the *papas*, looking past me into the distance. '*Deuts*?'

'English.'

'Ah, Benny Xill.* Are you interested in jokes?' It seemed a strange preoccupation for a man of the cloth.

'Jokes?'

'Jokes,' said the *papas* and pointed up into the sky. The sleeve of his cassock fell to the elbow and revealed the long yellow arm of a woolly vest. I looked up at the clouds. I sympathised with the belief that Creation is a massive practical joke, but that it was held by an Orthodox *papas* was harder to swallow.

'I have a telescope. From Dixon's in London.' Then he added in English, 'Stargazer. Four inch. *Spessial*.' The penny dropped. Not jokes but stars, the difference of an 'r'.

'You in London?' I asked.

'My nephew works for Olympic Airways.'

---

*As in loch again.

It was time to pop the question. What was it to be? Greek or mime? The potential for misunderstanding was about equal in both. As we were standing in the middle of the street and all eyes were on us, I chose Greek.

'Would you like my *kaka*?'

'Your what?'

'My *kaka*. In my house much *kaka*. You want *kaka* in church?'

The coal-black eyes began to burn. I persevered.

'In my house much goat *kaka*. Prrrp. Prrrp. *Kaka*. You want it for the church? For roses?' I suddenly had a horrible suspicion that Barba Vasilis had played a joke on me and that giving manure to a priest was an ancient insult. But it was a false alarm. The black eyes turned back to the horizon and he nodded.

'Put it behind the church. Next to my garden. Good evening.'

'How shall I get it down?'

He shrugged again and stalked off on his patrol. In the café everyone else shrugged too. It was the *papas*'s manure now and of no interest to anyone else. I could not go back on my gift, so I had to pay Dimitris the builder and Adonis his labourer to load it onto panniers on their donkeys and take it down to the pick-up parked by the cemetery. For the same price they would have dug it straight out of the house and saved me three days of hard labour, acute lumbago and hands like skinned sausages. The only consolation was that I would never have found my old front door key.

The treasure lay heaped up against the back of the church, gently steaming. Every morning it seemed to have shrunk in the night and I could only think that it was settling. One night I couldn't sleep and went into the kitchen for a glass of water. Out of the window I saw waxy-fingered Elpida sneaking back into the yard with two buckets of manure. The heap was all gone in a week, scattered at night through the gardens of the village. The next time I walked past his house behind the church, I was glad to see that the *papas* had taken some for his own tomatoes.

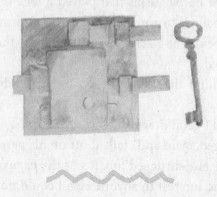

Island of dreams

very Thursday I so look forward to Friday when I will be with the family again. On Friday afternoon I think of Arfa strapping little Harry into the child seat, where he spends a lot of his day, awake or asleep. They drive to the school and pick up the other three and supplies of bags of bilious yellow corn curls, called *garidakia*, and cartons of tepid chocolate milk. They set off for Evia along the National Road, the patched and potholed four-lane, third-world, second-rate highway to Salonica.

After twenty minutes they turn off on a little road that meanders through vineyards and orchards and pine forests across the hills, with views of Evia over the water, and down a steep winding road to the tiny port of Scaly Orifice, or Skala Oropos as it is more generally known outside our family. Here the Gulf of Evia is half an hour wide by little ferry. While they wait for the next boat, the mob demands its pay-off for not fighting in the back of the camper and lines up for ice lollies at the kiosk by the quay.

The ferry is a big white landing craft. They reverse on board, the deck hands chanting *ela piso piso piso* – come back, back, back – into the magical ship's aroma of old diesel, disinfectant, dead fish, stale piss, sweat, new paint, seaweed, salt, sea breeze and coffee. The engine shudders and thrums, the boarding ramp becomes the bow door rising shut, and with hoots and bells the screws churn up the black and oily water.

Out in the Gulf the breeze freshens and the family turn their backs on Attica. The sea works its magic. The worries and stress of the mainland sink into the dregs of the wine-dark Aegean, until someone finds that they have left their shoes or their security blanket or their homework behind.

Loudspeakers crackle the theme tunes of Greece. *Never on Sunday* (da di-di-di-di-di-di *dum-dum* di-*dum-dum* di-*dum-dum*) or *Zorba's Dance* (da-*dum* di-di-di-*dum* da-*dum* di-di-di-*dum*). If ever there was a prize for an overworked tune these two would lead the field. Not long before we first went to Greece, *Zorba* was banned by the American puppet junta because it was written by a com-munist, Theodorakis. You could go to jail for humming it. Now it makes up for lost airtime.

After horseplay on the stairs, swinging over the deck rails, hanging from the awning frames, the children shove past each other into the shady saloon for more bribes, lemonade and stale cheese pies. It is too early for tourists. Men in traditional island dress – leather jacket, check shirt and jeans – play cards and drink beer. An old granny skulks in a corner with a live chicken in a basket. The children hide the crusts of their cheese pies under the seats and mesmerise themselves with an old-fangled arcade game, new to Greece, a blob of light simulating a tennis ball that zigzags across the screen and makes a popping noise when you 'hit' it.

Arfa says that computer games will never catch on and tries to entice them to a game of shove-drachma football on the table. The granny comes over and interrogates her: where are they going, how much does her husband earn, how much rent do they pay in Athens? 'You've got lovely children,' she says, 'but why did you marry a foreigner?' Arfa, who has been making serious efforts to learn Greek, has been smug about this question for twenty-five years.

They go out on deck to watch themselves arrive. Eretria is a natural little harbour overlooked by its acropolis and ringed by scrubby, green-pocked hills. They chug past a spit of wooded land with a sign saying 'Island of Dreams'. The port is cluttered with blue and white fishing boats, some of them with their owners hunched over yellow nets getting things ready for the evening's hunting. A man slaps an octopus against a wall below a sign prohibiting the slapping of octopuses and the rhythmic smack, smack, smack echoes across the water. Plastic bags drift in the shallows like jelly-fish. Or jellyfish drift in the shallows like plastic bags, it's hard to tell from the deck.

A port policeman holds back the scrum of foot passengers returning to Athens. They seem desperate to leave the island with their tatty cases and parcels, pushing each other out of the way like refugees from an imminent disaster that they are keeping secret from the new arrivals.

Twenty yards from the quay they stop for a dozen *sou-vlakis*, little cubes of pork grilled on a sharp stick, drenched in salt and lemon juice and topped with a chunk of bread. The last cube is a piece of gristly fat and the world divides between those who relish it and those who retch on it. Bartering fat cubes or squirreling them under the seat cushions, they take the coast road south. The beach is lined with hotels and tavernas and discos and pizzerias, still shuttered for the winter. On tattered signs Zorbas dance their haemorrhoidal jig. Da-dum di-di-di-dum. Further on the family pass olive groves shimmering silver in the breeze and fruit orchards and small fields of crops divided by dry stone walls. Then rocky foothills to the left and an exquisite blue sea to the right.

They get stuck behind a Pepsi truck, farting fumes as it labours up a winding gradient, past a round cement silo belonging to the Herakles Cement Company. It is painted cream and adorned with the black silhouette of the hero, his lion skin flopping over his forehead in a widow's peak. The landscape is scribbled with political slogans and signs, stencilled on fences and buildings and outcrops of rock and the road itself, as if there weren't already enough symbols in the world – the green rising sun of the socialist party PASOK, the blue flaming torch of New Democracy and the red hammer and sickle of the two Communist parties, the internationalists and the allegedly independent Eurocommunists.

Aliveri is waking from its siesta. The first men shuffle to their café chairs on the pavement, leaning on sticks and clacking beads. A lignite train from the mines that feed the power station on the bay clatters over the level crossing at the entrance to the town. In the queue an antique blue bus belches blue smoke, pick-ups klaxon the first three bars of the *Marseillaise* and *Colonel Bogey*, stereos bray Greek and American pop.

Outside the town is a square tower on top of a conical hill. Such stone towers are ten a penny. Ancient Athenians and Spartans and Corinthians built them, as did Alexander's generals, Roman governors, Byzantine despots, Frankish crusaders, Venetian mercenaries, Catalan adventurers, Knights Templar, Turkish pashas, Moorish pirates, mountain brigands and the *palikaria* of the War of Independence. Then they went out of fashion. German *Gauleiter*, Greek Colonels and Nato commanders preferred reinforced concrete bunkers.

I wait in the café. Three hours after leaving Athens the camper stops and I am jumped on and tickled and scragged until I buy the children off with ice creams to tide us over the last part of the journey to Kyria Sofia's taverna in Limanaki, where we spend a riotous weekend. By Sunday afternoon I so look forward to Monday when they will leave me in peace to get on with the house.

Evia's heyday was three thousand years ago when its seven city states were thriving and independent. Chalkis, or Halkida as it is now known, means copper and that was the source of its wealth. The plain between Chalkis and Eretria was famous for horses and the cattle after which the island was named. Evian warriors had a reputation for old-fashioned courage. They didn't use cunning stratagems or throw spears like cissies but fought like men, hand to hand with swords. Evians founded colonies in the Aegean islands and Italy. Reggio Calabria was founded by Chalkidians. Cuma north of Naples got its name from Kimi.

Since this golden age Evia had got lost in the backwaters of history. Why don't we talk about Chalkis and Eretria in the same breath as Athens and Sparta, Corinth and Thebes? Until we went there we had never heard of them. Yet it was a large, fertile and populous island close to trade routes and seaways. Perhaps people who bred horses and liked to do things the old-fashioned way weren't smart enough to prosper in the growing sophistication of the Greek world. Perhaps it was because they had a talent for backing the losing sides in the interminable wars between Athens and Sparta and Thebes. When they sided with Athens, Thebes won. When they sided with Sparta, Athens won. When they rose up in revolt, they were smacked down again. In the end Philip of Macedon, Alexander the Great's father, swallowed them all in his Macedonian empire. Evia became known again for what its name means, happy cattle, and its fertile plains grew grain for Athens.

A hundred and fifty years later Macedon was swallowed up by Rome. The Romans were fond of the swirly green cipollino marble from Karystos at the southern tip of Evia for their baths, but otherwise they left few records of the island. The Roman empire split and Byzantium took over the east. We can skim thankfully over the next eight hundred years along with local historian Tassos N Petrisa: 'The emperor Justinian fortified Halkida in the fifth century.

There then follows a period of some centuries during which very little of importance seems to have happened.' Happy cows.

In 1209 the Pope's crusaders captured Constantinople. The Republic of Venice took over Evia, which they called Negroponte. It ranked as a kingdom, like Crete, and its flag was one of three flown in St Mark's Square. Halkida, which the Venetians also called Negroponte, was already a wealthy and cosmopolitan trading centre. A symptom of and probable contributor to this was the largest and oldest Jewish community in Greece, known as Little Jerusalem. The Venetians made the city their centre of operations for all the Aegean: the laws of the island were written in their dialect and they had a church and a warehouse in every large village. The island was divided into three baronies owing allegiance to the king of Salonika. The Venetians held the ports and numerous minor Frankish nobles occupied the interior, which they adorned with their castles. For the next two hundred years they engaged in confusing and readily forgettable skirmishes, invasions and wars with Albanians, Turks, pirates, each other and the rulers of a resurgent Byzantium.

On 29 May 1453 the Ottomans captured Constantinople. For the next fifty years they whittled away at Venice's empire. In 1470 they took the city of Negroponte with the greatest massacre the island had seen. The kingdom became the fief of the Capitan Pasha, high admiral of the Ottoman Empire. It was renamed the Pasalik of Egripos and included Athens and Thebes.

For the next four centuries again nothing much happened. In the words of another local historian, Alexandros Kalemis, 'In 1470 Evia surrenders to the Ottoman hordes of Mohameth and has to bear the Turkish yoke until the revolution of 1821.' Actually Evia was liberated on 13 June 1830.

From time to time I decide to learn classical Turkish and the Arabic script it is written in and to rediscover Greece from the Ottoman point of view, decisions that last about five minutes until I think of other ways to spend my time. There must be letters and reports from the pashas of Egripos and Aliveri and the scribes of the Capitan Pasha when he came on state visits. Perhaps some Anatolian Leigh Fermor had a bestseller among the *chatterati* of Topkapi with his *Travels in the Egripos*. There must also be things written in Greek by clever Greek administrators, who ran the empire.

Whisper it softly, but many Greeks, including clergy, welcomed the Ottomans. On the whole Muslim rulers have been much more tolerant of infidels than their Christian counterparts have. As long as their subjects paid taxes and provided recruits to the harems and armies of the Sultan, they could have whatever religion they liked. Only when they joined religion with revolt did scimitars and stakes come out. Orthodox Christianity was under far greater threat from the Roman variety imposed by Venetians and Franks and Catalans. Jews too were safer from pogrom under the crescent than the cross. This is not a line of thought that goes down well in Greek company.

The War of Independence began in 1821. Out of this Balkan saga of courage and heroism, chaos and confusion, massacre and betrayal, brigands and warlords, Great Power rivalry and Ottoman infirmity, a new Greece was born. Evia played its part. A hero of the revolution, Kriezotis, took his name from the village of Krieza, just down the road from us. Actually he came from another village and by rights should have called himself Argyrotis – all the received information about this confusing time needs to be carefully picked apart.

The Halkida revolutionary committee raised money and the nationalist consciousness. The Crispi and Cohen families were active members, not least to promote religious freedom in the event of an Orthodox theocracy. In fact a secular republic was created in 1828 and lasted until its president, Kapodistrias, was assassinated in 1831. It was replaced by a monarchy in 1833. Emulating its British protector, a German king was installed, the Bavarian Otto.

We decided to explore the square tower in the middle of the amphitheatrical plain that we could see from the house. Chivalry was the theme. The knights accoutred themselves in various bits of cardboard and plastic and stick.

'I don't want to be a damson in this dress again, I want to be a knight,' said Kate.

'All right, you can be Sir Pegoraro de Pegorari, Baron of North Evia,' said Arfa, who had been reading up on the mediaeval history of the island.

'And me,' said Harry.

'You can be Sir Gilberto de Villardoin, Baron of Middle Evia.'

'And me,' said Jim.

'Sir Ravanos de Lecarzeri, Baron of South Evia.'

'Maam, you're making these up,' complained Jack.

'I'm not, promise. Genuine thirteenth century. As you're the eldest, you can be Sir Boniface de Montferrat, King of Salonica, who was in charge of all of them. He reported to Venice. They took over after the crusaders plundered Constantinople.'

'Yebbut who do we fight?' asked Jack, getting to the crux.

'The other French and German and Spanish and Italian knights who tried to build castles here. They fought all the time.'

'Yebbut what about the Greeks?'

'They kept small and quiet. The Emperor of Constantinople was Belgian. His name was Henry. They fought him too.'

We set off in the camper down into the valley and along a maze of dirt roads through fields of vines and melons to the tower. We parked at the bottom of the hillock, as the slope was steep and covered with a jumble of rocks and cut stone, all that remained of the winding road that led up to the main entrance. It was stoutly built with massive stones, about four storeys high with authentic-looking crenellations. It was probably a Venetian signal tower, one of the chain that ran the length of the island, and not much use thereafter except to watchmen who guarded the fields. We disturbed the present chatelaine, a large white owl, who flapped off crossly when we went in.

We had a good view of the lake and its emerald shore. In the middle was a tall, conical island topped with a jumble of stone and marble ruins, all that remained of Dystos, one of the seven independent city states of ancient Evia. Hidden in the mountains beyond were the 3,000-year-old Dragon Houses of the Heroic Age, massive bunkers made out of giant slabs of rock that these days would need heavy cranes to lift. Who built them and how and why are still a mystery.

The hills around the lake were dotted with little Byzantine chapels. On the shore at the closest point to the island of Dystos was the Serai of the Pasha of Aliveri, a summer palace with the remains of a handsome stone tower and stables and outbuildings. High in the blue sky above us the vapour trails of a flight of fighters traced the Greek flag. If we squinted we could make out our house across the plain. It was thrilling to feel that we were part of this landscape full of stories.

It was too hot for jousting, so the Knights of Evia sat in the shade of the wall.

'This was probably where they kept Aghios Ioannes prisoner,' I said.

'Nah, we want to hear about knights, not religion stuff,' said Jim.

'Religion's boring,' said Kate.

'Bo-ring,' said the chorus.

'Don't you want to know how he was condemned to be

skinned alive and put on a spit and roasted and torn into little bits with red hot pincers?'

'Oh, all right then.'

'He was born in Egypt about eight hundred years ago. He was made a priest by the Bishop of Alexandria and went with him to Constantinople. That's what they called Istanbul before the Turks got it. While they were there the Crusaders arrived. They were Catholic knights from France and Germany and England. The Pope had sent them to throw the Muslims out of Israel, but they thought it was too difficult so instead they attacked Constantinople and set fire to it and massacred the Orthodox Christians.'

'Why did they do that?' asked Jack.

'To steal their treasure. That's why knights went on Crusades. Poor Ioannes was stuck in the Archbishop's palace and he was likely to be killed by the knights too. So he ran down to the kitchen yard, where there were some sheep waiting to be made into dinner. He tied a sheepskin round himself and opened the back gate. He hung on to the underneath of a big fat ram and it ran through the burning streets to safety.'

'Odysseus did that.'

'Very good, Harry. And so did a lot of other heroes.'

'Why didn't the knights kill the ram?' asked Jack.

'They were busy killing the people.'

'And they're easier to catch. Especially the girls. Halee-laleeloolah,' crowed Jim.

'So Ioannes escaped from the city and tried to get back to Egypt. But he kept getting blown off course and having adventures. Finally he was shipwrecked on Evia. Round here was ruled by the Franks then. These were Catholic knights from France. After they ruined Constantinople they took over a lot of the Greek lands and tried to stamp out the Orthodox Christians. Ioannes knew what sort of people they were, so he ran up into the mountains in case they tried to stamp him out too. He lived in a cave and avoided other people. He kept a few sheep for milk and used to preach to them, like St Francis did to the birds and St Anthony did to the fish. If anybody came near he pretended to be dumb in case they betrayed him to the Franks.'

'What's betray?' asked Harry.

'Snitch, stoopid,' said Kate.

'So people crept up and hid in the rocks and the trees to listen. Then they found that if they wrapped themselves in skins and joined the real sheep, they could get closer.'

'Was he short-sighted like you, Dad?' asked Kate.

'He probably knew.'

'Why would they want to listen to a boring sermon?' wondered Jack.

'His sermons weren't boring. They were probably funny. Egyptians have a great sense of humour. Anyway, he was the only Orthodox priest left and although the people told the Franks they had become Catholic, they were only pretending. So he got to be famous. His woolly congregation grew and grew. He started to do miracles. His speciality was club feet. Then someone snitched on him to the governor of the island. It wasn't only against the law, but it sounded like witchcraft, dressing up as animals to go to mass. The

Frankish priests in Halkida spread stories about pagan goings-on in the mountains at night. So the governor sent soldiers to arrest Ioannes and after a big hunt in the mountains they caught him and locked him up in this tower.'

'I bet it wasn't this tower,' said Jack.

'Why not?'

'You're always telling us stories about places we know to keep us interested.'

'Anyway, the governor said he should be treated like a sheep or a goat and hung up and skinned and put on a spit, except he was not to be killed first. They came to the tower to get him, but he had disappeared and in his cell was a live sheep.'

'How?' asked Jack.

'It might have been a miracle. Or somebody might have bribed the guard to smuggle him out.'

'Did they kill the sheep?' wondered Kate.

'I think they did, just in case it was still Aghios Ioannes in disguise. And then they put it on a spit and had a barbecue. But that wasn't the end of things. For hundreds of years afterwards people heard Ioannes preaching to the wild goats high up there in the mountains. They dressed in animal skins and went to listen. They say it all died out when the Turks captured the island three hundred years later. They threw out the Catholics and gave Orthodox Christianity back to the people, so there was no need. But that's why Aghios Ioannes round here always carries a baby lamb.'

'Can you still hear him in the mountains?' asked Harry.

'Probably. If you listen hard enough.'

'You tricked us, Dad,' said Jim.

'How?'

'You said he would be skinned alive and torn to pieces.'

'I didn't. I said he was condemned.'

'That's a cheat.'

Raising the roof

〜〜〜〜

Nektarios was the man to put a new roof on the house. I found him on top of the baker's. His glossy hair was oiled and slicked back, as if he had just come out of the shower. Unlike most of the village men, he was clean-shaven every day. Nevertheless, his dapper appearance was marred by red-rimmed eyes and cheekbones etched with purple veins, for he was in constant struggle with a hangover. I called up to him. He shinned down his ladder and listened patiently to the speech I had prepared. He shrugged his shoulders, pouted his bottom lip and began a litany of reasons why he could not start work until the end of summer.

'How can get my truck up that mule track... I have just got the contract for the cooperative in Drossia... I promised to roof a church on the other side of Aliveri...'

I heard him out. It was part of the ritual. Ask a Greek tradesman to change a tap washer and he produces a score of reasons why it is impossible. It is to do with asserting dignity and independence, not being at someone else's beck and call. Doing that person a favour in the face of overwhelming difficulty restores the balance of power. Knowing this doesn't make it less irritating, however.

'My brother has to have an operation and can't help me... the Ellenit people are on strike... my mother has to go into hospital in Athens... my wife is pregnant...'

Most Greeks hate to do anything alone. It frightens them. To live alone, to work alone, even to take a walk alone is a misfortune. But at the same time, they live on rivalry. One of the reasons they stick together is so there is always someone to get the better of. So I smiled and nodded and said I was sorry to have troubled him and it was OK because I'd heard in the café about a good roofer in Aliveri, who was short of work. It came out more like roof pimp than roof expert, but Nektarios got the message.

'Bah. He couldn't put the lid on a cardboard box. I'll come up this evening.'

At sunset I watched him pace over the fields up the hill, ignoring the path. He stooped to pick something up. When he arrived, red-faced and breathless, he pressed a wild orchid into my hand. He wore one behind his own ear, which gave him a raffish look. I put mine behind my ear too, which was not strictly appropriate as it means the wearer has been drinking and I usually saved my daily ration until nightfall. Nektarios pointed to the ruin of the house next door and laughed.

'The stick I took in there. Po-po-po.' I did not understand the phrase, literally 'the wood I've eaten', but the accompanying sign language was clear enough.

'You lived there?'

'Nine children. Parents. Grandparents. We had two rooms and one for the animals.'

'Now there is no one.'

'They are all still there. No one ever leaves. Not even the Old Ones.'

'Who are the Old Ones?'

'Eh. The Old Ones.' He looked away as if he has already told me more than he should. He kicked a stone with his foot and it skittered down the rocky path towards the chapel.

'Like the stones,' he said. 'They change their shape and they change their colour but they are always there.' He put a finger to his lips. 'Don't tell the *papas* I said these things. Aren't you afraid to be up here on your own?'

'Why?'

'Hearing things.'

'What things?'

'Voices.'

'What voices?'

'The voices floating in the air.'

'What do they say?'

'Anything. Except prayers. Prayers go up to heaven. The rest stays down here.'

I was out of my depth. This was not the conversation I expected from a roof pimp. I had a nasty suspicion that my Greek was letting me down again and substituting the fantastical for Nektarios's plain and practical words. But all I could do was press on.

'Do you hear them?' I ventured.

'What?'

'The Old Ones.'

He shrugged like a man used to hearing things, which,

given his fondness for the bottle, he probably was. He took the flower from behind his ear, tossed it away without a glance and began his inspection of the house. He walked round it, looking up at the roof, tutting and shaking his head. From the top step by the front door he shinned up the stone wall like a lizard. He took out his car keys and jabbed them into all the beams and rafters he could reach. His face had the lugubrious expression of the expert in search of the worst. I looked through his eyes and felt embarrassed. How could I have bought such a dump?

Spanning the two longest walls were three vertical triangles of chestnut beams. Across them were laid horizontal rafters. On top of the rafters and at right angles to them was a layer of dry reeds, like bamboo, that made the ceiling inside. On top of the reeds were heavy split stone slabs, like slates. In time slates slip off. Wasps and beetles chew away the inside of the rafters so that they explode at a touch like puffballs. Water trickles down unprotected walls and washes away the mud and water between the stones. The roof falls in and the walls collapse and the thistles grow. Then along comes a foreigner. Dapper Nektarios clambered down and delivered the verdict.

'You'll need a cement ring round the top of the walls. You'll need new beams, which you can get in laminated pine. You'll need a chipboard ceiling. And you'll need ten sheets of Ellenit.'

Ellenit is corrugated sheets of asbestos cement, like on Barba Mitsos's roof. Greece was one of the world's biggest producers of asbestos and one of the last European countries to ban it.

'I don't want Ellenit.'

'You don't want Ellenit?'

I tossed my head back with a disdainful tut to show that I was not a foreigner to be walked over. I knew that it was out of the question to replace the stone roof. The craft was lost. Each slab was larger than a concrete paving stone. The weight needs seasoned beams and skill in setting them up. Every fifteen years or so the stone slabs have to be taken off and turned over. But I refused to have corrugated asbestos.

'Onions I want.'

'Onions? You want onions?' It was Nektarios's turn to feel out of his depth. I would have said tiles but for a missing vowel, *keramidia* for *kremidia*.

'Yes, onions. Not Ellenit. Onions.' I was firm and not to be bullied.

'Why not? You can have onions. And potatoes and garlic and whatever you like.'

I hoped I had misheard. If not, Nektarios was barking mad. I felt uneasy at being alone with him in the gathering dusk and he probably felt the same about me.

'And I don't want chipboard for the ceiling.'

'No, no chipboard. Certainly no chipboard.'

That threw me. Where was the rhetoric? Where were the histrionics? It did not occur to me then that he was humouring the crazy foreigner. But I pursued my advantage. I wanted a ceiling of yellow reeds harvested from the lake and laid across the beams.

'Squid I want.'

'You want what?'

'Squid. I want the ceilings made of squid.'

This time it was an intrusive 'ar', *kalamaria* for *kalamia*, that made the difference.

'You don't want Ellenit and you don't want chipboard. You want onions and you want squid. Do you want a roof or a *meze*?'

I was sure he said *meze*. What the hell had *meze*, which means appetiser, got to do with anything? He must have been hungry, which is why he was beetling off down the path past the chapel without so much as a good evening. I put my orchid behind my ear and followed him to the village. These Greeks were very odd.

I walked into the café twenty minutes later. It went quiet and everyone looked at me. I was used to this by now. Unlike most British, who don't know where to look if they catch the eye of strangers, Greeks are happy to stare. At a table in the corner, Nektarios and Ajax the butcher and Dimitris the builder were sniggering at some private joke, so I didn't interrupt them but sat down at a table on my own.

Yannis waddled up to me, grinning all over his face, and took my order for an ouzo. As he walked back to the counter there was a guffaw from Nektarios's table. When Yannis came back with the ouzo, instead of the usual cube of feta and an olive on a saucer, there were bits of tinned squid and onion. I dug in my pocket for change, but Yannis jerked his thumb towards Nektarios and company.

'With their compliments.'

There was another guffaw when I raised my glass to toast them and Ajax waved me over. I carried my saucer and glass and hoped that they were not going to share their joke because I would probably not understand it. Ajax slapped me on the shoulder.

'*Also mein Freund*, you want tiles and reeds. But those old ways are difficult and dirty. The rats and hornets love them.'

'They're for barns and sheep pens,' said Dimitris, 'and the tiles never lie flat on the reeds.'

'And who's going to cut the reeds down at the lake and strip them?' asked Nektarios. 'The reeds are strong, but they move and leave gaps so the mortar falls inside the house. Up there you need everything tight shut, you don't want to leave cracks for anything to get in.'

'*Ach Gott*,' exclaimed Ajax, 'let the man have tiles if he wants them. I can get you some beautiful ones in Aliveri. French tiles from Romania, nice and flat. I can get you a good price. *Spessial, sehr spessial*.' Ajax tried to look innocent, but when he sensed a profit his nostrils flared.

'Bah, French tiles,' countered Dimitris, 'you want Roman tiles. My godfather in Halkida imports them straight from Italy. Very good price and easy to lay.'

'Why not Greek tiles?' I asked. Greek tiles are curved and tapered so that one end can fit inside the other. They are laid in rows alternately curved side up and curved side down so that they interlock.

'Greek tiles?' queried Ajax, '*Warum?*'

'We are in Greece.'

'What's that got to do with it?'

'They look paradisical.'

'Paradisical?'

'He means traditional,' said Nektarios, who had tumbled to the secret of running a mental spell-check on anything that sounded bizarre.

'So what?' countered Ajax. 'We don't live in the past.'

'They look beautiful,' I ventured, struggling for a justification that they could not refute.

'*Um Gotteswillen*. They are ugly. Greek tiles are never the same size and the colour varies even from the factory in Athens. The hand-made ones are worse. We're not ignorant peasants here.' He used the more contemptuous word *vlachs*, the nomads from the north. 'In Germany they call them *Mönch und Nonne* tiles. Monk and nun.' He rubbed his two forefingers together side by side and everybody laughed.

'Don't they make tiles on the island?'

'Bah,' said Nektarios, 'there was a man down in Aliveri. He made them by hand so every one was different. His old kiln couldn't make the same colour each time he fired it up. He went out of business. Serves him right. He should have modernised. We like foreign tiles. They're bigger and the red is brighter.'

And they stuck out on the landscape like acne. They would weather after fifty years or so, but I didn't have that long to wait.

'Look,' I said, 'I want a roof that looks as if it's been there a hundred years.' They looked at me in amazement, but I pressed on. 'In England we like things to look old. Old doors and old glass and old roses cost more than new ones.'

'The old days are gone, thank God,' said Nektarios and slapped his stomach. In Greece the old days mean poverty and hunger. Oxfam, the Oxford Committee for Famine Relief, was set up in response to famine in Greece in 1942.

'He wants second-hand tiles,' explained Ajax, his nostrils flaring. 'I'll find you some.'

'Where?' asked Nektarios, who was annoyed at losing commission on a set of new tiles. 'On top of people's houses? What do they do if it rains?'

'You know there are enough tiles lying around on the island to cover Aghia Sofia and still have some left over. I'll take him up the mountain. We'll find plenty. We'll go tomorrow. OK, Johnny?'

'Eh,' said Dimitris, 'they have to be cleaned. Every one will have to be wire brushed by hand. It's cheaper to buy new.'

'He'll brush them,' said Ajax, 'he wants to do something useful. Real work. Isn't that right?'

I nodded, relieved that he was on my side, although it sounded like an insult. I stabbed the last piece of squid and swallowed it whole.

I arrived punctually at Ajax's house at eight o'clock. He was still in bed. Eleni looked drawn and tired and smelt of baby milk. She was wearing a long, flowery house-coat and her hair was pinned up in an untidy heap. She told me to go round to the balcony at the back.

I sat down at the imitation cast iron patio table. Up on

the hill I could see my house with its two blank windows staring sightless. Eleni came out with a cup of Nescafé and a glass of water on a tray. She had combed her hair and changed into a clean white frock and she smelt of perfume.

Ajax lurched out in furry leopard-skin slippers, jeans and a string vest, which raised lozenges on his belly. Black hair sprouted from his chest and neck and shoulders. He rubbed his face with the backs of his hands and finger-combed the glistening quiff that flopped over his forehead. He sat astride a chair, his burly arms resting on the back, and groomed his handsome moustaches.

'Eleni, let's have a beer. Johnny will have one too. *Engländer trinken Frühschoppen, nich*?'

'Not so early. The coffee is very nice.'

'You're right. It's too early for beer. Eleni, he'll have a whisky.'

I tried to put out of my mind the thought of ruddy-faced Ajax coming home in the small hours and pawing Eleni with meaty hands. He had the biggest Mercedes in the village and the biggest freezer and the biggest wine barrel and the biggest herd of goats and the most beautiful wife, who had given him not one son but two, may they live for you.

'You're a great man, Ajax.'

'*Was sagst du?*'

'I'm sorry. I was speaking English.'

'*Ich sprech' kein Englisch.*'

'I was saying you're a good man to help me like this.'

'*Nichts zu danken.*'

Eleni came back with a bottle of Glen Gorbals and olives

and two glasses. She did not sit down with us but stood like a servant. Ajax poured two whiskies and clinked his glass against mine.

'Our health,' he said and drained it in one gulp. Not wanting to seem standoffish, I did the same. I was ashamed that I didn't have the nerve to turn down the drink, but actually it tasted quite good. You could get the habit. Ajax stood up, clapped me on the shoulder and went away to get showered and dressed.

'Do you see me up there?' I asked.

'No. Why should I look up there?' replied Eleni, her eyes flickering up the hill.

'You were born there.'

'Eh,' she said.

Eh is not in *Greek-in-a-Week* but it is a vital word, a verbal shrug, resignation and defiance.

Ajax strode out, perfumed and glistening. We got into his Datsun pick-up. Our first stop was half a kilometre down the road at the house of Dimitris the builder. Two mixers, a compressor and a pick-up were parked outside on the road. The house looked permanently incomplete. Steel rods sprouted from the roof, a heap of breezeblocks might or might not have been an extension in the making, shuttering propped up the concrete veranda. The yard was a warren of breezeblock sheds roofed with Ellenit. Washing lines strung apparently at random fluttered with the clothes of eight children. Rusty oil drums full of cement and lime and plaster and rubble, piles of bricks and sand and gravel and steel bars lay around without any apparent order or arrangement. Goats and chickens wandered among them finishing off any green stuff that struggled through the lime and cement dust.

Dimitris's wife Roula was busy with a long stick chasing a yelling little girl round the oil drums. She was a big-boned woman with close-set eyes and the voice of a siren, not one of the sweet-voiced sea nymphs that lured Homer's sailors but an air-raid siren. All the village women had voices that could carry over several fields. I heard them at noon like a flock of angry seabirds, calling their husbands and children in to eat. Roula had the loudest voice of all, a high-pitched yodel, which she also used in normal conversation.

'Where's Dimitris?' shouted Ajax. Mother and child stopped in their tracks, wide-eyed and panting.

'The place,' she shrieked and pointed her cane at a wooden privy in a corner of the yard next to a vegetable patch. 'The old shit-bag's been there all morning.'

Ajax acknowledged this intelligence with a wave of his hand, which was the signal for hunter and hunted to resume the chase. Roula was a split second faster off the mark and she caught her victim by the hair. I followed Ajax over to the privy accompanied by the sound of screams and the thwack of the stick on tender flesh.

The privy was the only part of the house that looked finished. It was patriotically painted blue and white like a sentry box. The door was decorated with heart-shaped holes. Ajax banged on it with his fist.

'Come out you constipated bugger,' was his greeting.

'Constipated?' came the reply. 'Mother of God, if only I

was. Just for a week. Or a day. Just one little day.' Dimitris's voice sounded muffled and distant, as if he had fallen into the pit. 'What do you want? Can't you see I'm busy?'

'No we can't, thank God. The foreigner wants your old tiles. You don't need them.'

'What do you mean? Are you mad? They are my grand-father's,' replied Dimitris.

'Your grandfather doesn't need them. We buried him last year, for God's sake. The foreigner will give you five little drachmas each. You need the money.'

Ajax hectored and wheedled, the church bell tolled for the liturgy, Roula yodelled for her children and whacked them when they came, Dimitris grunted and farted behind the door and finally we settled on seven drachmas.

'I'll pick them up tomorrow.'

'Pay me now, then. Tell Roula we agreed on four.' The door opened a crack and a hand emerged. Ajax peeled off the notes, handed them over and the door slammed shut.

'Watch what you use for paper,' he shouted and thumped the door in farewell.

We set off in the pick-up on the road to Lepoura. On the outskirts of Neohori, we turned into a narrow track through a dense thicket of mountain oak and down to the bottom of a dry valley. We slowed down by a jumble of stone buildings, the largest of which boasted a handsome Ellenit roof, and parked next to a Toyota truck.

We pushed open the rough wooden garden gate. Bright

nails and shards of pink tile were scattered on the ground beneath the eaves. In the corner of a potato patch was a neat stack of tiles, faded and moss-mottled. Ajax pointed to them and winked at me. The windows of the house were shuttered, but the front door was open and dark shapes moved behind the blue and white stripes of a fly curtain.

'*Ho*, Thanassi,' shouted Ajax. A middle-aged woman dressed in black came to the threshold. 'Where's Thanassis? I came to see him about his tiles.'

Without a word, the woman beckoned us inside. Amber candles flickered in the gloom and the air was heavy with beeswax and sweetness. Three old women, dressed in black with shawls over their heads, stood beside a table. On it lay a man in a dark suit and white shirt buttoned up to the neck. His eyes were closed and his arms were at attention by his sides. One of the women held up his right leg, stiff and heavy, while another pushed the foot into a shiny shoe. The third woman waved the flies away from his face with a newspaper.

'God help us,' exclaimed Ajax, crossing himself three times. 'Condolences. Holy Mother of God. What happened? Heart?'

The middle-aged woman clutched her breast and rocked on her heels and in a high-pitched monotone gabbled a plaintive lament. I couldn't take my eyes off the dead man. His jaw was tied up with a white cloth, so he looked as if he were suffering from nothing more serious than toothache. It was my first dead body and I waited for the appropriate feelings. I didn't know what feelings to expect, which was worse than realising that I had none. It was all so matter-of-fact. The new widow sighed the final strophe of her lament.

'He breathed out heavily three times and his soul departed. Do you want a coffee?'

'No thanks,' said Ajax, 'we've had one. We have work to do. We have to load the tiles.'

'What tiles?'

Ajax jerked his thumb towards the corpse. The two women were tying his feet together with cord, as if they were afraid he would leap off the table and run away.

'Thanassis sold me the tiles. God rest him.'

'How much did he ask for them?'

'Four little drachmas.'

'The fool. They're worth ten.'

'Bah. New ones cost ten. I shouldn't have agreed on more than three. Thanassis got the best of me, may his soul be with God tonight.'

'He doesn't want to sell. He's keeping them for the pigsty.'

'He changed his mind. His very last words to me were Ajax my friend, you can have them for twenty. Then I can buy Voula that necklace I saw in Halkida...'

With that the widow burst into tears and Ajax turned to the body and crossed himself.

'I won't go back on his word,' said the widow, crossed herself and took up her threnody again. 'Thanassi, what have you done to me, have you no pity for me?'

I followed Ajax outside. I held the gate open and he reversed the pick-up as close as he could to the tiles. There were five hundred and by the time we finished I was pouring sweat and my hands were rubbed raw and stained red. We were fastening the tailgate when a green truck arrived. It had a loudspeaker on top of the cab and a canvas body supported by a metal tube frame. Two men got out, exchanged greetings with Ajax and unloaded a simple coffin from a pile of potatoes.

We followed them back inside. They put the coffin on the floor beside the table and bundled Thanassis in. His head clunked against the edge and fell on one side and fluid dribbled out of the corner of his mouth. The woman with the newspaper used it to wipe his chin. I helped them lift the coffin back on the table. A woman tucked a white sheet round the lower half of his body and placed an icon on his knees. They tied his hands together with a strip of white linen and put a long white candle between them.

Meanwhile, the widow brewed coffee and put ouzo and glasses beside the coffin. Ajax peeled money from the wad that he kept in his back pocket, watched closely by the other men who counted every note. He restored the wad to his right buttock, dug into his trouser pockets and looked at me.

'Got any change?' he asked, so brusquely that I didn't dare ask why. I came up with a few ten drachma coins and held them out on my palm. Ajax took all of them and dropped them on the dead man's chest like the tip you leave on a taverna table. He bent down and kissed the icon and then the marble forehead. Thankfully, I was not expected to do this. I obeyed with alacrity when Ajax said 'Let's go'.

*B*ack along the narrow track up the side of the valley and through the thicket of oak and onto the road, the pick-up laboured under its new load. We passed more trucks coming the other way. Men sat in the cabs and women in black rode behind, holding onto the bars and peering out like calves on the way to the slaughterhouse.

'Did Thanassis really sell them to you?' I asked, picking a coffin splinter out of my palm.

'He would have if he'd been spared. Don't worry. You got a good price. So did he for where he's going.' Ajax hummed a few notes and started to sing. His voice was pleasant.

'The world is a meadow and we are its grain... and Haros the harvester gathers what's his...'

'What's that song?'

'Haros,' he said and mimed scissors with his fingers.

'Charon?'

'Charon, Haron, the same. You know, whenever I have a problem getting it up I think of old Haros asking for his fare and boum, I'm like a stallion.' He guffawed and launched into a pop song about unrequited love with many slurs and vibratos and quarter tones.

We spent the rest of the day jolting over potholed roads and along rutted dirt tracks in search of tiles. We went higher and higher into the mountains. It was like driving over a Turkish carpet. The fields were covered with an intricate pattern of closely woven red, yellow and blue flowers against a fresh green background of new grass, guarded by stripes of meandering grey stone walls and the dark green scrollwork of oleanders. The hills ahead were a mosaic of flowering shrubs and streams and midnight blue rock spangled with turquoise and cobalt. The mountain rose like a mihrab in a tapering arch of richly chased ivory to the dome of a faience blue sky. Brightly coloured birds perched among the almond and olive blossom.

Ajax pointed to a hoopoe on a telephone wire, preening its brilliant yellow plumage and flourishing its crest. He joined the fingertips of his right hand and kissed them.

'Good eating, on the spit with a little fresh cheese.' He took his hands off the wheel and pointed an imaginary gun out of the window.

'Vlam. Vlam.'

We skirted the mountain until we saw the sea on the other side. Every time we saw a little stack of tiles, Ajax tried to buy them. Sometimes he was successful, sometimes not, but each time we had an ouzo and discussed the price of meat and how many lambs and kids were available for market. I realised that our expedition was not just for my benefit. The tiles were a pretext for Ajax to sound out the supply of meat for his new chiller without driving up the price.

By early afternoon the springs of the pick-up were groaning and I had heartburn and a headache from ouzo to go with backache and the agonising rawness of my hands. We reached a tiny village at the end of a potholed road where it widened out into a square, three sides of which were formed by single-storey whitewashed houses and a small church. The fourth side was a low wall that over-looked a precipitous drop down the hillside to the turquoise sea below. In the middle of the square was an ancient Aleppo pine that shaded a few metal tables and chairs belonging to a coffee-ouzo-everything-emporium. Fixed to the trunk of the tree with wire was a large metal litter bin embossed with the words 'City of Detroit', doubtless the gift of a villager in exile, since it was unlikely that the two communities were twinned in any more formal way.

There was something else odd about the square that took me a minute or two to put my finger on. There were no other vehicles or motorbikes, no television sounds, no music. And, most obvious of all, no people.

'Where is everybody?' I asked as I got out of the Datsun.

'America,' replied Ajax.

Detroit had a good bargain for its litter bin. I spotted a man watching us from the shadow of a doorway and a woman looking out of a crack in the shutters of another house. They were old and dressed in faded black. I followed Ajax into the coffee-ouzo-everything-emporium. Despite the promise of its name, the place was bare. Blue-painted shelves reached to the ceiling, but there was little on them except dust. One wall offered nothing more than a bundle of rubber sandals tied up with string and a car exhaust pipe, another memento of Detroit perhaps.

An old man, wizened as a nut, shuffled out of the back room and eyed us suspiciously. Ajax began a long negotiation for lunch and finally persuaded him to open a tin of sardines and fry some eggs, which we ate beneath the pine tree under the gaze of hidden old eyes. The meagreness of lunch was compensated for by tumblers of tart wine to wash it down. We wolfed the food in silence and then Ajax retired to sleep it off. He sprawled across the front seat of the Datsun and his snores echoed round the square. I was too sore and bloated to sleep and sat on the wall looking down at the sea, swallowing air and burping to relieve my indigestion.

To the right the bare rock of the mountain rose steeply to its summit. A stream tumbled past the wall and into a deep gorge overhung with trees whose foliage was speckled with blue flowers too far down to identify. It was a savage, romantic scene and I peopled it with klephts, the guerrillas of the War of Independence against the Turks. Recalcitrant janissaries would have hesitated to follow the goat paths up the narrow defile to the muskets of the fierce mountain men.

My reverie was interrupted by a bent old woman wearing the traditional yellow scarf of the island, now faded to calico. She had a squint and one eye was milky white. She carried a blue supermarket bag filled with rubbish, including eggshells and a sardine tin. With an impatient flourish, she tossed it over the wall and it plummeted into the void. Dismayed, I followed its flight into the trees below, where it joined myriad other scraps of fluttering blue plastic. My klephts evaporated.

'*Deuts*?'

I said nothing. I wasn't in the mood for pleasantries. She didn't give up and treated me to the customary grilling: where do you live, do you have a wife, what work do you do, how much do you earn, what rent do you pay... She reminded me of an old custom of the Greek islands, now only a folk memory, by which old women who became a burden to their families were taken to high places and thrown off like so much rubbish. There are many peaks and precipices throughout the Aegean called 'Granny's Leap' or something similar. But she survived, detritus from the days of famine and emigration, like my old tiles.

By the time Ajax had hammered out his calculations, preening his moustaches and looking innocent, the cost of my second-hand tiles was the same as new and I still had to clean them. I spent days sitting in my yard in the sweet spring sunshine, working on a tan and brushing old mortar

and moss and spiders from the tiles with a wire brush.

New beginnings

It was a time for new beginnings. Fresh green fields were stippled with colour and every cranny in paths and walls big enough for a thimble of earth held a flower. There were rustlings and slitherings, the whip of a tail and the scuttling dart of green, as snakes and lizards came out with the flowers from the underworld. The wind was from the south, not yet tasting of desert and suffocating with ancient dust, but warm and kind. It would soon bring birds, fattened on the fruit of Africa. Men were cleaning guns and laying in tiny shot for songsters instead of the heavier stuff they used on winter game.

The face I had seen in the buddleia when I was digging out the dung was no satyr. After a few days, Dionysos plucked up the courage to come out in the open. He was the son of Haralambos, the builder's merchant. He was in his early twenties. He had his father's nose and forehead, but the rest of his face was crumpled and squashed. His body was stunted and bandy-legged. Summer and winter alike, he shambled round the village barefoot in white sailor's trousers and a hooped blue and white shirt, like a refugee from the Club Med in the north of the island. He walked with a stoop, his head on one side looking curiously at things that took his fancy.

He never spoke or made any sound. Like a sacred cow, he went where he pleased and people behaved as if he weren't there. He stood in the middle of the square for hours looking up at the sky, ignored by everyone except drivers, who made a detour round him. He wandered into people's houses and if he was in the way was shooed off or given a titbit and led by the hand to the door. You would be sitting talking at a table in the café and suddenly you noticed him standing beside you, bending down as if to listen or staring inside an empty coffee cup. The Greek word for such a person is sun-touched, attributing to the sun what we attribute to the moon.

'Born on Christmas Day,' said waxy-fingered Elpida darkly as she shovelled *keftethes* onto my plate.

'Rubbish,' retorted canny Barba Mitsos, 'he was born in January.'

'What do you know?' she snapped. 'It's Christmas in the old calendar.'

Children born at midnight on Christmas Eve are doomed to become *kalikantzari*, imps with hairy bodies and swarthy skin and the legs of an ass or a goat. They are allowed into the world for the twelve nights of Christmas, when they play tricks and make mischief. They don't like fire or black cockerels and they are not very bright. If you meet one you should give him a sieve and he will count all the holes. As they can only count up to two, it will keep him busy until daybreak, when he will have to scamper back underground.

'It's wicked to spread those stories,' said Barba Mitsos. 'No wonder the children run after him.'

I too was an oddity to the villagers, yet I felt welcome. They already gave me countless kindnesses. If ever a man lives alone, even for a day, the first question is always 'Who cooks?' All I had to do was walk into the square and invitations were pressed on the man with no woman to look after him.

I was sometimes irritated by the unrelenting inquisitiveness and criticism, but there was no shortage of help or advice or just someone to talk to if I needed it. It was hard to imagine a foreigner descending on an English community and being welcomed with such immediate acceptance and hospitality. My heart was heavy when I thought of London, where friends and neighbours are no more than fellow passengers, good manners pass for kindness and 'community' is social workers' jargon. All I had to offer in return was entertainment, something to gossip about.

After work I had a shower and joined the rest of the village in the square at one of the tables outside Yannis's café. One side of the square was formed by a big new church. It was faced with grey stone, pointed black in a crocodile-skin pattern and roofed with bright red tiles. In front of the church was a massive plane tree with marble benches, supplemented in good weather by tables and chairs from the café opposite. The official name for Yannis's establishment, stencilled in black above the door, the letters cramped a little at the end where he ran out of space, was a coffee-ouzo-everything-emporium, like the one in the deserted village.

He was licensed by the state to sell charcoal and paraffin. These present-day barbecue essentials were the main means of cooking and lighting in country areas until the 1970s and were still a state monopoly. He was also the unofficial sub-post office. The postman from Aliveri dumped the mail on a shelf beside the coffee grinder for addressees to collect at their convenience. At the same time you could riffle through the pile to see what correspondence your neighbours were getting.

On the third side of the square was officialdom. On the ground floor was the office of the President of the Village Council. His name was Eleftherios, but he was always addressed as Mister President. His day job was agricultural supplies and machinery. On the floor above was the police station. It was rarely occupied, as Sotiris, like all good policemen, hated crime, so went to great lengths to avoid it. He preferred to keep order in his vegetable garden in another village down the road, where he had married into a local family. Making the corner between him and the barber's was Haralambos's building supplies and hardware store.

On the corner between the council office and the church was the ramshackle smithy where fat little Banos laboured over his fire and his anvil, mending tools and turning rods and sheets of steel into fences and gates that he called *fer forzai*, the French for wrought iron. Summer and winter he worked in vest, shorts, sandals and nothing else. A mat of luxuriant body hair from his chin to his toe knuckles was his only protection against sparks and filings.

Ajax's butchery was on the fourth side. Next to it was a little lock-up shop where Kyria Anna sold newspapers, stamps, lottery tickets and football pools. She also had a telephone, which is why Aussie Alekos parked his big grey Opel taxi in front under the mulberry in the expectation of calls from Aliveri bus station. He was not available on Friday and Saturday evenings because he was also the barber. His shop was next door to the café and a virtual extension of it. A man could stand up from his ouzo at an outside table and take his place in the barber's chair without interrupting his conversation.

Making up the last corner was Kyria Dimitra's bakery, known as the *fourno*, the oven. Kyria Dimitra looked like a Greek goddess. Not an aristocratic goddess of classical sculpture, but an earth goddess of the prehistoric Aegean. Great hips to give birth to demigods, swollen dugs to suckle them, a big belly and colossal thighs to steer the plough, brawny arms to reap and winnow and massive hands to knead. Her two sons were on Samos defending Greece against the Turks and from the way she described them they were standing on a headland in crested helmets and sandals staring down the ancient foe. She had inherited the bakery from her father Theodoros, along with a wine vat built on the side. This was a six-metre cube filled with juice every autumn, left to ferment with resin until January and drained from a tap at the bottom for the rest of the year. Some years it was vinegar, other years it was nectar. That year it was somewhere in between.

In addition to bread and wine, Kyria Dimitra provided the communal oven. In those days you cooked on gas rings or the stone oven in the yard. Few people had electric stoves. Every morning, at about half past nine, a procession of women carried the midday meal to the *fourno* in big roasting tins or earthenware dishes, which they collected some time after noon, leaving appetising vapour trails of roasts and pies and stews criss-crossing the square.

The villagers' remaining commercial needs were provided by travelling salesmen, who hawked their wares from crackly loudspeakers on top of battered trucks and tricycle vans. Fish was a regular, as were the fruit and vegetables that the villagers did not grow themselves or were out of season, Arcadian cherries or Cretan tomatoes for example. Household goods, clothing and fabrics came through from time to time, although most people bought these in the Saturday market in Aliveri. My favourite was the honeyed seduction of the underwear salesman. I have a photo of a little gaggle of women in black dresses and yellow scarves with distaffs and spindles in their hands rummaging through nylon fabrics in a huckster's van.

In the 'little evening', half an hour either side of sunset, the square milled with any villager who could walk. We men strolled to the café in clean shirts and slicked-down hair. We sat outside, flicked worry beads and made a coffee last two hours. Women sat under the plane tree and in front of the church. Young people found errands that took them from one end of the square to the other and back again. It was not as deliberate as the systematic evening patrols in Spain and Italy but, in its disorganised Greek way, it was the same idea.

*B*efore the new church in the square was built, the little one near our house served Horio. There may have been a church or a temple for much longer than the present building. A marble column and scraps of ancient brick were built into the walls. The church had been restored and renovated many times since then. Above the front door three porcelain plates were set into the plaster showing Britain's King George and his family. Evia is predominantly socialist with a communist streak, but our village was an island of royalism, transmuted in these republican days to the right-wing New Democracy. The church's original stone slab roof had been replaced with red Ellenit. The green metal door had opaque glass panels and a wrought-iron cross clumsily welded in the middle. It squealed on its hinges and grated on the floor.

The main icon on the iconostasis, the wall that enclosed the sanctuary, was Aghios Ioannes. His beard was white, his eyes tearful and his mouth turned down like a fish's. He held a white lamb. It was a cheap reproduction, paper pasted on board and varnished. Around it was a withered garland of flowers and in front hung a shiny metal oil lamp. With him were the Blessed Virgin, St Peter and a glowering head of Christ. An old wooden lectern was the only furniture in the room.

Every evening Antigone, the daughter of genial Spiros the carpenter, came up to light the lamp in front of the altar. She was about eighteen, plump and big breasted, with a round face and streaky blonde hair. She wore jeans carefully torn at the knees, off-the-shoulder T-shirts and a new-fangled Sony

Walkman. She had been born in the house opposite ours by the light of oil lamps and washed with water fetched from the spring a hundred yards downhill. In 1964 the family were the last to move down the hill to electricity and water. Spiros now kept chickens and doves in the house.

First Antigone fed the birds. Very carefully, because of her nails, she lugged a bucket of corn and scraps to empty into a trough made of an old tyre, poured water from a jerry can into another tyre and collected eggs from inside the house, which she put into the bucket to take back down. I waved to her, but she always looked the other way.

One evening I followed her to the church. Although she left the door open I pushed it further, scraping the floor with a tooth-grinding squeal so that she wouldn't be startled. She had washed her hair. It was damp and smelt of shampoo and conditioner and tint and streaking stuff. She had probably spent all afternoon doing it while the rest of the house was asleep. She was busy with the lamp, topping the oil up from an ouzo bottle that was kept with matches and wicks on the window ledge, next to the icon. It was odd seeing someone dressed for the urban jungle at such ancient chores.

'You like pop music?' I asked in a loud voice because of the Walkman. I could hear the beat like a noisy pacemaker. She shook her head and I shouted louder. 'You – like – pop – music?'

She shifted her chewing gum from the incisors to the molars and shouted back. 'I hate it. My father makes me listen to this all day.'

She giggled and I felt stupid, but she had the courtesy to slip the headphones down round her neck. U2 echoed round the chapel. She floated on the oil a new *kandili*, a piece of pink waxed string stuck through a tiny flat cork.

I tried again, abandoning youth talk. 'This church is very old.'

'I know. Thank God they cleaned it up. It was so creepy before, all dirty and full of spiders. You couldn't see because of the old glass in the windows. And there were these old wall paintings with staring eyes. Ugh.' She exaggerated her shudder so her breasts shook.

I pointed at the icon. 'The first St John in this church didn't look like that.'

'Really?' she asked. Her eyes were a dull, cow-like brown.

'He had the head of a goat.'

'How do you know?'

'I read it in a book. Some people who came here a long time ago wrote about it.'

'They must have been dreaming. There's no saint with a goat's head.'

'Why not? There's a saint with a dog's head.'

'That's St Christopher. Everyone knows that.'

In the Orthodox Church St Christopher, patron saint of travellers, the giant who carried Jesus across the river on his shoulders, is said to have come from a North African people with dogs' heads. There are icons and carvings of him all over the Aegean, a normal-looking saint with the head of a friendly retriever. His devotees and those named after him deny any connection with the dog-headed Egyptian god Anubis.

'I suppose your parents were married here.'

'It must have been a real bore. Now there's a *kentro* in Aliveri with good music.'

The word *kentro* is untranslatable, at least by me. It means a glorified taverna where they lay on parties and receptions.

'Were you baptised here?'

'Of course. And my brother. They had a big party for him and my father fired his shotgun. When I was baptised they passed around Turkish delight. It's not fair.'

'How do you know?'

'That's what they always do.' She picked up the matches. The box was damp. Two of them smeared pink stuff down the sandpaper, but the third caught fire.

'Are you at school?' I asked. She tutted. 'What will you do now?'

'Anything as long as I don't have to live here. My brother's married. He and his wife live in Athens. They're computer programmers. My mother lives with them to look after the baby.'

'Do you want to be a computer programmer?'

'I want to be a croupier on a cruise ship, but I have to stay here and look after my father. It's so boring.' She turned and faced me. Why does chewing gum look so insolent?

The cassette finished and there was an angry hissing from the headphones. She led the way out. I went back to my tiles.

Sassy Antigone, like passengers waiting for the ferry, was rushing to leave the island and the past. What was I doing trying to recreate it? What was the point of gentrifying old buildings, old stories, old saints? I should be living for the present. I closed my eyes and heard the familiar English voice, so practical, so common sense: 'It's too late now. Get on with it.' So I got on with coating myself in terracotta dust. I wouldn't have minded one of those new Walkmans though.

Hector, scourge of the Greeks

~~~~~~~~~

One of the compensations for missing my family was not missing Hector, our dog, who had arrived about 18 months before we bought the house. One day I had woken up at dawn, hadn't been able to get back to sleep and had gone for a walk on Mount Parnis. It was a grey, drizzly morning and I should have stayed in bed. It had the same raw feeling of getting up in the dark to go away on holiday or slipping out of the house before your girlfriend's parents catch you, but without the excitement.

After an hour I reached a ridge and took a breather. Everything looked glum, from the grungy green holm oaks to the grizzling grey sky and the whine-dark Aegean. There was no sign of life, not even a flock of sheep with its ferocious, hiker-hating guard dogs. I headed back home on a tarmac road, keeping my spirits up by trying to hum *Hearts of Oak* and simultaneously whistle *The British Grenadiers*, like my father could. A useless accomplishment but a satisfying one.

On a bend, where the road widened, I came to a fly-tip. It was the usual agglomeration of fridges and stoves, old tyres, little mounds of builders' rubble and plastic bags, good for ironic photographs but otherwise an eyesore.

I heard a whimper. *In my daydreams I carry on walking.* It sounded like a baby in pain. I stopped. *In my daydreams I turn away and walk on.* I stood at the edge of the tip and listened. Nothing. *In my daydreams I shrug my shoulders.* Out of the corner of my eye I saw a blue plastic bag twitch. *In my daydreams I give it a kick.* I picked it up. The top was knotted and I tore it open.

Inside was a tiny black-and-white-and-brown puppy, his eyes barely open, trembling in the palm of my hand. He whimpered. *In my daydreams I toss him into the thorn bushes for the weasels.* I wetted the tip of my little finger on my cagoule. He licked it with his tiny soft pink tongue. Again I wetted my finger and gave him suck. *In my daydreams… if only, if only, if only…* I tucked him inside my cagoule next to my shirt. He grew still but for the beating of his tiny heart. I felt a surge of warmth like a new mother whose baby is laid on her breast, but it was only the little bastard pissing on me. I carried him home feeling like a shepherd in an ancient tale who finds an infant abandoned on the mountainside. Such stories rarely have a happy ending.

The children were thrilled. Up to now our pets had been a succession of rodents, carried off by disease, accident or neglect. Although we can't remember their names at the precise time of these events, they were sure to have been something like Fluffles or Snuggly. A tour of the headstones in our extensive pet cemetery was not so much nostalgic as nauseating. We had never had a real pet before, the kind that chases sticks and goes for walks and rides in the pram dressed in baby clothes.

Arfa was less ecstatic. 'Who's going to clean up after it? Who's going to feed it? Who's going to take it to the vet?' Rhetorical questions to which, despite fervent promises to the contrary, we all knew the answer.

'Ah, he's so sweet.'

'What's his name?'

'Muffly. Can we call him Muffly? Can we? Can we?'

'No, let's call him Snuffles.'

'He hasn't got a cold.'

'Chuddly then. Cuddly Chuddly.'

In hindsight I wish we had given him such a name. Like Spielberg calling his shark Toothy or his T. Rex Trixie. At the time I preferred something more noble, which I wouldn't be embarrassed to call out in public when we went for walks. I insisted on my rights as finder and christened the dog Hector. It was a good classical name, although not a favourite of Greeks at the font since he was the chief warrior of the Trojans. Chaucer called him the 'scourge of the Greeks', which turned out to be appropriate. But the real reason was one of the favourite nursery rhymes of my childhood:

Hector Protector was dressed all in green,
Hector Protector was sent to the Queen,
The Queen did not like him nor yet did the King,
So Hector Protector was sent back again.

This sorry tale of hope and rejection made me cry when I was little and still made me sad when I read it to the children. Calling our foundling Hector was some sort of reparation. It never occurred to me that the King and Queen might have been on to something.

The first task was to deal with the ticks and fleas. I put my clothes in the hottest wash and stood naked in the garden to dust myself down with the powder that Arfa collected from the hardware store. Then we attended to Hector. We bedded him down next to the boiler in the kitchen in an olive basket with an old cot blanket and surrounded him with sheets of newspaper. Later on he developed the knack of scraping away the paper with his paws before relieving himself and then putting back the paper. Getting to the fridge was like tiptoeing through a minefield.

He was too young to have been taken from his mother and I prepared the children for the worst. Or the best, as it would have turned out. We suckled him on goat's milk and egg yolk. He thrived. He opened his eyes and began to toddle around on rubbery legs. He grew tiny teeth and exercised them on our fingers and toes like a sweet little baby piranha.

He lay in wait behind the door and with a growl leaped out and savaged us. This was no little kitten chasing after a paper ball – he drew blood. We learned to wear proper shoes and long trousers in his company, which was an inconvenience in hot weather. He went through the children's toys like a shredder and could scatter the insides of a cushion round the room faster than you or I could plump it. Oddly enough, he never molested the white wool flokati rugs.

From the size of his feet I should have been prepared for how big our sweet little puppy would grow. But not how ugly. It was like the ugly duckling in reverse. His head grew long and thin, with close-set eyes. He carried it low as though he felt continually in disgrace, which he was. His ears were ragged and lop-sided and covered with ticks. His hair grew coarse and wiry. It was like stroking a nylon brush. His body broadened out from narrow shoulders to bony haunches and his hind legs were longer than the front, so he walked with a permanent skulk. His tail was pointed and whippy and curled over his back like a scorpion's to flaunt a puckered grey bum-hole in a nest of clingers and a glimpse of dangling *marrons glacés*. When the children dressed him in baby clothes he looked like Red Riding Hood's wolf in grandma's clothes.

He soon grew out of a collar and lead. I bought a choke chain, not that it did much good. He had a galvanised wind-pipe. I fashioned a three-handled leash so that the children could take him for walks. If fewer than three of them took him, they were dragged in the dust like Greeks behind his namesake's chariot. Although I could manage him, I only took him out at night so we would not be seen together.

Training was a challenge. He treated 'Sit' with contempt and 'Heel' as a target. Chastisement was even more diffi-cult. He growled back at verbal reprimands, snapped at the hand that tapped his nose and tore to bits the rolled-up newspaper. He recognised Arfa's status as pack leader, but his relationship with the rest of the litter was more rough than tumble as he jostled for seniority in the snapping order.

'Daaad, Hector bit me again.'

'That's not a bite, sweetheart, there's no blood. That's his way of being friendly.' This was a big mistake, as it set a precedent.

'Maam, Harry bit me.'

'I was only being friendly.'

Ugly, vicious and uncooperative, Hector was the antithesis of the family pet in all but one respect: defending our territory. Like most of the houses in the neighbourhood we had a 'Beware of the Dog' sign on the gatepost, but in our case it was no bluff. One glimpse of Hector and you had second thoughts about coming in on aesthetic grounds alone. Gardeners, tradesmen, postmen and our friends waited for the all-clear before setting foot inside. Not that their bottoms were safe even then. Foiled by the chain link fence, the dog lurked in the bushes by the gate and as soon as it was open a crack he was through. Local lads soon realised that I was a soft touch for trousers. Hardly a week went by without a stranger at the gate holding a torn pair, Sunday best usually and probably caught on a nail.

Our Greek friends advised us to chain him up like their dogs, but one of the many sources of British superciliousness towards Greeks was how badly they treated their animals and look how they keep their dogs chained up all day.

So we let him roam free in the garden.

Hector was a great hunter. He practised his skills on balls, skipping ropes, toy planes, Frisbees and visiting children. He should have been a British dog of the kind that are encouraged to savage foxes and stags and badgers and hares, to the disgust of foreigners, but he had to make do with less sporting prey. He kept the garden free of living things, including cocky crows and pigeons that were rash enough to land on his lawn. They flapped away insolently when Hector bolted from the bushes, but they reckoned without his speed. He could jump six feet and catch them on the wing in a squawk and a flurry of feathers. When he had caught them he had no interest in finishing the job, however. It was the catching not the killing that drove him. Once they were disabled with broken backs or a wing torn off, he left them to writhe and flop on the terrace.

When he got out of the garden he came back with exotic victims, a snake or a rabbit or more usually one of the neighbours' chickens. It was my job to finish them off and stick them in a garbage bag before the owners traced them.

'Must you use the children's cricket bat?'

'They haven't got a baseball bat.'

'It's not funny.'

'You think I enjoy it? I think I'm whacking the wrong animal.'

'You brought him home.'

All our discussions about Hector ended with this damning phrase. He was my problem, but I was too cowardly to face up to the responsibility. Every time he got out I was afraid that he would be run over or shot by a chicken owner or poisoned by meat laced with strychnine, which is the Athenian method of dealing with strays, a fear that was also a hope. Just as we took the children to play with friends who had chickenpox, I took Hector to visit dogs infected with calazar, an incurable wasting disease that makes them weak but docile.

Finally, I had a golden opportunity. The occasion was a sunny afternoon in March. Hector had escaped that morning and we were enjoying the opportunity of a game of French cricket without him running off with the ball or yapping and scratching at the door of the basement, where we locked him in. The first few times he ran away we scoured the neighbourhood to find him, but even if we spotted him he never came when we called and was impossible to catch. He returned in his own good time.

But he had never come back like he did that day. My first thought was that he had been discharged from orthopaedics. The lower half of his body and his legs were encased in plaster. He limped one foot at a time, each step obviously agony. His whippy tail was tucked between his legs and his head hung as low as the plaster would let it.

'Maam, Hector's been turned to stone,' shouted Harry, whose current bedtime reading was Medusa with her boar tusks and head of writhing snakes. She turned to stone anyone who looked at her and was a change from the Mister Men.

After the initial shock, we deduced what had happened.

An essential ingredient of Greek life is *asvesti*, slaked lime. It looks like plaster of Paris. You dilute it with water into the milky whitewash that makes island houses such a brilliant white. It is a disinfectant and stings the tiny feet of flies, so you use it on the walls, floors and ceilings of the kitchen and the toilet. You paint steps and thresholds so that people can see them in the dark. You paint it on tree trunks to stop insects climbing up and motorists crashing into them. You decorate the pavement so that it looks nice. Diluted to the consistency of thick cream, you add it to mortar to make it sticky and to rendering so that it clings to vertical surfaces.

Hector must have been in hot pursuit through a building site and waded into a bath of *asvesti*. It bonded with his bristly hair like fibreglass. A Plimsoll line ran neatly round his body from just under his tail to just under his neck. Above it was Hector. Below it was the petrified dog found in the ashes of Pompeii.

In addition to the incapacity, it must have been really painful. I knew from personal experience that *asvesti* stings and shrivels the skin. We tried washing it off, chipping it with a hammer and tugging at little bits with pliers, but dogs are intolerant of body waxing and in any case it would have taken us days. Much as I resented the expense, I loaded Hector into the camper and took him to the vet.

Monika Papadopoulos was from Stuttgart and had a thriving practice attending to the pedigree pets of the smart set. Nevertheless, she swallowed her pride and laid our dog down on her operating table. She selected a syringe, pushed the needle under the skin of his shoulder and emptied half the vial. Hector drifted off into a deep and peaceful sleep. I took a long breath and with a lump in my throat suggested to Monika that she put him out of his misery for good. *In my daydreams she pushes the plunger the rest of the way. Good night sweet prince and flights of doggy angels sing thee to thy rest...*

'Vy? He is a helsy animal.'

I didn't have the courage to pursue it. She got busy with scissors and a packet of Bic razors. It took her an hour. She larded Hector with foul-smelling ointment and I carried him out to the camper, still dozy. His family welcomed him home with disappointment and horror.

When he staggered to his feet he was truly grotesque. Below the Plimsoll line his greasy skin was grey and raw and blotchy and scarred, like the slimy black skin of a steamed Dover sole, as repulsive to the touch as to the eye. Without hair his legs were long and knobbly, his belly sagged and his tail was clenched so hard between his legs that he limped. He had been ugly enough to start with, but now he looked like a mutant specially bred to frighten little children. Visitors blenched at the sight of him.

In the days that followed he slunk around, cowed and resentful, looking for places to slump and slurp his tender privates. We banned him from the terrace and anywhere else we ate or drank, for no better reason than that he put us off our food.

One evening I was sitting with my feet on the balcony rails enjoying the sunset over Mount Parnis. The children were hiding somewhere from bathtime and I was enjoying the tranquillity. Out of the corner of my eye I saw Hector slink like Gollum up the steps from the garden. I didn't have the strength to send him away and pretended not to notice. He disappeared behind me and I waited for the disgusting sounds of his personal hygiene.

My hands were dangling down beside the chair, as they do when they don't have a book or a glass to hold. I felt something warm, damp and soft against the fingers of one of them. Hector was licking my hand, tentatively at first as if he feared a rebuff – which was certainly on the cards when you thought of where his tongue had been – and then with greater assurance. It took me back to that morning less than a year ago when the little pink tongue of a helpless puppy had licked the tip of my finger. Now look at him. While he carried on licking my palm, I stroked the top of his nose with my fingers and he made little grunting noises. Arfa came out of the sliding doors onto the terrace with the ouzo.

'What's the matter?' she asked.

'Nothing!' I said brightly, wiping the tears off my cheeks with the heel of my free hand.

Nevertheless, the old Hector grew back with his hair. Soon enough he was the scourge of trousers and chickens again, the bane of ball games and toys. He was an untamed force of nature from the mountains and he made suburban life intolerable. He was to meet his destiny on Evia.

On my first visit home after the tile expedition with Ajax, Arfa and I had a classic marital row. It was the one in which each side accuses the other of having the easier life: 'It's all right for you... you never think of all I have to do... look what I have to put up with... why don't you stay at home all day and look after the children... why don't you hump tiles around and haggle with Greeks all day...' When we had exhausted the predictable stuff, Arfa announced that Hector was the last straw, he was my dog and he was going with me to Evia. Otherwise she would set him free where he belonged on Mount Parnis to fend for himself. I put up token resistance, saying that I had nowhere to keep him, he would antagonise our new neighbours by biting their children and killing their chickens, he would have to stay tied up or locked in the car and so on.

'He goes or I go,' she said and that was it.

With a heavy heart and full of premonition about Hector's fate, I bought a massive chain and a collar you would have thought went out with bear-baiting mastiffs. I tied him in the back of the mini out of reach of the upholstery, but I needn't have worried about him savaging the seats on the way. He was sick all over them.

It was like taking him home. At the cemetery he leaped out of the car and stood with his nose in the air, tail quivering. While I mopped out the car, he ran this way and that on the end of his chain, revelling in sights and smells that he had surely been too young to remember when I had found him on the mountain. He dragged me up the path to the house like a bloodhound closing on a fugitive.

I tied him to the olive tree, which was not a success because he ran round and round it and throttled himself, and then to a massive iron staple cemented into the stone wall of the house just inside the basement door. This was convenient, as I could barricade him inside at night when I finished work.

There was no question of taking Hector down to the village. I had my pride. I decided to keep him hidden like an undesirable relative in a Victorian novel. It was also for his own safety. Country folk, who live and work with animals, have no compunction about shooting any that prove to be a pest. At ouzo time I shut him in with an old door and left him with a bowl of dog food. I could hear him howling from the cemetery. When I went back the next morning with a bone from Eleni to salve my conscience, he presented me with two dead rats and a half-alive one for me to finish off.

I had to admit that he was company. As I brushed my old tiles he sat on his haunches beside me, vibrant and alert. He didn't pull at the leash or whine or yap and I was beginning to feel quite well-disposed towards him. I was so far deluded not to shut him away when sun-touched Dionysos first appeared. I had watched enough Disney with the children to know that this gentle child of nature would have an affinity with animals. I imagined him taming the beast with a glance and a whisper. But as soon as Dionysos crossed the boundary of our property, Hector leaped at him with a savage snarl and he scampered back into the bushes.

I usually made sure that Hector was firmly barricaded in when stylish Barba Vasilis came by with his sheep. One fateful morning I was so engrossed in my tiles that I didn't notice him until it was too late. Hector made his usual lunge. The chain brought him up short, pop-eyed and slavering, the bark choked out of him by the massive collar.

'A fine dog,' said Barba Vasilis.

It often happens that when you look at familiar things through someone else's eyes you see them as you have never seen them before. Full of trepidation, you send your child off to tea at another house. When the other mother tells you how polite and charming and helpful your offspring has been, you assume that she has mixed yours up with someone else's or has very low standards of behaviour. Then perhaps you see your child in a new light. But not this time. To my mind Hector's appearance and behaviour were as appalling as ever. I could not begin to see what Barba Vasilis saw in him to admire.

Worse was to come. Wherever Barba Vasilis was, his sheep were not far behind. They appeared scuffling and chomping from behind the chapel just down the hill. When Hector saw them he forgot Barba Vasilis. He was transfixed. Not only his tail but his whole body quivered. He saw chickens and pigeons and trousers and footballs all lumped into one woolly mass of irresistible temptation. He shuffled backwards and half crouched. A noise between a growl and a rumble started somewhere deep in his belly.

'Heck-tor,' I said in the warning tone I used when one of the children was about to be naughty. It had as much effect. The dog launched himself towards the sheep. I closed my eyes. What a horrible way to go: garrotted or even decapitated by his chain. Fat chance. His throat held. The chain held. The iron staple held. The wall gave way and he was off, dragging a lump of mortar behind him. I ran after. It was like chasing a kite that a child has let go.

In Britain sheep-worrying is a serious offence against the law and the countryside code. Collies learn to mince round their charges without alarming them. If a slavering dog were to charge at them with a bronze bark, a clanking chain and a thumping lump of rubble, a hysterical person waving his arms and yelling not far behind, they would reasonably take flight and have their bottoms bitten. Greek sheep are made of different stuff. In the mountains ferocious dogs are on their side. They protect them from wolves and rustlers and passers-by.

Barba Vasilis's sheep did not live in the mountains, but they had dog sense in their genes. Instead of bolting, they huddled and faced Hector full on. He braked and confronted them. This had never happened to him before. He was not used to being stared down. There was something in his own genes too. It was why he spared the wool flokati rugs at home. He slunk up to the flock, sniffed and lay down with his head on his paws. The sheep went back to their chomping.

'A very fine dog,' said Barba Vasilis. 'Do you want to sell him? My brother-in-law has animals on Dirfis. His dogs all have calazar.'

It was done the next day. Yannis from Dirfis came at the end of the morning. I said I wouldn't accept payment, which he and Barba Vasilis took as another sign of foreign madness. Hector scrambled into the sheep-smelling pick-up without a backward glance. It was such a relief to get him out of our lives, but at the same time I felt a pang of regret.

In my daydreams, hiking in the mountains, I am attacked by a pack of wolves. They are about to pounce when ferocious sheepdogs appear and drive them off. The ugliest brute, their leader, lopes up to me and licks my hand...

Divine intervention

~~~~~~

One evening Spiros the carpenter came up at sunset instead of his daughter Antigone. I hoped I hadn't caused a scandal by engaging her in conversation. In Victorian times in Britain a lady was 'compromised', in other words her reputation ruined, if she was seen unchaperoned in the company of an unrelated man, and so it still was in rural Greece. If so, her father was in no hurry for a confrontation. He fed the chickens, tidied his yard, disappeared inside the house where there was much squawking and fluttering, and took his time over plodding down to the church to light the lamp.

I worked diligently on my tiles and watched out of the corner of my eye as he pulled the squeaking door shut and came up the path towards me. The slope accentuated the hollow-chested stoop that he had acquired from a lifetime bent over saws and planes. For the same reason, his muscled arms were out of proportion to the rest of his scrawny body. His unhealthy yellow face was deeply crinkled and his breath came fast and shallow. His pride was a thick walrus moustache, which, contrary to local practice, he did not dye black but left to its natural colours, a motley of greys and gingers with yellow nicotine and blue marking pencil and red cough linctus and whatever he had eaten for his last meal, all sprinkled with gold sawdust.

'Hello neighbour,' he said, casting a rheumy eye about our ruin. I relaxed. 'What do you do for water up here?'

'I don't have any. I can give you a whisky though.'

He looked puzzled, but wasn't going to look a White Horse in the mouth. I rummaged in my tool bag and brought out a bottle and a couple of taverna glasses. I poured and we toasted each other. Spiros knocked his back in one go, sucked his moustache and tried again in pidgin.

'Water. Need water. Water for building. Cement.'

In the old days women went up and down the hill to the spring with pitchers or leading donkeys loaded with skins. But in the old days they did not have to feed a voracious cement mixer. Spiros's answer was to have mains water laid on by the village. He said that I was entitled to it as I was going to live there and, since we were neighbours, offered to help me apply to the village council.

'Neighbour?' smirked Barba Vasilis the shepherd when I told him. 'They want you to lay on water so they don't have to bring it in jerry cans for their animals. Make sure you get them to pay their share of the cost.'

An afternoon meeting was arranged in the café with Eleftherios, President of the Village Council. He was a pear-shaped man grown fat with the cares of office. The only energetic parts of him were his narrow, hooded, politician's eyes, darting constantly from side to side even when the rest of his body seemed still immersed in its afternoon sleep.

Spiros was there and several others who kept animals in the ruins. Aussie Alekos the taxi driver from Melbourne, who kept rabbits further down the hill from me, appointed himself advocate and interpreter. He insisted on translating everything into garbled Strine. Once we had ordered coffee, the conversation went something like this.

President (in Greek): '*Kyrie* Johnny, I understand you want village water in the old village?'

Me (in Greek): 'Yes, please.'

Alekos (in Strine): 'Lookere myte, you wanna worder pype upper the Old Plaice?

Me (in Greek): 'That's what I said. Yes, please.'

Alekos (in Greek): 'Yes, Mr President. What are the formalities he should complete in order to effect mains water?'

President (in Greek): 'Will he have a permanent residence?'

Me (in Greek): 'Yes. We intend to live here.'

Alekos (in Strine): 'Lookere myte, this erser youse, you wanna live int awler toime?'

Me (in Greek): 'I just said yes.'

Alekos (in Greek): 'He says, President, that since he intends to live there permanently, that is to say all the year round, President, and that he understands that in the interests of public health as well as a matter of entitlement...'

So it went on. In the end it was less confusing for me to stay with English. In any case it didn't matter what I said, I was only the catalyst.

After an hour's discussion about the route the pipe would take, which to English ears sounded like a blazing row, Yannis tore a page out of his exercise book and they drafted a formal petition to the President to be typed up in his office and forwarded with the President's recommendation to the district authorities in Aliveri. These functionaries would examine it, redraft it and forward it with their own recommendation to the headquarters of the Nomos – the Department – in Halkida. I was assured that the officials dealing with such matters lived only to serve the public and wanted nothing more than to demonstrate their diligence and efficiency. Eleftherios promised that approval would be back in a trice and that by the end of the month I would be washing and showering and inviting my friends round for swimming parties. In anticipation of the good life, we parted on the best of terms.

Ten days later I went to the President's office to find out what progress had been made. He slouched in a wing chair behind a large and empty desk, bleary and unshaven, belly bursting out of the waistband of his silvery suit trousers, eyes flickering restlessly from side to side. Opposite him was an elderly farmer. I was not interrupting anything. Their only occupation seemed to be warding off the pangs of solitude by breathing in each other's cigarette smoke. The rest of the room was piled with sacks and machinery parts and half a dozen pot-bellied stoves that bore an uncanny resemblance to their distributor.

Behind the President was a map of the island with the districts luridly coloured in and a framed picture of Lord Byron. The hero posed in front of the Parthenon wearing pantaloons, a hussar's jacket and a helmet like a coal scuttle, several sizes too big for his head, adorned with a crest of what looked like chicken feathers. Taking courage from my heroic compatriot, I took a deep breath of the musty and dispirited air of bureaucracy and asked what had become of my application.

With immense effort, the President leaned forward and opened the top drawer of his desk. It was stuffed with papers. He shuffled among them, squinting in his smoke, and found my hand-written petition. He handed it back to me and said he was sorry but he was not in a position to forward it to Aliveri because my house was outside the village building zone. I was furious. Ten days! Why hadn't he told me before?

Stylish Barba Vasilis the shepherd was cynical. 'He's too idle even to ask for a bribe.'

Genial Spiros the carpenter was fatalistic. 'There's not enough pressure in the pipes to go up the hill.'

Dyspeptic Dimitris the builder was idealistic. 'Better to dig your own well.'

Dapper Nektarios the roofer was pessimistic. 'I can do nothing until you have water.'

Yannis the café owner was constructive. 'Fetch Aristotle the hydrologist.'

Canny Barba Mitsos took me to see Aristotle. A mile from the village on the road past the lake, we turned down a narrow track through fields of beans and melons to a small house of whitewashed breezeblocks and Ellenit. In front was parked a large blue Ford tractor and a water tank on wheels. Appropriately to his calling, the hydrologist was knee deep in water, slopping around in one of the ditches that criss-crossed his property as he rearranged a complicated network of blue and pink hoses. He was a jolly man with a moon face and a tatty straw hat. We began the courtship necessary to get anyone to do anything.

'I'm sorry... I'm watering... I can't stop... I have to pick beans for the market in Aliveri tomorrow... my back is hurting... I don't have my equipment... you'll have to ask my wife...'

She was bent double in an orchard of peaches and walnuts, massive bottom in the air, rooting for carrots in the dark, damp soil. Without bothering to stand up she shrieked, 'Of course he can't go, he's too busy, in any case it costs five hundred.'

I reached for my wallet, but Barba Mitsos put his hand on my arm and winked.

'His balls are full of water,' he whispered and then shouted to the woman. 'All right. We're going. Costas in Drossia will do it for two hundred.'

He was answered by a shriek from the orchard. 'All right, he can go, but he's to be back in an hour.'

With the sigh of a put-upon professional, Aristotle climbed out of the ditch and washed his rubber boots in a leak from a hose. He picked up a piece of rusty wire about a metre long and we drove back to Horio. He seemed glad to get away and joked and gossiped about wells and springs and water tables. He was curious to know if it rained much in England. When I told him it did, he rhapsodised about the exquisite melons and grapes and peaches that must grow there without watering. I saw no point in disillusioning him.

At the house, Barba Mitsos and I stood respectfully under the olive tree as Aristotle looked critically at the lie of the land. He teased the wire into a semi-circle and, with a solemn expression, moved to the far corner of the yard beside the remains of a rat-eaten mattress. He pushed his straw hat to the back of his head and stood with his eyes closed for half a minute, the wire hanging down from his hands in a curve. He opened his eyes and with a flat-footed, bow-legged gait paced up and down, covering all the ground, muttering to himself, holding his arms straight out in front of him, his eyes fixed on the wire that turned round and round in his hands. It revolved in slow circles, sped up, slowed down, stopped, started again.

He halted where the wire turned fastest, halfway between the house and the olive tree. He closed his eyes, faced the house and turned the wire four times. Then he faced the olive tree and turned it seven times.

He opened his eyes and looked at us as if he had woken up from a dream. He was no longer the jolly bumpkin. Flesh melted from his moon face, unblinking eyes sank into their sockets and his face became a ritual mask crowned with a golden halo. I had thought it all a bit of a joke, a ridiculous charade, but now my amusement evaporated.

In a solemn voice, Aristotle intoned, 'Right here… four metres down, three metres deep… not enough for a field of crops... enough for a family and a tree and a few vegetables... what more do you want?... water is never bad... always good... the water of life... always trust the water... I recommend a concrete cistern bitumen sealed... it's the blood of the earth... the water was before the earth and before the moon... you'll need a good pump... you are born in water and made in water and will rise again in water... American pumps are best, try the Briggs and Stratton... give back to the earth what is the earth's and it will reward you... village water is bad and it comes from Rodi and they are all donkeys up there... water washes the living and the dead and the in-between... I have to pick my beans before it gets dark...'

The incantation ceased and abruptly he tossed away the wire. He became jolly again. We drove him home and he invited us in for a glass of Sprite. I offered him five hundred drachmas, which he waved away and his wife took instead. On the way back to the village Barba Mitsos complained that two hundred would have done. I gave him five hundred for his own trouble.

'I hope he's right,' I said.

'Eh. Get Zenon to dig a hole with his machine. If there's water you're in luck. If it's empty you can use it as a cesspit and fill it yourself. You can't lose.'

I went in search of Zenon the excavator to dig my water hole. I also wanted him to level the mule path for vehicles, despite my guilt at being the first person to bring the internal combustion engine to our unspoiled hillside. I belonged to Friends of the Earth and Greenpeace and Save the Planet, but my principles were no match for a Datsun pick-up.

Zenon lived on the edge of the village. The house was not difficult to find. Parked in front of the door was a bright yellow digger with a large-toothed shovel at one end and a smaller-toothed bucket on the end of a hydraulic arm at the back. It was personalised with a bright red clenched fist painted on each side of the cab.

An old woman opened the door. She was doubled up as if endlessly searching for the groat that was lost. She contemplated my muddy trainers and addressed my knees, while I wondered if it would be more polite to squat or stay on my feet looking down at her hump. Zenon had gone to his sister's in Aliveri. As hopefully as astronomers who send messages to other galaxies, I left a message that the foreigner required his services.

Although I never saw her face, I got to know the bent widow well over the next few days. If I had not seen the digger parked in a slightly different place each time I called, I would have doubted the existence of the elusive Zenon.

There was nothing anyone could do until I had water and a road, so I sat in my yard with my tiles and through the scrawping of the wire brush listened to the sweet sounds of the countryside rising from the village on the crystal-clear air. Yodels and whoops of siren women, explosions of laughter and shouting, the grinding gears of the Aliveri bus, chunderings of diesel compressors, the first ten notes of *Waltzing Matilda* from Aussie Alekos's taxi, a score of radios blaring different lyrics to the same tune, different words with the same complaint of unrequited love. Over all this were blasts of *bouzouki* music and the frenzied loud-spoken hollerings of travelling merchants. From further away came the scream of warplanes and the boom of blasting at the cement quarry.

At two o'clock when people went to bed, the noise gave way to more rustic sounds, the bleating of goats and the leprous clanging of neck bells, the crowing of untimely cocks, the song of other birds, secret rustlings in the grass and leaves, gentle sounds ripped apart by the despairing bray of a donkey. At the peak of the day, around three o'clock when the sun was at its hottest, these sounds died away leaving nothing, the abyss between two heartbeats. Then the stirrings and rustlings began again. At five o'clock the voice of the village rose into the jaded air and was joined by the babble of television.

Laying down my wire brush at last, I sat in the gathering dusk under my blossoming almond tree and an Islamic moon, breathing the scent of summer flowers and mountain herbs, and wallowed in the nostalgia of ancient television programmes melting into the soft night air – *I Love Lucy*, *Bilko*, *Benny Hill*. When Perseus the Gorgon slayer strode the sky, I strode down to Yannis's for an ouzo.

A word about ouzo. It starts off, like grappa or marc or raki, as the alcohol distilled from grape skins after wine making. Then, with slight variations according to which label you read, it is distilled again with some or all of aniseed, liquorice, coriander, cloves, angelica root, mint, wintergreen, fennel, hazelnut and cinnamon. Aniseed, the main ingredient, has medical and magical properties. Like all herbal nostrums, there is something for everyone. Over the millennia it has been recommended for indigestion, sexual performance, breastfeeding, flatulence, bad breath, water retention and averting the Evil Eye. Ouzo turns cloudy when you add water because diluting the alcohol turns the aniseed oil into microscopic crystals.

Yannis stocked several brands with labels to suit every taste: the elegant 12 on a red and black background, a pretty cheerleader in a short white skirt and red top, a classical goddess, a bottle shaped like an amphora. Some of them were in boxes or wrapped in cellophane or gift-wrapped with ribbons. He kept them on the highest shelf near the ceiling, along with Amaretto and Dubonnet and Campari and other exotic brews, the equivalent of the back of the drinks cupboard at home, Eurobeverages from the duty-free that never taste the same as they did on holiday and gently ferment in the dark until they are recycled via a bottle stall or a tombola to the back of someone else's drinks cupboard.

His customers drank real ouzo from twenty-litre wicker demijohns that he decanted into half-litre jugs. There was no label, no list of ingredients, no indication of alcoholic strength. Like fancy bottled ouzo it probably turned white when you put in an ice cube or a splash of water, but how would we know? In Yannis's café it would be like putting Coke into single malt. You filled a shot glass, tossed it back, slammed the glass on the table, gasped and lunged for an olive or a bit of tomato. The finer points of tasting? Bouquet – you could smell a glass from across the table. Tongue – the blisters went in a few hours. Back of the throat – fire from your nose to your oesophagus. Palate – dead. Aftertaste – the kind of aromatic high you got from drinking bottles of traditional cough mixture before they banned it. No wonder the villagers preferred whisky when they could afford it. Nowadays more Scotch is drunk in Greece than ouzo. More ouzo is drunk in Germany than in Greece.

I was brushing the thousandth tile when the elusive Zenon finally arrived on his motorcycle, bucking and revving in a cloud of blue smoke up the rocky, pitted track, daring himself not to put his foot down for balance. The bike was East German, a Zündapp 500cc. He wore a brown leather jacket and a matching old-fashioned dispatch rider's leather helmet, strings dangling down his cheeks. He was slight and wiry and had red curly hair, which spoke of Celtic incursion into the gene pool. A Pelasgian invader? A Macedonian prince? An Irish tourist? Redheads are called children of Alexander. He gunned the engine, killed it and leaned the bike up against the olive. He stood legs apart among the ruins in his helmet and leathers like a Russian tank commander.

There were no preliminaries. 'Where do you want the hole?'

I pointed at the ground under his feet. He kicked it and frowned as if he expected it to yield to his toe as easily as it would to the blade of his digger.

'Hard. Too hard. You need a compressor. And a jack-hammer. Krak. Dynamite. Boom. In any case I can't get the machine up that track. It's too narrow. There's nowhere to turn without knocking all those ruins over. Fta. And where shall I put the dirt? I can't eat it. You can't eat it. Yach. Despite what the government says. I'd like to see them take a mouthful. They care nothing for the people. They're out for themselves. Filthy capitalist pigs. Oink.'

'Can you make the road as well while you're here?'

'Impossible. The track is all rocks. You need dirt to pack down. Vlam. Where do I get the dirt from?'

'How about the dirt you dig up from the well?'

'How am I supposed to get it down there? With a tea-spoon? I've got to do a road for the council in Kidoni and a well to dig for Aristotle…'

Everything is difficult, but nothing is impossible. I waited for Zenon to finish his rigmarole and name his price. Political conviction had not blunted his commercial instincts. His price was outrageous. However, I was proud of my improving haggling skills. It was a question of mentality rather than technique, overcoming English embarrassment about money and a fear of giving offence. I halved what he said. He stuck at his price. I split the difference between it and my first offer. He stuck at his price. I split the difference again. He stuck at his price. I agreed and we shook hands. I felt foolish and foreign and angry that he did not have the common decency to knock off just a few per cent.

He brought the excavator the next afternoon and began to dig between the stairs and the olive tree. He stood at the controls in his tank driver's hat, naked to the waist, peering through the windscreen over the top of the hydraulic arm. He shouted encouragement to the sharp metal teeth as the machine bucked and groaned and gasped blue smoke. After a metre he was through the topsoil and biting into soft, ochre rock.

I stood at the side of the pit peering for a gush of spring water, a trickle of moisture, patches of damp, but the rock remained dry. At four and a half metres, which was the limit of the machine, we gave up.

'So much for Aristotle,' I said to Barba Vasilis later as we gazed down into the hole.

'Did you believe there was water there?' he asked. 'Did you really believe?'

'No.'

'Then what are you complaining about? Believe in nothing, lose nothing,' he counselled and polished his nails on a lapel.

Sea stories

~~~~~~~~

It was warm enough to swim, not for Greeks of course but for anyone used to British beaches. Driving over the hills behind the house, from the top you can see miles along the cliffs and craggy headlands facing the open Aegean. This is a wild coast, open to deep-sea rollers, with few safe ports or beaches. In summer the Melteme from the north whips up white horses and brings cool sea breezes into bays like those around Limanaki, the little harbour, where we are going now. The dirt road winds down the mountain to the mouth of a ravine, a reedy river, a beach and a village in the middle of a wide, sheltered bay. It is a lovely place, spoiled only when we were there by us and the orange blob of our camper.

About a kilometre out to sea in the mouth of the bay is the little island of Gameela. This is an Arabic word via Turkish and means both camel and beautiful, which says something about Bedouin aesthetics. It is narrow and steep-sided and does look a bit like a sleeping camel, complete with hairy hump.

When we first came to the bay there were two dozen little stone houses along the shore. They were shaded by *tsitsifies*, jujube trees, which look like olives and thrive on salty air and brackish water. Men dragged their boats up onto the beach when they came back in the morning and mended the nets in the afternoon. They went out every night except when the moon was full and fish swam to the moonlight instead of the gas lights in the bows of their boats. Women sat outside the front doors of their houses spinning wool with distaff and spindle or working at looms in the shade inside. They did not wear the Evia yellow scarf but solid black, because of a boating disaster when a dozen children on a school picnic drowned in 1922 or because all the men were lost in the Melteme in 1895 or because in 1823 the Turks took away the women whose husbands joined the War of Independence. It depended on whom you asked.

Twice a day a bus lurched down the potholed road to take children to the school in Lepoura. Once a day when there was no full moon a truck came down for the catch. Once a month a BP diesel truck drove onto the beach to refill a communal fuel tank by the water's edge. When it got stuck in the sand, all the boats were hitched to the back and thrashed the water to foam while the truck whisked up the sand in a tug of war, which somehow gave the wheels enough traction to escape.

When we bought our house the place was beginning to be discovered by Greeks from Halkida and Athens. They were not interested in swimming or sunbathing. They thought that lying around in the sun with no clothes on was madness and swimming was for catching seafood. The main purpose of tourism, and of almost everything else in life, was to eat. To cater for them Kyria Sofia had built a concrete terrace round the jujubes in front of her house for a dozen tables and chairs. The menu was salad, chips and whatever her husband brought back in the morning. The kitchen consisted of two gas rings and a charcoal grill, on which she produced some of the finest meals we have ever eaten. She had also built an extension at the back for three simple rooms. This is where we stayed at the weekends while we were doing up the house.

Kyria Sofia provided one of my most memorable meals. It was pouring with rain, so I couldn't do anything at the house. I was out of books and didn't feel like getting sucked into an ouzo session in Yannis's café. I had exhausted the wet-weather charms of Aliveri the day before. I drove down to Limanaki, expecting no more than a morose walk along the beach before I went back to bed for the afternoon.

Walking past Kyria Sofia's taverna, I saw her through the glass doors and went to wish her good day. Her two children had just come back on the bus from school. The three of them were sitting draped in blankets in the middle of the room around a pot-bellied stove that barely took the chill off the air. She waved me over to sit down with them.

On her lap was a loaf of bread, on one side of her a plastic flagon of wine and on the other a basket with *gopes*, the cheapest and least prized of all the white fish. It was all that her husband had come home with that morning. There were just enough to make a decent meal for them, but there was no question of not sharing. She sprinkled coarse salt on the top of the iron stove and laid the fish down for a couple of minutes each side. As the Greek saying goes, 'Fish, chicken and women with the hands'. We picked the meat off with our fingers and threw the bones into the stove. I can still taste them as I write this twenty-five years later. Hunger is a good sauce and so is hospitality.

'Tell us a Fingers Bumcrusty Dad, go on, tell us...' The adventures of the hairless and sublimely fat international master criminal Jeremiah 'Fingers' Bumcrusty and his accomplice Ebenezer 'Soapy' Flannel helped to while away the interminable hours of waiting for ferries to arrive, planes to depart, destinations to be reached and above all the eternity between the ordering and serving of food in tavernas. One Friday evening we were sitting under the stars and a string of forty-watt bulbs on Kyria Sofia's terrace waiting for our kilo and a half of baby red mullet.

'I'll tell you about Kyria Sofia and the camel instead.'

'Bo-ring,' said Jack.

'There aren't any camels in Greece,' said Harry.

'Yes there are. There's that peeling one by the Corinth Canal.'

Kate was right. For many years the main attractions of the Corinth Canal were a permanently moulting camel and the excellent *souvlaki* stalls. As for the famous canal, once you've seen it you've seen it.

'This was when Kyria Sofia was a young girl. Before she opened this taverna. She couldn't make up her mind who to marry. She was a pretty girl and lots of boys wanted to marry her. One of them was Costas, but he never said very much. Sofia liked him the most but he was too shy to ask her out.'

'This is a rubbish story,' said Jim.

'No, it's good,' said Kate from across the gender divide.

'One evening in September all the men went out fishing as usual. Silent Costas fished with lines by himself. He used his father's boat.'

'Where was his father?'

'He'd been a dynamite fisherman but one day he'd held on to the dynamite too long. Anyway, after an hour or so a big storm blew up. The little boats scurried back in first, followed by the bigger ones. All except for silent Costas. The last anyone saw of him he was pulling away at the starting string of his motor. Then the mist and the spray closed in and waves piled on waves and it was every boat for itself. The storm lasted all night and through the following day. The waves came right up to where we're sitting now. The whole village watched out for Costas on the top of the cliffs over there. But all they saw was the wreckage of his boat washed up in the evening. Still the storm blew and blew and the women of the village all crowded into his house to keep his mother company and say prayers. The next morning the wind dropped, the sun came out and white horses galloped over the blue sea again. The villagers went back on the cliff and waited for the sea to give them back their boy.'

'Is that it?' asked Jack.

'Sofia spotted him first. Way out to sea. Actually she spotted what he was riding on. You know what it was?'

'How do we know? You're telling the story,' said Jack.

'Costas had been blown right out to sea by the storm. The wind howled and lightning flashed and the waves were as high as houses. His little boat could hold out no longer and was smashed in pieces by an enormous wave. Like a lot of fishermen, Costas couldn't swim. He thought he was going to drown and all he could do was pray with all his might to Our Lady and Aghios Ioannes. Just as he was going down for the last time, a camel swam past. He held tight to its hump and so he was saved.'

'Camels can't swim,' said Jim.

'Why are they called the ship of the desert then?' retorted Harry.

'Too right, Harry. Aghios Ioannes came from Egypt. It was probably the best he could do. Sofia could just see its head like the head of the Loch Ness Monster and his hump. And then she saw Costas sitting on top of the hump and waving his arms. She got in the boat that went to fetch him. His lips were all cracked and salty from riding the camel in the sea for two days, but the first thing he said was "Will you marry me?"'

'You made that up,' said Jack.

'You ask Kyria Sofia when she brings the fish. Or go and ask Costas over there.' Costas was quietly gathering up his lines in a basket and sticking the hooks in the cork rim round the edge.

'I bet he got shipwrecked on Camel Island out there,' said Jack, 'so what you said isn't true.'

'All stories are true. The truth is just tweaked a bit to make them more interesting. Look, here come the fish.'

'I bags the eyeballs,' said Jim.

I tried to get the family involved in the house. Like hunting or growing your own food, building your own house satisfies a deep instinct. I hoped that heaving rocks and earth and slates and wood with their bare hands would leave a lasting impression. The fun of heat and sweat and blisters and fatigue lasted about ten minutes.

To counterbalance the deep resentment of this primitive experience, Arfa and I introduced them to our passion for sailing. In my case it was a theoretical passion rooted in *Treasure Island* and *Captain Hornblower* and the odd bank holiday outing in rowing boats on park lakes. When I first met Arfa she told exciting tales of dinghy sailing on her exchange in Spain, luffing and jibbing in the teeth of gales and hanging over the water on a trapeze, so I deferred to her in practical navigation. I caught up with her by an afternoon's lesson in London docks soon after we were married and assumed that the essentials were unforgettable. I am tempted to say like riding a bicycle, but I have the example of Arfa who every time she mounts the saddle looks as if she has to learn all over again.

We bought a second-hand Mirror dinghy. When it came to giving her a name I lobbied for *Argos*, but the children saw this as a ploy to indoctrinate them with more classical mythology. With its maroon hull and yellow decking and angry red sails the popular vote was for *Bumboil*, but this was overruled by the Guardian of Taste in favour of *Blister*.

It was no accident that the boat had red sails and was called a Mirror. It was promoted in the early 1960s by the left-wing *Daily Mirror*, a tabloid daily with a red banner. Its mission was to bring sailing to the people. The boat came in a kit with pre-cut plywood panels, which you slotted together and joined with fibreglass tape. They said it took 120 hours to build. The fleet is now 70,000 worldwide, but there must be a lot more still lying around in garages and lofts with bits glued together the wrong way round. There was a big black M for Mirror stitched into the sail, which we told Kyria Sofia stood for Mole and she was impressed that we had a monogrammed boat.

The Mirror's revolutionary design was by Barry Bucknell, the father of British DIY and television programmes about giving your home a makeover. His shows went out live and the ceilings and wardrobes that collapsed on air were legendary. Inspired by Barry, our generation ripped out old-fashioned Victorian fireplaces and dirt-trapping plaster cornices and flowery tiles and replaced them with Contemporary. His dinghy and his pump-action screwdriver moulded our leisure pursuits as much as the Dansette record player on its spindly black legs. He died recently aged 91, but he will live on whenever I hoist the mainsail or put up a shelf. We explained all this to the children.

'Daad, when we grow up will we have our own memories or will we just have yours?'

So we shut up and hoped that their nostalgia for the Mirror would be more exciting than ours. It was certainly a memorable moment when we first lifted *Blister* off the roof of the camper onto the sands of Limanaki. I was in tears because the stern landed on my foot, Arfa was in tears because I yelled at her for dropping her end, Jack was in tears because the boom fell off the roof rack and whacked him on the head – a foretaste of things to come – Jim was in tears because Jack had punched him for laughing, Kate was in tears because she was being made to wear sailing shoes she didn't like and Harry was in tears because everyone else was. We wailed round the boat like a Viking funeral.

Sailing is an excellent family activity that teaches teamwork and fosters togetherness, according to *Dinghy Sailing for Fun*, published by the *News Chronicle*, priced at 2/6. It had been hanging around our shelves since before the decimalisation of the pound, but I saw no reason to splash out on a metric version.

'Is that what it's supposed to be?' mused Arfa when she saw the title. This should have given me a clue to her innermost feelings about the sport. The *News Chronicle*, by then defunct, was a middle-class paper that sponsored a rival boat called the Enterprise and made no mention of how to rig a plebeian Mirror. So we had to work it out for ourselves. This led to more accusations and tears as we tried various combinations of pulleys and stays.

'Kate, give me the sheet. Hey! Where are you going?'

'To get the sheet. Maam, Dad wants a sheet. Single or double, Dad?'

'Tell him we only have a picnic blanket.'

My vigorous explanation that sheets were the soft ropes that you fix to the bottom of the sail to control them certainly fostered family togetherness. With one voice they made me promise not to shout at them again or they would never get in the boat, ever.

The Mirror is more complicated than the archetypal yachts that landlubbers doodle, in that it doesn't have a long upright mast but what we mariners call a gaff rig. Trying to puzzle it out, I accused Arfa of not pulling her weight.

'Don't hide your light under a bushel, darling. Come and help.'

'It's OK, darling. You're the best at rigging boats.'

'Daad, what's a gaff?'

'A big mistake,' said Arfa, smugly.

'That's with an *e*. G-a-f-f-e.'

'Like I said, darling,' said Arfa sweetly. 'Does your ship have front-wheel steering or have you rigged it the wrong way round?'

All we had to go on from our advisers at the *Chronicle* was the definition 'Gaff: the spar on a mast, on which the head of the sail is bent.' At least this cleared up the mystery of why we seemed to have a stubby little mast and two booms.

'Daad, what does bent mean?'

'Er, the mast is in two pieces, son. So it's bent at the top. You need it a bit crooked to catch the wind.'

When I found out that bent means knotted, I didn't have the courage to confess. When they found out they had no such inhibitions, but by then my cover was blown. I got off to a bad start by my technique for getting into the boat. Launching from the beach against the prevailing onshore wind meant that I usually had to hold *Blister* until the crew got in, push it out until I was waist deep and then spring agilely over the stern. Being overweight and under-coordinated, this did not go well. In the early days we drifted back to shore with the skipper's head in the bilges and his legs waving in the air and the boat heeled over in the capsize-ho! position.

'Daad, you told us you were good at sailing.'

'The sea's different in England, son.'

Finally we got the hang of it, although I was too nervous to venture out of our sheltered bay into the rolling swells of the deep. I preferred light airs, as we sailors say. The boat didn't rock and roll around so much. The gentle slap-slap of ripples against the bow, licking round the boat with happy gurgles, lip-smacking, creaming round the stern, a few bubbles from the rudder showing we were making headway, were excitement enough. I was happy to see the dinghy bobbing around in the shallows. Unlike our orange camper, which disfigured the scenery, it wasn't a blot on the seascape. The little red triangle gave it focus, contrast, movement, a sense of scale, like a figure or a cottage in a romantic landscape.

One day we took advantage of a dead calm to picnic in the shade of the cliffs. For once Arfa came along, but it was only much later that I connected this with the weather conditions. We paddled gently over to a natural grotto. The water was Perspex clear, like looking through a diving mask. We gazed down at the lovely intestinal hues of the rocky bed five metres down, purples and greens and greys, silk-shot with darting fish and sinuous fronds of weed.

'Heave-ho my hearties, let's park and have our picnic.'

'Do you mean heave-to, Dad?' asked Jack.

'Er, that's what I said.'

'You said heave-ho.'

'Heave-ho is what you say when you pull the anchor up,' said Jim, 'It's in the *Hardy Boys*.'

'Good point. We'd better do our anchor drill.'

'Oh no, not more lessons…'

'Very important, the anchor. It's your handbrake. What if we drifted? There's nothing between us and Turkey. It's a long row back.'

While Arfa got out the sandwiches, I laid out the anchor and its coil of rope on the foredeck.

'It's vital that the end of the rope is well tied to the boat. The best place is the foot of the mast. You feel a real fool when you toss the anchor overboard and it sinks to the bottom with the rope and you sail on regardless.'

'Has that happened to you then, Dad?'

'Me? What a silly idea. Now watch.'

Tying the rope to the boat is good advice as far as it goes, but it's only half the story. The other half is tying the rope to the anchor.

'But Daad…'

'Please don't interrupt.'

'Dad wait…'

'See, firm as a rock.'

'Dad!'

'Make sure the rope's not knotted or snagged.'

'Daaaad…'

'OH FUDGE!'

I used a different word. I got into trouble for it then, so I won't repeat it now. We peered down through the ripples at the anchor plummeting to the sea bed and nestling with its chain in a cleft between two rocks. I still have souvenirs of the occasion, the scars on my knuckles where I punched the mast. When I got over the sulks, I took a mask and flippers back to the grotto. The anchor did what it was designed to do, held on to the rocks like a limpet, but I won in the end. My ears were popping for a week.

Bringing back Arcadia

apper Nektarios and his mate lanky Adonis drove up my new dirt road in a Mitsubishi pick-up to start work on the roof. Adonis was in his thirties. He was blonde and tall and thin and had a lazy, shy smile. Although he looked more like a tubercular poet or an artist, there was great strength in his slender body. Every evening he sat in the café and quietly drank away his wages in Amstel.

The pair enjoyed demolishing what remained of the old roof. The stone slabs were kept in place by their own weight without nails or other fixings. The two men sat astride the ridge and, with warning whoops, dislodged them so that they slid to the ground and cracked in pieces. After a dozen slabs had smashed, I interrupted them on the pretext of a morning whisky. When they came down I explained that I wanted to use the stone for the floor downstairs and a terrace outside. They gave me the look I had come to know so well in the last few weeks, the same one they gave sun-touched Dionysos.

'You know how long it would take to hand them down one by one? We don't have time to waste. We'd need a crane.'

'They didn't have cranes when they built the house.'

'How do you know? Were you there?'

'I read it in a book.'

'Bah, books.'

We argued, all three of us talking at once and waving hands and slapping thighs and turning on heels. When I first came to Greece and saw these violent displays of vituperation, I expected weapons to be drawn and blood on the street. Coming from England it seemed so distasteful. Now I was used to it I enjoyed the crude rhetoric and the adrenalin it produced, although I always came off worst. Like haggling, it has to be learned at a mother's knee.

The argument was reaching a crescendo when I realised that we were knee deep in sheep. Barba Vasilis stood watching us, leaning on his stick and gently teasing his trim moustache. He took advantage of a lull in the shouting.

'These stones are worth something. I know a man in Aliveri who buys them for fifty each. You're throwing good money away.'

Enlightenment spread over their faces. We agreed on a small bonus for each slab they stacked unbroken. When they were out of earshot up on the roof again, I give Vasilis his morning tot and asked if there really was a man in Aliveri.

'You speak Greek but you don't know our mentality. Who would want these old stones? They are Titans who built these houses. They had no engines. They used bone and muscle. We degenerates, who take pride in our superiority, can't understand that. There's no strength any more and no passion. Bah. This is the cementolithic age.'

He downed his drink, summoned his flock and ambled away up the path into the hills.

By the end of the next day the house was roofless. I was dismayed by the broken slabs lying heaped about the walls, blackened ceiling reeds in a spiky heap and cemented together with gigantic papery wasps' nests, beams honeycombed with woodworm and piled like old bones. The warm, dark rooms were open to the sky. Rubble covered the basement floor. The house looked shrunken and pathetic and exposed for what it was, a pile of old stones and a few wormy beams.

Barba Mitsos the melon farmer said that in the old days such a house took four masons and two labourers ten days to build, sixty man-days. In the two hundred years since it was built our house had withstood storms and earthquakes and the more patient enemies of rain and insects. In one day I could push over the walls single-handed and nothing would remain except a rocky field. The house had been a promise, a link with something that I only vaguely understood, and now there was no more than rubble.

I could see Ajax's house from mine. At the back was a slaughtering yard and a holding pen for condemned animals. At the side he kept a lawn, a little piece of Düsseldorf, where it could be seen from the narrow road that ran down the side of his property. He put a white plastic fence around it to keep out goats and children. Once a week he got out an electric mower and made it stripy. It was the first lawn in the village. Lawns were a recent innovation in the countryside, where using land for anything but food was a waste. The Greeks use the French word, *gazon*.

In the morning Eleni shook rugs and bedding over the balcony. Then she came out with food for the chickens and washing for the line. In the evening she milked the goat and picked vegetables and watered the fruit trees and the *gazon*.

As the weather got warmer domestic life moved out onto the balcony. At the end of siesta Ajax scuffed out in slippers, trousers unbuttoned, idly scratching himself through his vest, and sat down at a white plastic table where Eleni served him coffee. Then he went back to the shop or sat in the café or drove off in his red Mercedes. On the rare occasions that he ate dinner at home, he brought the television outside and watched it while she served him. More often than not he left her to watch it alone. I could see her face in the green glow of the screen. Moths, snatched in the light, flashed round her head like fireflies.

Every day I watched their self-absorbed activities as you watch a hill of ants, knowing their purpose but ignorant of their reasons. In one of my ramshackle conversations with Barba Vasilis, he mentioned his niece.

'May she live for you,' I said, leaning on my shovel and grateful for the rest. 'Ajax is a lucky man.'

It came out less like 'lucky' than 'stuck up on the wall', but Vasilis was developing the necessary linguistic gymnastics and got the drift.

'Eh, she was on the shelf. She was twenty before she let us marry her. None of the men were any good for her. She had fancy ideas about going abroad.'

The thought of beautiful Eleni disposed of like a chattel was shameful but titillating. 'Where did she want to go?'

'Athens,' said Vasilis and spat on the ground as if he had said Gomorrah or Ankara or some other ungodly place. 'My wife's niece had a beauty shop there.'

'Did she go?'

'Bah. The business went bankrupt. You should see my wife's niece. Ugly as a goat. What an advertisement.'

'So you married her to Ajax the butcher.'

'He lived in Düsseldorf. He left the village to work for his cousin. They're all butchers in that family.'

'So how did Eleni marry him?'

'After fifteen years in Düsseldorf he came back to the village to marry. Eleni jumped at him so she could get away to Germany. It was a big wedding. Fifteen hundred people. There was food for everyone. Mind you, his father was the butcher so it was easy for him.'

'When did they come back from Germany?'

'They never went. The day after the wedding his father died. Ajax took over the shop with his bride and his Mercedes and his big ideas and his fancy cuts. We ate Wienerschnitzel for a month before we got tired of it. Six months later she had the twins.'

'May they live for you.'

'Thank you.'

'Other children?'

'He won't have any more. Two's enough these days. That's the end of it, thank God.'

'Thank God,' I repeated piously.

That was the end of it. Poor Eleni. I wondered what she thought of us moving into a place she was probably desperate to get away from. Eventually I had the chance to find out.

Waxy-fingered Elpida sent me to buy meat. She was weaning me off *keftethes*, which are round meat balls, and on to *soutsoukakia*, which are oval meat balls. Eleni was sitting behind the counter wistfully chewing the end of a pencil over a magazine of logic problems. When I came in she jumped to her feet and slipped the magazine under the counter like a guilty secret.

'A kilo of mince please.'

For once kilo came out right and nothing to do with chemistry or sleep or bellies or ruptures or any of the other words like kilo that usually complicated my shopping. Without a trace of puzzlement, she opened the door of the new chill room that my money had paid for. It was empty, the bright metal walls dulled with a thin coating of frost. Meat hooks hung from racks in the ceiling. I am not sentimental about eating animals, but I shivered at the sight of the waiting, empty room.

A breath of cold air followed Eleni as she returned. She dumped a hunk of marbled red meat on the counter and sliced off lumps with a long, thin-bladed knife. She switched on the mincer and fed chunks of meat into the funnel, tamping them down with a brass pestle. The bottom of the machine excreted long pink worms onto a stack of greaseproof paper.

'How can you live up there? There's no electricity.'

'We like the simple life.'

'Do you have a simple life in London? Tell me how you live.'

Where do you start? She had never been further than Athens. I conjured up an afternoon in Tesco's and she marvelled at the enormous trolleys and the length of the aisles and the fifteen varieties of everything. I loved watching her eyebrows and the corner of her mouth twitch as she tried to remain unimpressed by these wonders.

A couple of days later I offered to buy the braising steak that Elpida was going to turn into *stifado* with the help of the year's first crop of little onions. This time I took Eleni with me on the underground and double-decker buses. I described the weather, how it hardly snowed and rained less than people imagined but how it was grey and chilly most of the year.

Over the days that followed she was entranced by the English countryside, vast bright yellow and green fields, unalleviated by hedge or pond or tree, in which extraneous flowers and weeds and birds and animals had been eradicated by chemicals. She could not picture a countryside without farmyards, where all the cows and chickens were locked away in sheds, and she thought I was joking when I described country villages where a loaf of bread was made in the city fifty kilometres away and beans came from Africa and churches and pubs were abandoned.

Her fascination with all this was nothing compared with her amazement when I described the way we lived. She could not understand why it was rude to ask personal questions, for example about what people earned or spent or paid for their houses. I tried to explain privacy, but it was impossible. It wasn't that she didn't understand the concept, she thought it was an aberration. She didn't understand why you went to strangers in a bank if you wanted money for a house or a car. What was your family for? The idea that tax evasion and otherwise cheating the government were looked down on she found peculiar, considering that politicians were thieves and liars and that the aim of government was to steal from one lot of people and give to another. She pitied people who lived alone, single-parent families, children growing up without their father or with someone else's, old people looked after by strangers instead of their children. She was shocked that we burned our dead, gave names to children without baptism, were married by a civil servant. She envied girls who married whom they liked and without a dowry.

'Po-po-po,' she said after every revelation. The romance of Tesco's and the Bakerloo line rubbed off on me. I was an alien with news of foreign parts. I liked the way Eleni looked at me with curiosity and compassion, abhorrence and excitement. One morning, I plucked up courage to ask what people thought of us.

'When you first came to the village we were disappointed. You are not how we imagine Europeans. You want to live like a *vlach* up there and you dress like a labourer and you drive a cheap old car. But we see now you are European. You are alone in the world. You do what pleases you. We want to be European but not like that. *Ti na kanoume?* What can we do?'

I needed five hundred reeds for the ceiling. Barba Vasilis inspected his long little fingernail and said that his sister Athina had the best reeds on the island. She lived in a small, low concrete and Ellenit house by Lake Dystos.

I found her in an overgrown garden whacking a bramble bush with a machete. She was a plump little woman in her sixties who flouted convention by wearing bright flowery dresses and pink velvet slippers with pompoms instead of black. In those days most women over the age of forty were in mourning for somebody. Her head sprouted green curlers and was shrouded in a mist of tiny, silent insects. She ignored them, but I swatted and slapped at mine. We went through the usual preliminaries.

'*Deuts?*'

I fell into the trap of shaking my head when I should have nodded my head backwards with a disdainful tut. So she repeated the question in a louder voice. '*Sind Sie Deuts?*'

'*Nein. Englesos.*'

'Ah. Thatser.'

In those days they said 'Ah, Thatcher' or 'Ah, Benny Hill'. These days they say 'Ah, Beckham' or 'Ah, Mister Bean'.

I pronounced the speech I had rehearsed about the reeds and asked how much. She hesitated, so I expected a ridiculous foreigner's price, which I would have to beat down. I was not disappointed. She held up a chubby finger with a sweet, innocent smile.

'One drachma? Each?' I spread my arms and tilted my head back and treated her to a histrionic tut.

'Alright, two for one drachma,' she said.

'OK. OK. Right. It's a deal.'

I could have kissed her. I had finally haggled someone down. I looked round for a neat pile of golden reeds.

'Where are they?'

'Over there.'

She waved her machete dangerously close to my stomach towards the reeds crowding her garden wall like extras from *The Day of the Triffids*.

'What do you want for that price? You have to cut them yourself. Are you afraid of water snakes?'

I forced myself not to run away as she went into the house to fetch a pruning knife and a pair of long rubber boots. They were several sizes too small and my heels would not go in, but I hobbled in them anyway for fear of snakes.

'Just make a noise and they'll go away,' she advised.

You could hear me singing and splashing all over the island as I started chopping at the reeds. The ones on drier ground near the house were too thin. The good stuff was in the marsh. I laboured and sweated as the sun rose higher in the clear blue sky. I could have done with gloves. The cane was covered in a green, feathery husk as sharp as razors. Hands cut by the reeds, feet sucking in the black mud, crippled by the boots, fearful of quicksand and snakes, I edged closer and closer through the stench of rotting vegetation and marsh gas towards the ancient city of Dystos on its conical island. Water rats and birds scuttled away and clouds of insects condensed around my head. Exhausted, aching, crippled, blistered and covered in bites, this was not how I imagined having a Greek island dwelling would be. I finally hacked the five hundredth reed and added it to the pile to lug back up to Athina's house.

Lunch was waiting on the veranda along with Athina's husband, Pericles. I can't describe him because I can't remember anything about him. Rare among Greeks, he was quiet and unobtrusive. It must have been a precious gift for ambushing duck or netting warblers or stalking eel with a trident or fishing frogs with a bit of raw meat on the hook. We ate the fruits of his labour. Little lake birds stewed in lemon sauce, bigger birds stuffed with cheese and roasted, deep-fried frogs' legs tasting like squid, chunks of shallow fried eel in lemon, a poached carp, peppery watercress, waterweed blanched and oiled... A sea eagle perched on a telephone pole to watch us for a while and then took off to find his own dinner.

I paid Athina for the reeds and lashed them in bundles on the roof of the car. My knots have never progressed beyond the granny and the reef, so half of them ended up slung over the sides and trailing on the road. Like Birnam Wood I crawled back to the house, peering through the fronds and swatting away little creatures that lived in them and had decided that the inside of the car was a nicer place.

'How much did you give her?' snorted Vasilis. 'But they don't belong to her. They don't belong to anyone. They are free to everybody. Bah. Athina was always crafty.'

So much for my haggling skills. Far from beating her price down, I'd beaten it up from nothing. But she'd given me an excellent lunch.

I had to strip the reeds, so I bought a pruning knife and

sat in a growing pile of reed husks, wondering how to get Nektarios to finish the roof. I had given him a third of the price as a deposit and he was in no hurry to finish. Like contractors everywhere, he had several jobs on the go at once. The best way to persuade him to start was to get up early and lie in wait at the café where he came for breakfast coffee and aspirin. This worked unless other suitors were competing for his favours, in which case I brought out the Scottish seducer and corrected his coffee, as the Italians say.

Anyone uninterested in the restoration of island roofs might want to skip the next couple of paragraphs. While I find this sort of thing fascinating, I can see that it could be boring.

While I finished stripping the reeds, Nektarios and Adonis built a rough scaffold around the top of the walls by poking timbers into holes in the wall that the original builders had left and nailing old floorboards over them. Meanwhile I negotiated with Aristotle the diviner for the hire of his water tank on wheels. Nektarios needed water for concrete, which he laid on top of the walls to stop water getting in and for the beams to rest on. When the concrete was set and the shuttering removed, he laid down three massive chestnut joists that spanned the house and were notched into the concrete. They formed the base of three equilateral triangles made up with a pair of rafters each.

The rafters were joined at the top by a sort of keystone made by a timber that hung vertically downwards almost to the horizontal joists. This allowed the rafters some play under the heavy weight of the roof. The tops of the triangles were connected by a ridge beam running lengthways. Parallel to the ridge were four rows of chestnut battens that also connected the rafters. The roof was hipped at the end, meaning that it sloped down to the short sides as well as the long sides of the house, so that long rafters stretched from the ends of the ridge to the corners of the walls and were connected by battens.

At the end of each day I painted the wood with preservative using a long-handled brush, trying not to look down from Nektarios's rickety scaffolding. Then they took four days to lay the reeds across the battens, fixing them with laths nailed into the rafters. When they finished in the evening I crawled over the reeds, straightening them and painting them with preservative as well. My hands were full of splinters and dripped blood. When we finished it looked like a Club Med hut, but there was a sense of habitable space inside, cool and light and enclosed. It had become a house again.

Then they began work on the tiling. They manhandled onto the scaffold long pieces of stone, which Nektarios trimmed with a mason's hammer and laid along the top of the wall for the soffits. At the end facing uphill he built the chimney. He wanted to use brick but, after an arm-waving argument, agreed to use stone. He was fussy about the mortar for the tiles. He said that the more cement you have in the mix, the more it expands and contracts with changes in the temperature and so loosens the tiles. He used an orange-pink sand to blend in with the terracotta. Adonis mixed it while I handed up the tiles on an improvised hod. First Nektarios spread mortar over the reeds and put down the bottom layer of tiles on their backs and overlapping end to end. Then he put the top layer face down on them and sealed the join with a dollop of mortar. He finished tiling at sunset on the second day.

After more than twenty years, we still sit outside and admire the roof as the sun goes down. The natural unevenness of the beams and reeds gently distorts all the straight lines. The curve as the pitch flattens out towards the eaves is deliciously sensual. It doesn't squat heavy on the walls like a stone roof but strains to lift off, airy and buoyant, taking the rest of the house with it like a balloon. The colours are exquisite, a palette of reds and yellows and pinks that reflect the moods of the day, fresh light pink in the dawn, ruddy and strong at midday, ochre and subdued in the afternoon, ripe and luscious in the evening. In the setting sun they glow with their own inner light like iron in a furnace.

You can see the roof clearly from the road to Aliveri, a warm and natural red against the dark green hills. Inside is just as beautiful. The chestnut beams gleam a rich brown in an intricate geometric pattern. The pale yellow ceiling behind them is smooth and warm and textured. We love our roof.

I was so happy that I gave Nektarios a whole bottle of Old McSporran. He was very touched and opened it right away. The three of us sat on the steps of the chapel and watched Spiros's white doves wheeling over the new roof. Nektarios held up the amber liquid to the setting sun.

'Oh mama,' he said, suddenly moved. 'My father and all my brothers were drunkards and wastrels and my dying mother made me promise on the hair of her head never to drink wine or ouzo or brandy or beer. Thank God she died before she heard of whisky. Oh my little sparrow, she used to say, remember the story. The God Dionysos came out of the east and showed the farmer Nimichos how to make wine. He planted his wand in the ground and touched it and it sprouted leaves. That was the first vine. Then he said "Nimichos, fetch me a lion and an ass and a pig." Nimichos caught a lion on Pendeli and brought the other animals from his stable. Dionysos told him to cut the lion's throat and pour the blood on the vine. Nimichos did this and Dionysos told him to cut the throat of the ass too and pour the blood on the vine. Nimichos did this too and Dionysos told him to cut the throat of the pig and pour its blood on the vine. That is why when you drink wine you become first like a lion and then like an ass and then like a pig. Stick to whisky, my friend, and you'll stay a randy old goat.' He cackled with laughter and picked a flower where it grew in a crack in the steps and stuck it behind his ear.

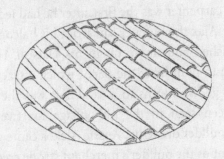

Rites and rituals

Our beautiful new roof glowing in the setting sun acted like a beacon. By the time Nektarios the roofer had finished his story, which is at least three thousand years old, men were gathering for an informal topping-out. In England if you put up a fence or add on a garage the neighbours pretend not to notice. They twitch the curtains or take a quick sideways look as they walk past. But in Greece they come round and tell you what you are doing wrong the moment the first sod is turned. And when it is finished they come and wish you health and good luck.

Spiros the carpenter was the first, after he had fed his doves and chickens. Ajax the butcher saw from his balcony that the roof was finished and drove up in his Datsun. He left the headlights on to illuminate the party, which attracted others from the village like moths to a candle. It was the first time lights had been seen in the old village for twenty years. Dimitris the builder drove up. Aussie Alekos came with a taxi load. Haralambos the builder's merchant strode erect over the fields. I caught a glimpse of sun-touched Dionysos hovering in the background.

In the dying light of day they walked round the house and inspected the work and reminisced about the stick they had taken in the nearby houses. I had three glasses, Alekos found a couple in the church and Spiros went into his old house for some chipped cups, so with my last two bottles of Old McSporran and a cheese that Ajax produced and a bucket of olives that had been lurking in a pick-up, we had the makings of a party. Ajax turned up the Datsun's radio and left the door open in case we were disturbed by the noises of the night.

'Why do you want to live on your own in a stable?' asked Nikos, the bus driver whose snorting blue Volvo plied between Limanaki and Aliveri twice a day in a cloud of dust and black diesel.

'He likes things the old way,' said Ajax.

'That's because he never knew them. If he'd lived in the old days he wouldn't want them back.'

'Ten people in one room and the donkey in bad weather.'

'No medicine, no schools, no electric…'

'Tell them what you got up to in the old days, Barba Fedon,' said Nikos and we turned to an old man sitting on an upturned bucket in the shadow of the olive tree.

Barba Fedon was well into his eighties and looked as if he had always been little and wasted and not simply shrunk by old age. He did not take advantage of the licence for shabbiness given to the old. His chalk-white death's head was topped with a chestnut-dyed comb-over and he was always carefully shaved and perfumed and dressed in a black leather jacket and pressed grey trousers and patent leather shoes. He was one of a quartet of regulars in the café who shared a copper kilo pot of wine and half a kilo of feta for breakfast before the rest of us had finished the first coffee of the day. Sometimes they stayed there until it was time for the afternoon sleep, dealing with copper pot after copper pot, while they played cards or *tavli*. I had never seen him with anyone who might have been a relative, even on Sundays or holidays.

I occasionally saw him going slowly but purposefully up the mountain on his donkey and coming back with a bulging plastic bag or a stick of wood or a scrap of rusty wire. Our relationship had got off to a bad start when he stopped to watch me levelling the earth outside the back door for a terrace. He asked me what I was doing and I said that I would like to plant vegetables but I didn't have the time. Unfortunately the word for vegetables and the word for sausages are confusingly similar and he thought that I was making fun of him. Since then his bright rheumy eyes flickered over my yard like an old magpie's and we exchanged 'good evenings', but he did not stop to talk.

'Come on, Fedon, tell us about the old days,' said several men, laughing and glancing at each other. Barba Fedon obviously had a party piece.

He cleared his throat and worked his lips and started his story. My Greek wasn't up to understanding all of it and I had to piece it together afterwards from Ajax and Vasilis and Mitsos. You have to imagine for yourself the men's guffaws, *bouzouki* music from Ajax's car, cries of owls, moths in the headlight beams, bats above our heads, the enticing glug-glug of a bottle and Barba Fedon's thin but vigorous voice wafting out of the darkness on a breath of cologne.

'Ah, the old times. You all think of the hunger and the sickness and the wars. Me, I think of the people and how we were and what we did. When I was a boy old women muttered over bird bones and red flannel and mothers fiddled with amulets and charms against the evil eye and girls played with grains of wheat and pomegranate seeds and buried them and wept and didn't wash and ran round in the full moon and bathed in dew and all that. The men were the same. We carved crosses and signs on our tools and saddles and guns and played with little leather bags of bones and God knows what. The eighth of January is St Domenica's day. The saint of midwives. It was a cold day and dull and there was snow on the ground. The men always stayed indoors on that day while the women went out to have fun on their own. But I said I was going to hunt hare on the mountain.'

'Ah, winter hare. On the spit.'

'Bah. In the oven.'

'With garlic purée. Has to have garlic purée.'

'*Op-pa*. Let Barba Fedon get on with his story.'

'I put on my greatcoat and my cap with the earflaps and the gun and a few cartridges I begged from my father and kissed my mother and left at dawn. But when I got to the edge of the woods, just up there, I hid my coat and my gun and crept down to old Dimitris's olive mill on the main road that Spiros now has for his woodwork. It was just a big shed with the press at one end and we used to have it for parties in the winter before they built the *kentro*.'

'We know all that.'

'Give the old boy a drink.'

'It was all locked up, but I knew there was a trapdoor at the back for the belt drive to the press from the old engine they had. I was always a skinny lad and I wriggled through that hole like a rat. I was scared, I tell you. A bird fluttered in the rafters and I nearly died. At one end of the shed was a platform with a chair draped in a white sheet. At the other were trestle tables. In one corner were empty wine barrels I had helped my father unload a few days before. I opened the nearest and threw in a bale of straw to sit on. I turned it round so the bung hole in the middle faced outwards and got inside. It soon got warm I tell you, even though I left the lid open a crack. The fumes made me drowsy. Only the straw pricking my bum kept me awake. My neck and my back were getting stiff and I decided to give up the whole stupid idea and get my gun and go up the mountain when the women came in. Five more minutes and I would have been off to chase hare and women the rest of my life.'

'Get to the good bit, Fedon.'

'Let him tell his story.'

'So in came all the women of the village except those too old or too young to bear children. There were about fifty of them. Some wore the old costumes and others Sunday best and they all wore yellow scarves. I saw two of my aunts and lots of cousins and my mother. And I saw Persephone, the priest's daughter, with two of her friends. She was fifteen and older than me, but I was in love with her. These three were quiet and shy while the other women giggled and chattered so I guessed it was their first time. They bolted the door and lit a stove and some oil lamps, which made my barrel even stuffier.

'Then there was a loud hammering on the door. Everyone went quiet. Four old women came in hobbling on their corns. Behind them came Thea Katina, Aunt Katina, the midwife. She was short and fat and had brawny arms for pulling babies out. She sat down on the chair on the platform and the women lined up to give her presents. A woman who had just had twins put a woollen shawl round her shoulders. They put a wreath of garlic and onion on her head and a string of dried figs and carobs round her neck. She ended up with a big onion in one hand and a giant leek in the other, a basin of water at her feet, a new pair of scissors, a knife, a fancy jug and bowl, embroidered towels and bars of soap that cost a lot in the old days. They all came up to kiss her hand. Persephone and her friends were the last.

'"My dears," said Thea Katina, "this is your first Domenica's day. A woman's lot is pain, pain from men and pain from children. Be a brave child of Domenica. Now kiss." They had to kneel down and kiss the vegetables. While this was going on they sang a carol about an angel coming down from heaven to help with the birth of Christ. I thought it was all ridiculous and I was uncomfortable and dizzy cooped up in my barrel.'

'We're going to sleep too, Barba Fedon.'

'Go and watch television if you don't want to listen.'

'They dragged out the tables and benches and laid out the food. Thea Katina was put on her throne at one end. Persephone and her two friends ran round the tables with jugs of wine they refilled from a barrel near mine. I have never seen women drink so much, not at weddings or Easter. They talked louder and louder and laughed a lot and started singing. First it was the songs they always sang when they were working and then the rude songs the men sang when they thought the women could not hear and then songs much worse than the men's, which I had never heard before. They made my ears burn, I can tell you. In between the songs they told dirty stories about the village men. My mother said my father had flippy-floppy balls like a ram on a spit and massaged them with olive oil.'

'I prefer butter, what about you?'

'Massage myself? Never. I get someone to do it for me.'

'Then they started to dance. There wasn't any music, because playing was man's work then, so they beat time on anything they could find. One of them thumped the top of my barrel and I nearly shat myself. By now it was really hot and they all shone with sweat and unpinned their hair and undid their bodices and corsets and waistbands. They put two poles under Thea Katina's chair and carried her round the room and she sprinkled them with water from her

~~~~~

basin. They sang faster and faster until they were jogging round the room and singing nonsense. All at once they stopped and heaved the chair up towards the roof. Thea Katina reached up and scrabbled round the beam. With a great shout she brought down something long and fat and showed it round like a holy relic on a saint's day. When I saw what it was I had to stuff my fingers in my mouth. It was a sausage. A metre-long sausage.

'The women didn't laugh. They stopped yelling and chanting and cheered instead. They put Thea Katina down in the middle of the floor. She put the sausage in her lap with the end sticking out over her knees. She called in a low voice "come women come" and they all crowded up like they do at church for the bread and tore off chunks of it and ate them.'

'I hope Eleni's not got salami tonight.'

'If not you'll give her some, will you?'

'I tell you, it was bad enough during the songs and dancing, but now I couldn't help it. I exploded like a ripe melon. I sent the lid of the barrel flying through the air. The singing stopped. Those eyes, how shall I ever forget them? They stared like basilisks at my poor head sticking out of the barrel. They tipped it over and dragged me by the hair in front of Thea Katina. I was too dumbstruck to say anything. She looked down on me like Christ in the cupola. "A man," she said in this terrible voice.'

For all the times he must have told this story, Fedon's voice was shaking.

'Go on. What happened then?'

'He never tells us.'

'But I'll tell you what was the worst. It was their cries like the baying of hounds.'

Fedon stood up from his bucket and stepped into the light. His eyes were moist, but whether from tears or laughter or the rheuminess of age I couldn't say. He smoothed down his comb-over and without saying goodbye he picked his way carefully through us to the path and down past the chapel. The rest drained their glasses and queued up to shake my hand and wish me *kalo risiko* before getting in their cars. I stayed to enjoy my roof in the starlight and watch the constellations trace ancient tales across the sky.

Thanassis, who sold me tiles, was my first dead body. Now I was invited to my first death. The host was stylish Barba Vasilis's father, Barba Petros, the oldest man in the village. They said he was a hundred but nobody was sure. In addition to his great age he was famous for introducing cigarettes to the village. Before then, everyone smoked the hookah.

'In his day he was a giant,' said Barba Vasilis. 'He could lift a rock that size with one hand and toss it on top of a wall like half a brick.' He tapped a boulder in front of him with his stick. 'Eh, the wood we ate. One whack and you felt you'd had a hiding. That was after he came back. Before we were born he went away to build the Panama Canal.'

He made it sound as if Barba Petros had cut the trench single-handed like some modern Hercules or the logger who stirred his coffee with his thumb.

'That was before the First War. The French came round the islands in a steamer collecting men. My father signed up. He had no idea where Panama was. He had never been off the island before. He told my mother there was digging to be done and he'd be back at the end of the month. He was away three years. They sailed round the islands picking up men and took them to Marseilles. That's where he learned to smoke cigarettes.' He said this as if Barba Petros had taken a course with exams and a certificate.

'They were collecting men from all over Europe. My father told us stories about the fights they had with the Sicilians. From Marseilles they went to Panama and he stayed until the work was finished. He came back with enough money to build a house, but he never told anyone where the rest went. And of course he came back with the cigarettes. He taught everyone to roll them [again I thought of classes in the schoolroom] but it was Yannis's father who made a profit from the idea and sold the tobacco and the papers. We used to have the Turkish pipe, but you had to be sitting down for that.'

Cigarettes are such an integral part of the Mediterranean diet that it is hard to imagine a time when people did not smoke them. Here I should make a distinction between the Mediterranean Diet, which is an invention of Californian hypochondriacs, and the Mediterranean diet, which keeps Mediterraneans alive into their nineties. The real Mediterranean diet consists of a cup of strong black coffee in the morning, a quarter pound of cheese and a couple of beers for elevenses, stews or a fry-up for lunch with eggs and chips and cheese, more meat and cheese at night and the odd cheese pie during the day when you feel peckish. Plenty of salad but also plenty of fried vegetables, a litre or so of wine, a few beers and a couple of ouzos along with whisky when you can get it. And don't forget a couple of packs of cigarettes a day.

'Every day of his life he had half a kilo of wine and a chunk of cheese for his breakfast. Now he doesn't have the cheese. Eh, soon he won't have the wine. You should come down and see him before he goes. They say it will be tomorrow or the next day.'

The next day at lunchtime I paid my respects to the local hero. A tiny old woman opened the door and without a query ushered me into a front room stuffed with heavy dark furniture. Barba Petros lay propped up on a large brass bed in the middle of the room, diffusing an aura of sweetness and stale urine. The shutters were closed and he was illuminated by a single bare bulb of modest wattage above the bed. The walls had gilt-framed pictures of heroes of the War of Independence, posturing with swords and muskets in tasselled caps and fustanellas.

I had come not a moment too soon. I abandoned hopes of hearing about the Panama Canal. Petros lay with his head back and his eyes closed and his mouth half open. His breath came in hoarse, irregular gasps. Shrunk and wizened he was lost in the bed, a giant laid low. Around him were waxy-fingered Elpida and half a dozen other women in black sitting on kitchen chairs. A woman fussed round with damp flannels and cloths, while another dusted the sideboard. They chattered in low voices but I couldn't tell what about.

Vasilis stood behind the head of the bed, his hands gripping the brass rail like someone in the dock. It was as if we were all on stage behind the curtain, waiting for it to rise. I wanted to leave, but more people were coming in behind me and pushing me over to the far corner of the room. One of them was green-eyed Eleni. She was surprised to see me and I was the only one she greeted before bending down to kiss her grandfather. She stood next to Vasilis at the head of the bed and joined in the general muttered conversation.

As the room filled up, the talk got louder and Petros's breathing became rougher and more irregular. Once it stopped for a couple of seconds, like a baby's sometimes does, and we all held our breath too. Then it started again and the buzz of conversation resumed. By now the room was full and the air was thick and stale. Fortunately there were no cigarettes in the hero's honour.

I decided I had had enough and wormed my way to the door, to find it blocked by Papas Konstantinos, wearing a stole and carrying a leather bag. The crowd parted to let him through to the bed and I stayed to see what he did. He had timed his entrance perfectly. Petros's eyes clicked open like a doll's and there was a collective gasp from the onlookers. He looked up at the ceiling, or rather through it. His face was radiant and full of strength and vigour, as if a beam of sunlight pierced the roof. He struggled to sit up and Eleni, tears welling in her lovely eyes, leaned over to help him. He smiled a beaming, toothless smile so full of joy that many of us could not help joining in.

'*Te quiero*,' I heard him say in a clear and gentle voice, '*te quiero*.' And with those words he closed his eyes, the light on his face went dim and he breathed a long sigh and fell back into Eleni's arms.

There was a stunned silence. Then Elpida started to keen in a throaty contralto and one by one the others took up her lament.

'Alas what an agony the soul endures when it is parting from the body, a man's body, a strong body like yours, Petros...'

My own reaction caught me by surprise. My chest swelled and my eyes were moist in pride on his behalf as if he had won a great victory. The feeling of triumph was bizarre but genuine. I stayed to watch the *papas* administer the Unction and then those of us who were neither related nor acolytes at the rituals of washing and dressing filed out of the room behind him, the men lighting up as they got outside. The church bell began to toll its terrible message.

Spiros the carpenter was waiting outside with a coffin. He asked what the old man's last words were. I didn't say they were 'I love you' in Spanish.

Elpida was behind me. 'He said *Kyrie, Kyrie*,' she said, 'Lord, Lord,' and they crossed themselves three times.

I had probably misheard. Elpida was probably right. In any case, I was glad for Petros that after such a long life he had found at last whomever it was he saw. But if he had said *te quiero*, it would have made a nice story.

After a coffee and a gossip in the café, I went back up to the house and tried to work. But I could not get Petros's expression out of my mind or the turmoil of feelings out of my heart. Or the terrible sense of finality. I wanted to be with my family and at about five o'clock I couldn't stand it any more. I ran down to the cemetery and got in the car. As I drove past the church the funeral procession was forming outside Petros's house. Tonight he would be in the ground with lamps flickering above him.

I got home in time to read stories to the children. In the small hours I held Arfa tight and told her about old Petros and how I never wanted to be separated from her for a single moment and that life was too short for absence and longing.

We will grow old together in a stone house with a red roof under the mountain by a grassy meadow dotted with olives and almonds. I will build a floor with mellow pine from Olympus and gleaming chestnut from Macedonia and a chair of silky beech seated with ochre rushes from the Acheron and a table with sea-washed oak from shipwrecks and a great bed of African mahogany perfumed with wild lavender and thyme with posts and bedhead carved with flowers and grapes and furnished with silk from Mistra and the down of countless birds of passage. When we are old we will sit hand in hand under a canopy of vines and look out for our grandchildren over a silver sea scored with currents, the wakes of invisible ships...

We wept together and fell asleep as the sky grew light. When she woke she reached over to touch me, but I was gone. I had to see Haralambos about the plumbing.

Making it up

~~~~~~

People who buy houses in nice places often end up running a guest house. Friends and relations who usually keep in touch through photocopied Christmas letters start to phone and write in the spring, just to see how you are and coincidentally to discuss their holiday plans. In our case word had got round about the standard of accommodation, so we had few visitors and those who did come did not stay very long.

Our friends Frank and Marcie from Pittsburgh were not put off, however. They were our first visitors and stayed with us at Kyria Sofia's fish taverna down in Limanaki. They had just finished converting an old barn and advised us on our new wooden floor.

Barba Mitsos said that in the days before imported chestnut and pine floorboards, the floor would have been made of earth laid on layers of reeds, supported by olive or cypress joists. The neighbours joined in trampling down the earth and poured on buckets of pig's blood to make it hard as concrete. It sounded jolly, but what about the smell and the flies? A waste of good food, said Elpida. In any case, it was hard enough to lure my craftsmen away from chipboard and plastic tiles onto wooden floorboards. In the interests of fake authenticity we thought old boards would look better than new Swedish pine, but there were none to be found on the island.

One of the most famous temples of Ancient Greece was Eleusis, pronounced Elefsis, about fifteen miles from Athens. It was allegedly the last place that the corn goddess Demeter looked for her daughter Persephone, who had been carried off by Hades alias Pluto alias Lord of the Underworld. Zeus intervened and let her have her daughter back, except for the four months of winter when she had to go back down to be Queen of the Underworld. Every autumn for thousands of years, until about 400 AD, secret ceremonies commemorating the death and rebirth of corn and promising life after death were held at Eleusis. The solemnities began with a procession along the Sacred Way from Athens. So I did my best to instil a sense of awe and timeless mystery in the two eldest lads as we sat in fumes and traffic jams on the way to the tips and salvage yards that now line the Sacred Way.

Frank came along to help load the splintery old boards. If I sat sideways at the wheel they just fitted between the front and rear windows and left a space for the boys to stand in their usual place, leaning up against the back of the front seats. Frank slept off jet lag and last night's retsina on the back seat under a low planking roof. Dangerously loaded, we laboured in third gear from Athens to Skala Oropos.

Everything was going well until we were halfway down the steep winding road to the port. I was musing on the past lives that had seeped into the wood and wondered what memories would season it in future. A scream from Jim pierced my eardrum. I stamped on the brakes. We fish-tailed to the unfenced cliff edge. In the mirror I saw Frank jerk up out of his doze. He banged his head on the planks and fell back dazed. Both boys screamed. Off brakes, steer into skid...

It probably felt more dramatic and dangerous than it really was. Scrunching to a stop, I jumped out and wrenched open the sliding door. Frank clutched his head. Where am I? Where am I? Jack had his hands over his ears. Jim screamed. He clutched his crotch. I made the diagnosis. As we drove along he had been idly whipping his zip up and down, as one does, forgetting that he had not put under-pants on that morning. He had meshed himself in the zip-per. Tiny bobbles of pink skin protruded all the way up the line of clamped metal teeth.

Frank saved the day. He had been a US Army medic in Korea and he took charge. After a scream to out-scream all the previous, we saw that the skin had not been broken, only savagely mauled. We continued on our way while Frank entertained us with similar cases he had seen. Another of life's dramas seasoned the old boards, another sentimental memory to relive, especially when Jim's friends come to stay.

We delivered the boards to Spiros for sanding and regrooving and told him the reason for getting old wood was that it was cheaper than new, which was untrue. I was already in trouble for buying chestnut beams for joists instead of straight pine. He grumbled that it would be impossible to lay the floor level. To prove him wrong, Frank and I did the work ourselves. The basement was only about two metres high so we could easily reach and it was simple enough to fit the chestnut poles, split in half lengthways to make a flat side, into the existing holes in the walls. The only problem was that chestnut is as hard as oak and as difficult to saw. My arms were like jelly before we finished.

When we laid the floorboards I realised what Spiros meant about a level floor. In addition to the unevenness of the wood the house had settled over the years, so the slots for the joists were out of alignment. Old floorboards are not flexible like new ones, nor do they take nails well. I hammered down one end and the other sprang up with a rattle like a diving board. We weighed them down with the heaviest rocks we could carry and soaked them with water. It worked, sort of, although there were gaps between the boards, which I explained to Arfa were expansion joints for when the walls settled in the future.

At last we could stand at the windows. The view was exquisite. We looked out on our little almond tree, whose blossom had been replaced by delicate leaves. All we could see of the old village was the church and the ancient olive next to it. Down the hill stretched an intricate jigsaw of tiny pastures and vegetable plots dotted with almonds and olives and mulberries. The village was screened by trees. We could see the church and the top of the plane tree in the square and Spiros's old olive mill. Beyond was the plain beside the lake, yellow and green with corn and melons and tomatoes

and darker green as it got marshier near Dystos on its conical hill. I could see crafty Athina's little house and the reed
bed where I had cut the ceiling. In the distance was the ring
of hills that made the plain a gigantic amphitheatre. Leaning
on the stone sill, we were in a box halfway between the stage
and the gods waiting for the play to begin.

One day Frank, Marcie, Arfa and I were sitting by the sea
with the children. As usual, we had the beach to ourselves.
We saw an old lady hobbling over the sand towards us with
a bow-legged waddle acquired from a lifetime of stooping
in fields. From her wrists to her calves she was dressed in
faded black and wore her scarf like a Tuareg, wound round
her head and face with only a slit for her eyes. We specu-
lated nervously whether she was coming to tell the women
off for their bikinis or for letting our pale-skinned little
children run around in the malevolent sun.

She stopped beside us and as she was little and bent was
on the same level as us sitting down. She smelled of liniment and fish. We gave her our bravest *kalimeras*. She had
eyes only for Frank, who was black. She held out her hand
and when he took it did not let go.

'You are the first black person who has ever come to our
village. Welcome and God keep you well and give you many
years and bring you back again.' She turned to the women.
'They are lovely children. May they live for you.'

After a dry spit to avert the evil eye, she took out of her
apron a dozen little dried figs, which she laid out ceremo-
niously one by one on our beach mat. 'May you be well,' she
said, turned away and waddled back to her spinning.

The four of us could do nothing but look out to sea. Kate ran up. 'Why are you all crying?' she asked.

For the rest of his stay Frank acted like an honorary ambassador, giving out *kalimeras* and shaking hands with strangers. Alas, he never came back and died of cancer a few years later.

Genial Spiros was to make the doors and windows using old frames that we scavenged from the house and the salvage yards of the Sacred Way. Every morning I went down to his workshop to chivvy him into making a start. Every morning he greeted me as if we hadn't seen each other for months. We sat under a feathery walnut tree and sassy Antigone slouched over with coffee in the best flowery china cups with rims scalloped like tulips. We discussed the world as if one of us had just come back from a long journey.

Spiros was the exception to the rule of migration from the islands and villages into Athens. His family was born and bred Athenian. His father lived in Plaka at the foot of the Acropolis and was a photographer, plying his trade round the Parthenon with a bucket of water, a box of plates and a large wooden box on a tripod. Every autumn, when the summer trade slackened, he brought his family and his gun to the lake for the geese that stopped over on St Athanasios's day, regular as clockwork. He paid for their holiday by taking portraits and wedding photos in the villages around.

The Germans occupied Athens, bringing brutality and famine. Although he had no family connections, he sent his wife and three children to Evia, which they associated with peace and plenty. They nearly died of starvation in a hunter's shack living off frogs from the lake and acorns from the mountains and what flour they could beg. The Germans squeezed the islanders for everything they could not hide. Without family and connections it was hard to survive. Money would have helped, but after six months none came from Athens. Spiros's father had stayed to take photographs of SS officers posing against the marble gods and heroes they emulated. But when the Germans discovered copies of his photographs in a raid on the headquarters of ELAS, the communist resistance, he was arrested and never heard of again. When the Germans finally left, the photographer's brother warned Spiros's mother not to come back to Athens from Evia because of a British purge against communists, including families of resistance heroes. The real reason was that he had moved his own family into his brother's house in Plaka.

Spiros found work with Nikos the carpenter and married his only daughter. He married well. Her dowry was a house in the old village and the olive mill. The olives now went to an industrial mill in Aliveri and he made the shed into a carpenter's shop for his German woodworking machines. He kept doves in the house opposite ours. During the day they chortled and grumbled and pecked at the grain and water brought up by Antigone. In the evening they wheeled in intricate patterns with a rushing and beating of wings over the heads of the women on their way to graves and shrines and chapels to light lamps and gossip. When their white wings turned to crimson in the setting sun, they came back to roost.

This was all very interesting, but when was Spiros going to finish my doors and windows? It was always tomorrow. I tried reasonableness, persuasion, pleading, threats, anger, all with the same result. He would take me by the arm, his punk moustache close to my cheek, and pull me into the workshop. There was a lintel on the planing machine, a box of hinges on the bench and a door plank on the saw.

'My friend, my compatriot, don't worry, you will have the finest doors in Evia. Do you have fine wooden doors in England?'

'How the fig do you think we get in and out of the houses?'

'What did you say?'

'Just an English expression, Spiros.'

'Here. Take these.'

I went back to the house with a handful of apricots or a couple of fresh eggs, disarmed and bursting with frustration. The next day the materials were all in different places but untouched. I asked stylish Barba Vasilis's advice.

'If you want your doors and windows made down there, why are you up here?' he queried, leaning on his stick.

'Why? I'm not making them. He is. I've got plenty to do up here.'

'He thinks you don't care. He thinks you come in the morning just to pass the time of day.'

'But I've given him money. A third of his price.'

'Bah. That's just commercial. Go and work with him.'

In Greece when you walk into a carpenter's or a metal worker's or a garage, the customer is often there watching the work being done. It is partly to make sure it gets done right and partly because you have embarked on a relationship that is more than commercial. So the next day I did not leave Spiros after coffee. By afternoon I had watched him plane and fit the wood for the window and door frames. The next day I watched him build two doors modelled on the oldest I could find in the old village. To one of them I fitted the ancient lock that I had found in the straw and laboriously dismantled and cleaned. It took another three days to make the windows and shutters. I put two coats of yacht varnish on the windows and took them to Haralambos to glaze.

'Don't tell me you got Spiros to make them. By the All Holy One you did. I recognise his work. There isn't a right angle in the lot. How am I supposed to cut the glass?'

Spiros came up to fit them. He scorned the spirit level and the plumb line, tapping his nose and twitching his moustache when I offered him mine. He relied on years of experience, the innate talent of a master craftsman, the natural feel of the simple man for materials and their relationship with each other. I put my level back in the tool box feeling humbled, an impoverished child of the cementolithic age. Spiros ran his hands up and down a frame, squinted with one eye then the other and it was done.

As a result, every door and window was at least ten degrees out of true. When he had gone I did my best to put them straight, but they were fixed with massive six-inch nails hammered into the stones. The windows did not matter so much, in fact it was an advantage to have self-closing shutters swinging to under their own weight, but the angle of the door was a nuisance. Because the frame leaned into the house Spiros had trimmed the bottoms of the doors so that they opened and this left a four-inch gap when they were closed.

'Mother of God, were you both drunk?' marvelled Barba Vasilis.

Looking back on what I have written so far, it gives a misleading impression of my mental and physical state. Apart from the odd tantrum, it reads as if I were healthy and balanced and enjoying myself. I should set the record straight.

At any one time I had at least five of the following: sunburn, diarrhoea, a succession of colds, coughs and chills, heartburn, nausea, vomiting, stomach ache, back ache, leg ache, arm ache, head ache, blisters, cuts, scratches, splinters, a bloody eye from a wood chip and styes from cement dust, torn muscles, strained ligaments, rash in the crotch, fungus in the toes, itch in the scalp, wasp stings, bee stings, centipede bites, spider bites and flea bites. My left thumb was swollen and blue from the hammer, my fingers lacerated by slipping screwdrivers, my thigh slashed by a saw blade. I had been stabbed all over by rusty nails, brush-wood thorns, last year's razor thistles. My face was the worst. I had a peeling forehead, a permanent red lump from banging my head on the basement lintel, cracked lips, a bright red nose, three permanently infected mosquito bites and an itchy new beard.

I regularly took aspirin, salt tablets, Alka-Seltzer and antibiotics and my tetanus immunity was working over-time. Most of the day I was dizzy from ouzo, wine, beer, whisky or the hangover therefrom, too many cigarettes, too little sleep, fatigue, sunstroke or heat exhaustion. I had chronic indigestion from the meats and fats, oils and acids of the Mediterranean diet. My mood swung from elation to despair a dozen times a day. Most of the time I was lonely, bored, frustrated and frightened of getting ill without a decent doctor. My head ached from speaking Greek and people haranguing me or ignoring me. I wanted to buy things without having to haggle and plead. I longed for the telly and a pint of Guinness. I wanted to go home.

I went back to Athens at weekends when there was a good party or a school event we couldn't miss. With a stiff-legged walk from too much heavy lifting, peeling sunburn, cracked lips, village haircut and bruised, shredded hands ingrained with dirt and coarse with cement, I looked like Arfa's bit of rough.

Our smart Greek friends took advantage. When we went to dinner they spoke perfectly fluent English out of cour-tesy. But over the liqueurs they would deliberately switch to

Greek. Someone would ask me how the house on Evia was getting on and I'd say in building-site vernacular something like 'Werl, we've got the friggin roof on but them buggers sit round on their arses all day' and the Greeks would fall about laughing. I had no idea what half the words meant. I thought I was being witty and amusing and didn't realise that I was being set up.

We walked home from such an occasion at one of Athens's best tavernas. I was basking in the afterglow of what I thought had been my sparkling conversation. It was a lovely summer night. Familiar constellations were lost in the lactescence of unnamed stars and galaxies. A nightingale, lover of the absent moon, sang unfaithfully to the bright Milky Way spilling across the sky. Cicadas chirred and Athena's owl coo-cooed. The garden breathed a cachou breath of night-scented blooms, gardenia and jasmine and japonica. Beside a fragrant loquat, Arfa broke our silence.

'Must you go on about your bloody roof?' she complained.

'Wah?'

'You're obsessed. You're a joke.'

'Wah?'

'You're never here and when you're here you're not. When we go there as far as you're concerned we're not there and you can't wait for us to go, not though you'd notice. When you used to go away you were here more than you are now and when you're not there you might as well be.'

'Wah?'

'You leave me here to cope with everything while you go and live out your fantasies. All you ever think about is sand and cement. I'm sorry we're in the way. I'm on the beach looking after the kids while you're in the café drinking ouzo.'

'Wah?'

'And what was this tonight about living off the land? Growing olives and tomatoes and keeping goats? What's happened to you? You don't know the first thing. You hate digging. You grow mustard and cress and the blotting paper goes mouldy. And what will the children do? Have you ever wondered why Greeks go to Australia? What makes you think you can earn a living when the locals can't make a go of it? We're townies. We've got degrees.'

'Wah?'

'I know the house is lovely. Why do you think it's so cheap to buy lovely little houses and farms all over France and Spain and Italy and Greece? Why do you think the natives leave their lovely places to live in slums? They're not stupid. Nowhere's lovely if you have no work and no money and no prospects. There's never any dropping out. There's only dropping in. Dropping out is dropping in and the out you drop in from ends up the in you want to get out to.'

'Wah?'

'Stop saying wah. Say something else.'

I flopped into a canvas chair. What could I say? I was tired and pissed and looking forward to a screw and a lie-in and here I was ambushed out of the blue. This is all I could think of:

Today I finished scraping the plaster and cement off the floor. It was hard work because it bonds with the stone. I had to use a chisel and a wire brush. It now shines like marble with streaks of quartz like diamonds. On Monday I'll trim slates for the window ledges and cement them in. When that's done I'll scrape the splashes of plaster off the woodwork and the reeds. Then I can clean it all up for varnishing. I'll do the floor first. Won't it look beautiful when it's mellow and shiny? And the beams. The varnish will bring up the chestnut. The lintels over the doors and windows are olive wood. I love olive wood...

But that would have been fuel on the flames. So instead I did what loving partners do when their life's companion is feeling isolated and aggrieved. I went on the attack.

'I'm sorry I've put you to any inconvenience when I've been slaving my guts out on my own so you all can loll around on an unspoiled Greek island...'

And so we continued through the balmy night as the universe wheeled around the pole above the peaks of Parnis. We laid out under the stars the old battle scars of marriage, the grudges and wounds, compromises and disillusionments, frustrations and disappointments that two people share when they make one life together. Relationships are built on trust and openness, self-sacrifice and kindness, but they also need envy and competition, selfishness and malice to give them spice and interest. Not forgetting lust. When the curtains billowed in the first breeze of dawn, we lay hand in hand on crumpled sheets.

'How do you put up with being married to me?' I whispered.

'The secret of marriage, Toad,' she replied, 'is low expectations.'

Lambs to the slaughter

I was looking forward to an easy day hacking plaster from the inside walls. We hadn't moved in yet, but I could make myself comfortable now that I had a proper house with a roof and floor and doors and windows. I bought a double gas ring from Haralambos and salvaged a metal table from his yard. Elpida gave me a chair and a few pieces of crockery. I could make filter coffee instead of the inch of sludge that Yannis served. I took a jug of it with half a loaf of sweet bread and some fruit to the top step outside the front door that served as a veranda-for-one. It was a delicious morning, warm and fresh. In the pure Greek light the view had the unnatural detail of a Canaletto, as clear in the distance as close at hand.

I was on my second cup and wondering what a third Cretan peach would do for my heartburn when a quaint procession made its way along the path. At the head sauntered Barba Vasilis, leading by a rope one of his yearling lambs, a fat male. Then strutted ruddy-faced Ajax the butcher, carrying a large canvas bag. At the rear plodded Spiros the carpenter, sucking his yard-brush moustache. I waited for them to say the first *kalimera*, which is the duty of the passer-by, and then offered them coffee. Ajax shouted that they were too busy.

'*Kein' Zeit, danke, viel' Arbeit.*'

I poured myself another cup. Barba Vasilis led the way to the old olive tree beside the little church and halted with the lamb. It stood patiently, its large, dark eyes worldly wise. Spiros tethered the donkey. Ajax dropped his bag on the ground and opened it. He took something shiny out of the bag and nodded to Vasilis. With practised skill they scooped the legs from under the lamb. A bleat turned into a gurgle as Ajax slipped the knife into its neck and sawed briefly. They stooped over the animal, holding its kicking legs at arm's length so that blood would not spurt over their clean shoes while Spiros pulled on the rope around its crimson neck. The donkey was indifferent and carried on grazing as if nothing had happened.

I froze, the coffee cup halfway to my lips. I closed my eyes and opened them again, but it was not a hallucination. I waited for revulsion or nausea or shock to strike – instead all I felt was boiling resentment that they had done it in the middle of my breakfast. I focused my anger on the red-handed butcher. Didn't he have a yard down the hill where he could do this sort of thing in private? Why did they have to do it in front of our house? Our church? Outrage turned to squeamishness. I wanted to run away and hide although the deed was done, but my legs were trembling and I forced myself to sit there to watch what they did next.

Ajax went back to his canvas bag, while Spiros untied the bloody end of the rope from the neck of the animal and used it to lash the hind legs together at the hoof. He slung the other end over the strongest branch of the olive tree and with Vasilis's help hauled the lamb up until its nose was a foot off the ground. It dripped dark blood into the spreading pool on the grass, food for ants and worms and other underground things. Ajax made a small cut in a hind leg next to the rope and pushed the rubber tube of a foot pump into the incision. There was a fat little Michelin man on the pedal and I loathed him for smiling. Ajax pumped and the carcase swelled. Air filled the scrotum to the size of two beach balls. During the killing the men had been solemn. Now the tension was gone they talked and joked.

'Hey, Johnny, don't you wish you had a pair like that?' shouted Ajax.

The pumping became more difficult. With popping and tearing sounds, the skin came away from the flesh underneath. When the carcase was the size of a bullock, Ajax stopped pumping and with his knife split the belly from scrotum to breastbone. The air rushed out with a sigh that echoed over the hillside and announced that the lamb was truly dead. There was no terror any more. It was just meat.

I put down my coffee and joined them to watch what Ajax did next. The intestines were greenish white and the liver and lungs a delicate, luminous purple. There was little blood, even from the heart. It had all soaked into the ground. There was a raw, metallic smell, vaguely familiar. I tried to ignore the slurp as the knife did its work and listened instead to the breeze in the olive trees and the scrunch of the donkey grazing. Ajax cut the large intestine at both ends, tugged it out and threw it on the grass. Spiros snapped a twig from the branch above him and wound the gut around it from the stomach end, forcing out the contents, first in black nuggets and then in green slime. At home a woman would do the job again more carefully, squeezing the tube between her fingers and washing it in plenty of water. It would be made into soup or wound tightly on a spit around other pieces of offal to make tasty *kokoretsi*.

Ajax carefully cut out the liver and kidneys and sweetbreads and heart and testicles and other delicacies and put them in a black garbage bag. He tossed the stomach on the grass. His bare arms were bloody to the elbows, but his white shirt, blue jeans and shiny black shoes remained immaculate. As he worked he whistled softly to himself. He took a small knife with a wide blade and cut through the skin at the hooves and joints. Starting at the hindquarters, he peeled it off like a glove. Loosened by the pump, it came off easily. The membrane underneath was creamy white. When he got to the head Ajax hacked off the twisted horns with a cleaver and with a final yank pulled the skin off the nose. Black, bulbous eyes stared down at the ground from the narrow head. Blood dripped from the nostrils.

Spiros finished rolling the guts and put them in the garbage bag. Vasilis picked up the stomach and threw it over the stone wall into the next field where it burst, spilling out yellow grass. Ajax untied the rope and lowered the carcase onto the ground. He chopped off the hooves with a cleaver. He wiped his knives and his hands on a clean patch of grass, finishing off with a rag from the bag. His hairy forearms were still flecked with dried blood and under his fingernails was dark red. I imagined those arms around Eleni, those hands exploring her. I also considered his proficiency at cutting throats with knives.

'Hard work,' I said, surprised at my own equanimity. 'Now come and have some coffee.'

'*Dank' schön. Zu viel' Arbeit.*'

Ajax went off to fetch his pick-up, parked down the track.

'Spiros is marrying his daughter on Saturday,' said Vasilis, 'he needs a lot of meat. Ajax is best man. Spiros, did you give Johnny an invitation?'

Spiros looked blank. He had not given me an invitation, nor had it apparently crossed his mind. I was too embarrassed to ask whom she was marrying. He wiped warm blood and fat and excrement off his hands and untied the donkey, leading it away so that Ajax could reverse the Datsun closer to the carcase. There was an aluminium box on the back, which Spiros opened. It already contained two carcases and lumpy black garbage bags. They heaved the third inside, head flopping, and slammed the door. The Datsun lurched down the path, followed by Spiros on his donkey. With a wave of his stick Vasilis went to find the rest of his flock.

Under the olive tree flies swarmed where blood glistened on the grass. The stomach in the next field writhed with them. I picked up the dainty little feet and threw them over the wall. I jammed the twisted horns into a crack in the olive trunk so that it looked as if they grew there.

I had never seen a life taken before. Less than half an hour ago this had been a living, breathing, sentient being. I waited to feel more than a mild distaste for what had happened, but nothing came. It was in the order of things. The animal was a passive participant in something incomprehensible to it. It deserved its fate simply because it was there. Anger against the men who did it drained away with the blood on the ground. They too were passive participants, although they wielded the knives and ropes. What troubled me most is that although I was an unwilling observer, I felt guilty for myself as if something in what I witnessed touched a shameful and repressed desire. And I hated Ajax for whistling.

Back at Barba Mitsos's that evening, a large envelope was waiting for me. Inside was a printed invitation to the wedding on the following Saturday of Spiros's daughter Antigone to Haralambos, the builder's merchant.

'Haralambos. She's marrying Haralambos.'

'So?' asked Elpida as she dolloped fresh cheese onto a square of muslin.

'But Antigone's so young.'

'He did well. She might be a virgin even if she's got those things in her ears all day. She's got the hips for children. Spiros is a fool, but he's respectable enough. He's given her a good dowry, a field of fifteen olives and the chicken house in the old village and an apartment in Athens. It's rented to Lebanese. Good money.' She tied the corners of the muslin into a knot and gently squeezed the pulpy mass into the sink.

'And Antigone? What does she think?'

'Eh. She made a good match. He's a good man. He had the only Mercedes in the village until Ajax came back. He's been abroad. He knows things. Whatever he got up to on his travels, there's never been any scandal about him in the village. He's been married. He'll know how to handle her.'

'But she's only eighteen and he's older than I am. There must be twenty-five years between them.'

'So much the better. She'll still be in her prime when he gets old. By the time she loses her looks he'll be too old to chase other women.'

'I hope he likes rock and roll.'

'He'll soon knock that contraption off her head.'

'She wanted to live in Athens.'

'He'll knock that silliness out of her too. Look what Ajax did for Eleni.'

Then something else occurred to me. 'Ajax is their *koumbaros*.'

The *koumbaros* is much more than best man. For a start, he pays for the wedding. For the rest of their lives he and the *koumbara*, in this case Eleni, are family, like godfathers to the couple, as close relatives as brother and sister.

'They are repugnant.' I meant to say 'rivals' but Elpida caught the sense, no doubt pleased to have collected another bon mot from the foreigner.

'Eh, they both think they're big men. And big men stick together.' She crossed her fingers, slimy with curd. 'Besides, they're family. Haralambos married Ajax's sister. She died when her sun-touched son was born. That's why Haralambos left to work in Arabia. He came home when old Dionysos his father died and took over the hardware store. It's time he married. He has no one to look after the house.' She edged past me to the back door and hung the ball of cheese on the branch of a walnut to ripen in the air.

I was depressed and angry, I hoped because I deplored the men's treatment of women, but I suspected because I wished I could be the same.

'What did Barba Mitsos do for you, Elpida?'

She laughed. 'What did I do for him you mean? He came at me with a stick once and I flattened him.'

The only drawback to Haralambos's eligibility, which had already put off the families of two potential brides, was his son Dionysos, Ajax's nephew, whose stepmother the new bride would become.

'Dionysos is no problem. Don't worry. Antigone did well,' said Elpida, washing cheese slime off her hands.

*H*aralambos came to do the plumbing. It had to be done before the walls were plastered and the basement floor laid. He was keen to show that he had worked abroad for foreign companies and knew the proper way to do things. It was so refreshing that he did not need cajoling and persuading and begging and bribing like the others but came on the day he promised. He arrived in a tipper truck with Dionysos riding behind the cab. He made no effort to involve his son and behaved as though he were invisible. I joined in the conspiracy to save them both embarrassment. I felt so sorry for them and thanked God for my own children.

Dionysos did not seem to mind. He chewed a crust of bread and watched while I helped his father unload the copper and the plastic pipes. He stood over us like a fussy clerk of works while we dug a trench from the basement to the hole that Zenon had dug. Haralambos laid pipes along it from the bathroom and the kitchen and I was glad to see that he used levels and lines and not innate craftsmanship to get the falls right. Then we put down pipes from where my water tank would be to the house. When the trenches had been filled he installed the plumbing.

We worked hard through the morning with a break at noon for bread and cheese and finished by three o'clock, the end of the working day. We sat on a bag of cement under the olive. Dionysos lurked in the shade of the almond tree, watching us. I poured whisky.

'How will it be to be married again?' I asked.

'A man has to have a wife.'

'You were lucky to find her.'

'Eh, luck. You go where the wind takes you. She's a good girl. She's young but she'll be a good woman.'

He leaned back against the tree and sipped his whisky. He nodded to the little church. 'You know that Ajax's uncle murdered his wife's lover? He waited for him outside that church and shot him in the head. He would have killed her too, except they stopped him in time.'

'What happened to him?'

'He was unlucky. The judge made an example of him. He got four years.'

'That's not much.'

'Too much for what he did.'

'Who was the lover?'

'The saddle maker. The father of Adonis. His wife Maria sings at the funerals. She lives just along the hill.'

'That's terrible.'

'It was. Everyone had to go to Aliveri to get their saddles mended. Then Barba Vasilis took over the business.'

'Does that sort of thing happen now?'

'He was the last. But who knows? You never know what the fates have in store.'

'It wasn't fate. They could choose. The saddle maker did not have to sleep with Ajax's aunt. Ajax's uncle did not have to kill the saddle maker. They could choose what to do.'

'Eh. Eros drove the saddle maker. Nemesis drove the butcher. They had no choice.'

He finished his drink, stood up and clapped me on the shoulder as if he had delivered the clinching argument. I let it go. He got into the truck and drove down the hill. Dionysos scampered onto the back and sat with his legs dangling over the edge, looking at me. I waved goodbye to him but he did not wave back.

As the crow flew mournful Maria, mother of Adonis and widow of the murdered saddle maker, was my closest neighbour. She and Adonis lived in a stone house almost as dilapidated as mine along the hill but reached by a different mule track. It was as if she lived up there in disgrace, spending the days in atonement for her adulterous husband, growing vegetables and flowers in the flinty soil of her narrow terraces, rarely to be seen in the village but only in the cemetery at dusk where she sat over one grave or another, gently crooning. She made grief her life's vocation and with her sobbing voice and talent for improvisation was much in demand for funerals and exhumations. She earned a living from performing the daily graveside rituals on behalf of relatives who lived too far away to carry out the duties themselves.

Now that Haralambos had laid the pipes, I needed a concrete cistern for the water to fill them. On a hot, hazy day I found Dimitris the builder repairing an old diesel pump in his yard. He looked worried. For twenty-five years I have never seen him look anything else.

'It's got the gut ache like me. I've got the gut ache all the time. And diarrhoea. Chronic diarrhoea for five years. The doctor gives me Librium and kaolin. Do you get gut ache?'

'Often,' I said and ran through a few ailments whose Greek names I knew.

The fastest way to a hypochondriac's heart is through symptoms. Within half an hour we were sipping ouzo and eating salt anchovies – good for the gut ache, brings it on a treat – and discussing the merits of bulldozing the houses in the old village and building something nice and modern. The artist in Dimitris looked down on crude work like building cisterns and messing around with old stone. He loved to render walls and finish them off square and shiny with marble dust or pour bright-coloured marble floors from a can and ride a polisher over them. He looked pained at the work I wanted him to do and rubbed his stomach.

We went through the ritual of negotiation. I knew all the techniques by now: cajoling, flattery, breaking off, walking away. I haggled all morning and as usual ended up agreeing to the price he asked in the first place.

It took two days to build the tank out of breezeblocks in the highest part of the field behind the house. Adonis hefted the blocks and mixed the cement. I rendered it myself and roofed it with Ellenit covered with leftover tiles. It held two tons of water, which Aristotle the hydrologist delivered with his tractor and tank. Now I could plant olives and almonds and mulberries and vines.

Anxious not to make a mistake and deprived of gardening books, I asked for advice.

'Dig the holes three metres apart and fill them with manure, so they get a good start,' said Barba Vasilis.

'Two metres at most so they share each other's shade and no manure so they don't get lazy,' said Barba Mitsos.

'Three metres and just a little manure,' said Spiros.

So much for the collective wisdom of country folk. I planted some close together and the rest far apart and some with a lot of manure and others with little and the rest with none and they have all done equally well.

I spent a week bribing Dimitris with promises of Lomatil and Kaopectate from England to start the plastering. I was dreading the ordeal of badgering him yet again when one morning I heard a tractor. It was Zenon towing a cement mixer behind his digger. Following him was Dimitris in Haralambos's tipper loaded with sand and cement. I ran out with refreshments and indigestion tablets in case they went away again.

Within an hour the mixer was chundering and Adonis was caked white with dust and running backwards and forwards with raw sand and cement and buckets of mortar, while Dionysos stood chewing his crust and peering into the revolving drum for the secrets of the universe. Inside the house Dimitris and Haralambos worked together with cloths tied round their heads and mouths, tossing trowels of rough plaster at the walls and smoothing it off with careless swipes.

While the mixer was there they built a bathroom in the basement, installed a kitchen sink upstairs and laid stone floors.

It did not seem right to install a cheap eastern European bog from Haralambos in our old stone house. Nothing at all would have been authentic or, if we were going up-market, a Turkish squatter over a pit in the yard, but we decided that our bowels should move with the times. We made a family outing to the Sacred Way and tracked down a fine Royal Doulton suite. We drove it as far as the cemetery and then Arfa and I lugged it over the fields in the middle of a thunderstorm illuminated by lightning.

For ten days Dimitris and Haralambos started at half past seven and worked until noon. After bread and cheese and a few glasses of wine they began again and worked until the heat of three o'clock. When they went home I cleared up after them and used the leftover cement and plaster for jobs of my own. My hands were soon wizened with cement where they weren't weeping from blisters as big as saucers.

In one of our lunch breaks it came out that Dimitris was a cousin of ruddy-faced Ajax. His mother was Ajax's aunt and grew up in my house. To postpone getting back to work, I encouraged him to tell me about his family.

'You know the man who built your house? He was my great-great-great-great-grandfather. He wasn't Greek. He was an Albanian. We all are. My parents' first language is Albanian. You find us all over Greece. We came here under the Turks. We are mountain people from Epirus in the north round Yannina. The Albanian speciality is mules and horses. In our language we have six different names for a mule. As far as the Turks were concerned, we were the animals. They moved us from field to field wherever we gave the best milk. That place doesn't give enough taxes, eh, plant some Albanians. So they sent my ancestor Yannis here. He was a giant and a good man. He and his brothers built all the houses here. They were the best saddle makers on the island.

'The time came to take back our own from the Turks. There was no fighting here because what could we do on an island? So we sent our best men to the Morea. Now the Pasha of Aliveri had to send mules and saddles to Athens for the Turkish army. He rode up here one day from the seraglio down by the lake with his men and found old Yannis sitting on those steps where you are sitting now. He was about seventy years old but he was still strong. The Pasha was a bastard like all of them. They never got off their horses so they could always look down on the Greeks. He said that if he didn't have twenty new saddles by sunset the next day he would impale the old man. You know what impaling is? A sharp pole up your arse. Twenty saddles. One saddle takes a week to make. But what could Yannis do? He prayed to the Virgin and then gathered all his relatives together and anyone in the village who could help and he gave them all jobs to do. But he kept the tricks of the trade for himself and his eldest son so they had to do the difficult work themselves.

'They worked all through the night and all through the next day with the Virgin helping and all they could think of was the pointed stake. At sunset the Pasha rode up with his soldiers. All the saddles were ready and he took them, without paying of course. Our people were overjoyed. Old Yannis had cheated death again. The old man went to bed and died in his sleep of exhaustion. It was his fate to die that day whatever he did.'

'It wasn't his fate,' I said. 'He chose to make the saddles. He could have gone into the mountain with his gun. Anything.'

'He was a dead man whatever he did,' said Haralambos.

'Anyway,' said Dimitris, 'that's not the end of the story. You've seen our saddles, haven't you? We hammer in five brass nails so the heads make the blessed crucifix. Before the Pasha arrived Yannis gathered all the old women and told them that he was not going to put the crucifix on the saddles for the unbelievers. Instead, he wanted to put the evil eye on them. The women did it in the church over there. Those saddles were cursed by Aghios Ioannes himself. But the Pasha didn't know and he put them in a galley along with other supplies for the army and sent them off to Athens.

'The ship never arrived. It was captured by Bouboulina. You know Bouboulina? From Spetse. She was a woman but the fiercest of all the admirals. She took the booty and sold it to the Greeks. So what happened to the accursed saddles? Of course the Greeks noticed straight away that they didn't have crosses and nailed them on and had them blessed by a priest and that took away the evil eye. But one of her customers didn't because he wasn't a Christian. He was a crazy Englishman like you. You know who it was?'

'Tell me.'

'Lordos Byron. He sat on Yannis's saddle and in six weeks he was dead of a fever. He was a dead man whatever he did.'

Greek dancing

~~~~~~~~

The wedding present was easy. No cake stands and fish slices at a Greek wedding, you give money. I sorted out some clean notes and bought an envelope.

We were pleased when Arfa was invited to help make *spanakopitas* for the wedding, spinach and cheese pies. It was a sign that we were beginning to be accepted. She was less pleased that she had to be at Elpida's at seven in the morning. These *spanakopitas* were not the dainty little filo triangles that you find on the canapé tray with cherry tomato halves spread with taramasalata and cucumber sticks for dipping in the hummus. They were slabs two feet square and three inches thick and enough of them to give five hundred guests a couple of decent slices each.

The women gathered at Elpida's because she had the biggest stone oven. Barba Mitsos had already stuffed it with brushwood and logs and thrown in a match. On trestle tables in front of it were bags of flour, boxes of eggs, laundry baskets of fresh spinach, jugs of olive oil, cheeses piled in pyramids like cannonballs. The women divided the tasks, mixing pastry, rolling and tossing it into thin sheets, washing and chopping spinach, mashing up cheese. Elpida raked out the burning wood and brushed out the embers and threw the finished slabs onto the floor with a wooden spade. Arfa's slender arms were an asset in a cocktail dress but a liability at a pita-making party, where brawny biceps were needed for kneading and pounding and lifting. She made herself useful doing delicate things with a four-inch paintbrush pressed into service as a pastry brush and tried to make sense of the wedding gossip that seasoned the pies with slander and scurrility. She came back to us knackered.

After the siesta we dressed up. The children demonstrated their extraordinary capacity to attract dirt simply by sitting still on a chair in clean clothes reading *Asterix*. Through the vagaries of the airing cupboard, all six of us were in white shirts and dark blue trousers with slicked-down blonde hair. We looked like some kind of sect. At five, after a last face scrub with a licked handkerchief, we ambled along to Haralambos's Texan ranch house and joined the queue winding up the steps and through the lounge and in and out of the bedroom.

There was plenty of time to inspect his collection of brass Arabian coffee pots and pictures of charging purple elephants in heavy gilt frames and Louis de Lebanon gilt curlicued furniture. We threw coins on the bed, trying not to hit a sleeping baby who had been placed there to tempt fate and as a reminder of the point of the whole business. The women appraised the quality of the needlework in the dowry clothes and linen laid out for inspection in piles on the padded pink dressing table and a Yemeni sandalwood chest. In the lounge we were offered little glasses of a sweet liqueur.

As usual, it was an ordeal for the children. Old ladies pinched their cheeks, tweaked their blonde hair and spat on them with spits of varying degrees of dryness to chase away the evil eye. 'May they live for you,' they said to us.

At six o'clock we gathered outside the church. The men were in open-necked, short-sleeved white shirts but the women, whether they lived on the island or came from Athens for the occasion, were dressed for a reception at the Athens Hilton, clanking with jewellery, glittering with lamé and sequins and helmeted with lacquered hair. Only a few old grannies wore the traditional yellow scarf of the island. Arfa skulked with the dowdiest women, feeling underdressed.

Car horns blaring different versions of *Colonel Bogey* and the *Marseillaise* announced the arrival of the bride and groom in the back of Ajax's red Mercedes. Behind were the bride's parents in Haralambos's white Mercedes, followed by a hooting and tooting procession of humbler vehicles. They made a couple of circuits of the village, horns still blaring, before drawing up outside the church.

Ruddy-faced Ajax stepped out from behind the wheel, resplendent in a light grey double-breasted German suit, embroidered two-tone blue shirt, white tie, white belt and white patent shoes. His curly hair was slicked down and shiny and his moustaches sculpted and oiled so they looked like a plastic stick-on. A beaming smile showed off the gold dental work that matched his rings and pins and chains and links. He held the door for Haralambos, who wore a cream Italian suit and bright blue tie held down by a thick gold chain. He stood smiling and upright, chest out and stomach in, as if waiting for the *paparazzi*. They ignored Antigone struggling to get out of the other side of the car in her voluminous white dress. She was shy and sweet and nervous and waited to be told what to do, quite unlike the sassy teenager I knew.

Ajax the *koumbaros* took charge. With beefy hands scrubbed clean and manicured, he cleared a way through the crowd and ushered the wedding party into church. Parents and relatives followed and then the rest of the guests, jostling like a bus queue. Eleni was *koumbara*, matron of honour. She was stunning in a simple emerald green velvet dress and with her hair done up in intricate braids. She led sun-touched Dionysos, her nephew, by the hand up the aisle.

By Orthodox standards the service was mercifully short. It took place halfway down the church on a kind of bandstand with a little altar and a canopy twined with flowers. I stood on the men's side, the right, choking on aftershave and incense and wishing that I didn't smell of goat and old lime. Our children wormed their way to the front. Yannis the chief cantor and Giorgos his sidekick batted the responses to and fro in deep nasal quarter tones, oblivious of popping Instamatics and howling babies and the chattering congregation.

With a shawl wrapped tight over his head, Papas Konstantinos looked like a surly prophet. At key moments he shouted for silence, swatted the microphone with his hand and tried to look stern. Although he officiated Ajax was the master of ceremonies, nudging everyone into place and giving them their cues. At his bidding the bride and groom exchanged rings. He and Eleni held the *stefana* over them, wedding crowns like white halos connected by a ribbon, and switched them and planted them on their heads. The *papas* led them in a dance hand in hand round the little altar while the rest of us sang a chanting, lilting hymn and pelted them with rice. Children liked this part the best and aimed for tender parts.

After the service was over we queued down the aisle for gauze bags of sugared almonds and milled around outside. Haralambos stood with Ajax to greet their relatives with manly hugs and clouds of cigarette smoke. Antigone stood a few yards away with her mother and Eleni and other women to receive chaste kisses, envelopes of money and the ritual congratulation: 'May you live'. I couldn't decide if her uncharacteristic modesty was tradition or boredom.

The wedding feast was on the forecourt of the garage on the main road just outside the village. The villagers were proud of the new illuminated Shell sign, which showed that they were European. It belonged to Haralambos's cousin Haralambos – first-born of two brothers, they had automatically been named after their paternal grandfather. It was the largest expanse of concrete in the village and still the tables spilled out into the road. The pumps were decorated with paper flowers and white garlands hung from the canopy. Two wine barrels were set up between the pumps and the office. The band was installed on the hydraulic inspection ramp and an open patch of concrete in front of it was spotlit for dancing. The tables around it were planks on trestles covered with paper tablecloths. When we arrived they were already laid with plates of crumbly feta and big, salty anchovies.

We sat down and salads were brought and slices of *spanakopita* thunked down like bricks on our plastic plates. I drank steadily from two-litre plastic Pepsi bottles of tart, fruity wine, enough not to mind when the lamb was served. A flock of sheep had been slaughtered under the village's trees, chopped into chunks and wrapped with potatoes in aluminium foil, to be sent to Dimitra's bakery in flat tin trays. Still alive yesterday morning, it tasted a bit like the carcase smelled, metallic and raw although it was well cooked.

Arfa and I had the children between us. On my other side sat Aussie Alekos: 'Cawn't stend the crick't b't the rugby's a grait gaim.' When we had exhausted Australian sport and English football hooliganism, he dished the dirt on the guests, starting with our host, the garagiste Haralambos.

'Bastard's a sly-bag. Scoots off to Athens when he was a kid and ends up delivering fuel oil to people's houses for one of the big companies. Say you order some oil, there's always some left in the hose when it's finished filling. Counter's at the truck so the customer pays for it. End of the day the company thinks the whole load's sold, but there's still some left in the truck from the hose. What does the bastard do? Offloads it in his own truck and sells it to his own customers. Twenty yeers he builds up his business. He sells it to the oil company he works for and builds this place with the money. Bet the dodger runs the same scam when he fills your car up.'

Around us was the dark. We sat in a pool of brightness from the forecourt floodlights, the giant yellow shell above us beaming its ancient pilgrim message into the blackness. The stars had disappeared and been replaced by moths zipping through the glare like meteors. By the time the band began to tune up, the paper tablecloths were sodden with wine. Silver foil and plastic plates blew in a fluttering breeze and underfoot was thick with soggy bread, paper cups and crawling children.

It was hard to know when the band finished tuning up and when it started playing. The tormented wail of an amplified violin cut through the hubbub like cheese wire. An electric *bouzouki* played the soundtrack to a nervous breakdown. The trilling clarinet, its bell wrapped round the ball of a microphone, aroused a secret and unwanted excitement, like pulling wool through front teeth. Drums and an electric guitar gave body to the din. A man sang a mournful dirge full of trills and quarter tones more evocative of a funeral than a wedding, a threnody for sheep and women and anchovies and children and men and chickens and goats and all living creatures who copulate and die for reasons of which they have no inkling.

With the crash of a tambourine the song broke into a frenetic rhythm, the three lead instruments gambolling up and down a Doric scale and the others keeping up with a frenzied, deafening beat. Out of the darkness ran sun-touched Dionysos in a white shirt, white trousers and white shoes. In the spotlight his face was white too, his hair brushed down in a black cap pulled tight over his head. There was a girlish look about him, with his slim waist, delicate arms and soft features that sat badly on his stocky hips and bandy legs. He raised his arms and began the most exquisite parody of a Greek dance. He bent his knees like a man adjusting himself at a urinal, shuffled, waved his hands and stumbled over his feet. He kicked the air and pirouetted into the bandstand. He tried to slap his feet and hit his calves instead.

'What's the matter with that man?' asked Kate.

'He's pretending to dance like an English tourist.' It was the best I could come up with.

Dionysos took a white handkerchief from his pocket, flapped it as though he was waving goodbye and with his other hand on his hip led a chain of invisible dancers – as graceful as he was clumsy since they were light as the air itself – round and round the floor, in and out of the tables and the petrol pumps, faster and faster. His face was solemn and unsmiling, in contrast to the audience, who were laughing. A few were stony-faced from pity or embarrassment.

Someone came out onto the floor and popped a flash at him. Little children shrieked and aped him at the edge of the pool of light. His father, Haralambos the groom, sat bolt upright and smiled a fixed smile. His new stepmother Antigone turned her face away from the dance floor and talked animatedly to her *koumbaros* Ajax. Of the bridal party only Eleni watched the boy, her eyes welling with tears.

The band finished the song, truncating the music with a savage chop. Dionysos made a low bow to mocking applause, but showed no sign of leaving the floor. The *bouzouki* started a steely, complicated riff and Haralambos stood up, still smiling with his mouth, although his eyes – fixed on the clarinet player, anywhere but his prancing son – were full of anger and embarrassment. Slowly and with dignity he walked up to the boy with one arm outstretched to take his hand. Dionysos skipped to the other side of the floor. Haralambos had no choice but to follow him.

Dionysos jigged and pirouetted while his father tried to corner him like a frightened goat. They skipped to one side and then the other, arms out sideways, improvising their own dance to the feverish music. Finally Dimitris the builder, who had been clapping and egging them on, gave Dionysos a shove with his foot that sent him sprawling into his father's arms. Haralambos gripped his wrist, still smiling. Dionysos was immediately docile and let himself be led away by his father.

I slipped away from my seat and followed, curious to see what punishment would ensue and determined to intervene if the lad was made to take stick, to eat wood, as an English traveller might stop a man beating a donkey. But Haralambos was not such a man. Once outside the ring of tables he shook the boy off and without a word waved him away into the darkness. He returned to his bride while Dionysos, with no backward glance, stomped off into the night, knees bent and elbows crooked. Hidden in the shadows I watched until his white shape disappeared.

'Pore little bagger,' said Alekos when I came back to my seat. 'Should've bin strengled at berth.'

The proper dancing began. First were the ritual wedding dances for bride and groom, parents and close relatives. It was Ajax's job to lead them and he was a good dancer despite his bulk, light on his toes. He came into his own in the dowry dance, leading them out of the garage office with sheets and towels and blankets draped round their shoulders. Eleni was the best dancer. She seemed to move less than the others, gliding as though her feet hardly touched the ground, insolent in the careless grace with which she bent her slender neck, swivelled her hips and tossed glances over her shoulder.

After the formal wedding dances came the free-for-all. Arfa and I were dragged onto the floor by Elpida. Despite her bovine bosom and elephantine hips, she danced like a young girl. I copied her, curtsying and swivelling and tripping and confident that I was doing a great job and not letting the side down. By not trying too hard Arfa did much better, her subtle movements evoking the dance rather than performing it.

'You dance like Dionysos,' said Jack when I sat down for a breather.

'Was your wedding like this?' asked Kate.

I thought back to our own wedding reception in a tent on a lawn on a wet Saturday afternoon.

'Just like this, sweetheart,' I said.

We put the children to bed in the camper and danced until dawn, jigging and shuffling and fortified by great swigs of the Pepsi bottle. The bride and groom left without ceremony, slipping away in the white Mercedes for a night in Halkida. When we left the dancing was still in full swing, Ajax in the thick of things, jacket off and sleeves rolled up, roaring with laughter and chivvying those sitting down to join in.

Et in Arcadia ego

~~~~~

*I*t was high summer. Strident pink oleanders defied the flinty heat while other mountain flowers were gone and the grass grew golden yellow. You looked for shade not colour, especially in the middle of the day, when sleep was the only escape from heat.

Fig trees look good but their pale, translucent green is reptilian and sinister and the rustle of their leaves is harsh. The broad fingers they hold over the eye of the sun let in stroboscopic spots of light like needles in the retina. Elpida said never to sleep under a fig tree because it gives bad dreams. Never sleep under a cypress either. The spiky dark trees are old and damp and cast little shadow when the sun is high. Their roots spread among the dead and give them shelter, but they are not meant for the living. It is best not to sleep under a plane tree because it sucks your water. Almonds shrink your balls and give poor shade. Holly gives you gall stones. Olives are good, except they toss about too much if there is a breeze. The best for a luxuriant and dreamless sleep is the silky shade of a mulberry.

We had unseasonal daydreams about fireplaces. The original one had collapsed in rubble on the old floor. One evening, on the way to the café, I saw Ajax on his balcony and asked his advice. We sat on white plastic chairs arranged so that we could admire the emerald green patch of *gazon*, corralled by its neat white picket fence. Up the hill the roof of my house caught fire in the rays of the setting sun, blazing like a beacon across the plain. Spiros's scarlet doves wheeled above it as if they had risen from the flames.

The back door opened and the twins toddled out to greet their father. They were in blue T-shirts and shorts padded out with disposable diapers. Ajax swept them up one in each arm, jigged them up and down, sang a song and danced round and round, until one of them puked mixed vegetables down his shirt front and the other burst into tears. He guffawed, patted their heads, sent them back to their mother and mopped himself down with a paper napkin from a holder on the table.

'Fine boys, may they live for you,' I intoned.

'Thank you.'

Eleni brought a tray with a bottle of Auld Reekie, a carafe of water, several glasses and an ice bucket decorated with cocktail recipes. She put the tray down and went back to the kitchen.

'Eleni, stay. Sit down with us,' said Ajax, 'You needn't run away like a Greek wife. Pretend we're in Düsseldorf. Johnny is a foreigner. The world has changed. Come, Eleni, you have this glass.'

She sat down and helped herself to a glass of water. Ajax poured whisky and served the ice Greek fashion, adding it with a spoon afterwards.

'To our health,' he said, clinking his glass against mine and tossing it down in one gulp.

'Eleni, where are the *mezedakia*? Come on. Don't sit there. Open some of that Bavarian smoked cheese. And the Leberwurst. Johnny, you must be sick of feta and olives.'

Eleni went inside obediently. Ajax poured whisky into tumblers this time.

'A lovely lawn,' I said, for want of anything better.

'*Schön nich*? We have to drag this place into the future. Look at us, stuck in the old ways. But take us out of here and put us in Chicago or Melbourne or Düsseldorf and see what we do. You know the Pap test for women? He came from Evia, from Kimi. His name was Papanikolaou.'

'You just need opportunity.'

'Not opportunity, Johnny, brains. It's all done with brains.'

'And luck.'

'Bah. Luck is what you make it. Do you think our ancestors trusted to luck? Luck is an excuse for failure. *Guck mal das Licht*. The light of Greece.' He pointed upwards over his head out of the darkness gathering on the ground and into the empty sky, luminous blue. 'Isn't that right, Eleni?' he asked as she came back with a plate of *delikatessen* cut into cubes and two forks. 'Eleni, get yourself a fork, come on.'

Ajax stood up and lumbered down the steps to turn on the lawn sprinkler. I took the opportunity of a break in his chain of thought to mention fireplaces. He urged me to get a ready-made fireplace in a new shop called Rustikana outside Aliveri. There were several designs, all copies of French château fireplaces, with flues and throats and traps and controls, manufactured under licence in Salonica and guaranteed not to smoke.

'He is my cousin. I will get you a good price. *Spessial*,' he said.

'Sorry,' I said firmly, 'What's good enough for the village is good enough for me.'

'But we all go to Rustikana.'

I went round all the ruined houses in the old village measuring and sketching fireplaces. With bribery and flattery, I persuaded Barba Mitsos the melon farmer to take up his mason's hammer again. The design was very simple. The sides were built up a metre or so in stone, a large piece of chestnut was laid on top of them to support a mantelpiece made of stone and the whole lot was plastered over. It was large and open for cooking and a roaring log fire in winter. It looked simple, elegant and well-proportioned, as if it had been there for ever.

'You have a house now. You have a hearth,' said Barba Mitsos, hiding his pride behind a little smile.

There was no fancy funnel-shaped gather or bend in the flue. The smoke went straight up the chimney. That was the theory. In fact it went everywhere except up the chimney. I spent two days burning rubbish and twigs and logs trying to make it work. I raised the hearth and screened the front and extended the chimney and put a cowl on top, all without success. The smoke billowed and hung in the roof or crept along the floor to the windows.

'What did I tell you?' said Ajax, smugly. 'You should have gone to Rustikana.'

'But why doesn't it work? What did they do in the old days?'

'We had black faces and red eyes. The smoke killed the bugs so we didn't mind.'

The fireplace did have one fan. Ajax brought his great-aunt Iphigenia in the pick-up to visit. She was born in the house at the turn of the century, the eldest of seven. She rocked from side to side on bandy legs like a toy cow walking down a slope. The stairs were an ordeal, sideways, one step at a time, sighing with pain at every step. She waddled into the room and stood in front of the hearth, gazing into my smouldering debris, and mumbled to it as if the rest of us were not there. Her warty, hairy face creased around her cataracts and tears ran down the craggy wrinkles like flash floods in a desert riverbed. Then she started a lament for her past in the same style and cadences as mournful Maria at a graveside.

'*Ai, ai,* the pies we had, spinach and cheese and meat and the kid roast or done in a stew with onions and the grilled chops and the liver and the pork done on the grill and tender casseroles with celery and herbs and the hare with crushed garlic and the quail baked with aubergine...'

By the time she had gone through the menus of her youth we felt quite peckish. She looked round the rest of the room and struck her flaccid breasts.

'*Ai, ai,* the times I remember. See that hole in the wall where the stone is missing. We put the eggs in there to keep cool. We hung hams and sausages on the wall over the fire to smoke. I slept outside on the step in the afternoon and in the evening we got the mattresses off the chest and laid them out and slept here, me by the window because I was the eldest…'

And so she rambled on, seeing the house as she knew it as a child, feeling that the years in between had never been, a ghost haunting herself as she lay on the step outside, dreaming restlessly about what her future held. As she sang she worked her arthritic fingers as if she were trying to grasp something, clutching greedily at the air by her side. She fell silent, wiped the tears from her face with her faded yellow scarf and looked at us as if we had suddenly appeared in her past like aliens from another world.

'*Kalo risiko*,' she said to us, 'may you and your children live long here and well. May the Old Ones keep you safe and the Virgin smile on you. Keep the back window shut at night. There's a terrible draught.'

She waddled out to the pick-up shaking her head. Three weeks later she died.

Basking in memories of his youth and strength while he built our fireplace, Barba Mitsos took on the job of lining the cesspit. Dimitris the builder said that a concrete lining was good enough, but Barba Mitsos disagreed. The theory of the cesspit was that the water seeped through the stones while the solids fermented and dissolved. With a concrete lining there would be nowhere for it all to go.

It was hard to find people to work with stone the old way. I could patch up the walls of the house myself, fitting stones into the holes by trial and error and knocking up grey mortar mixed with pebbles to fill in the cracks. But lining the hole that Zenon's digger had made was not a job for an amateur.

First I spent a day collecting stones and piling them at the rim of the hole. It is no fun collecting five-pound rocks in the heat if you are nervous about scorpions and poisonous centipedes. When the pile looked as though it would fill the pit and not leave room for sewage, Barba Mitsos said that he needed half as many again. Finally he was satisfied.

At seven in the morning he came up with a hammer in his belt. He pushed his straw *republika* to the back of his head, rolled up his sleeves, downed an ouzo and climbed down Dimitris's rickety ladder into the pit. It was my job to pass down the stones and supply ouzo and water every half an hour. Barba Mitsos rarely used the hammer. He hefted each stone a couple of times in one hand, scarcely looking at it but sensing its size and contour with his fingers before dropping it into place. He took a day to make a perfectly round dungeon four metres deep and three metres across that looked as though each stone had been cut to size.

'What a pity to fill it with shit,' I said as we admired it from the edge.

'Bah. It's only stones,' he said, but again he grinned with pride.

That evening I climbed down into the hole. It was cool and quiet. I sat on the floor until nightfall with my back to the wall, listening. I heard whispering that seemed to come from beneath my feet and round my head but was probably the evening breeze playing over the mouth of the pit. Above was a disc of pure blue sky. It blazed with sunset, darkened with twilight and then stars appeared and the twinkling lights of aeroplanes. Stiff and hungry, I climbed out and went down the hill for dinner.

Two days later Dimitris covered the pit with old floorboards, laid a rusty steel mesh on the lid and poured six inches of concrete on top. A tin can stuck through the mesh and the wood made a hole for the inflow pipe. When the concrete was set I covered my stone tomb in earth.

Every day on my way to the village I went past the cemetery. A platoon of brooding cypresses stood sentry behind a whitewashed stone wall patched with cement blocks. In daylight it was not an attractive place. The marble work on the graves was crude and botched. The plastic flowers on all but the most recent had faded to white resin in the sun. Bits of brick and stone and rubbish were scattered on the paths. At dusk dark shapes scurried along the concrete road, flittering and twittering, women of the village on their way to tend the dead. Sometimes you saw husbands and sons and fathers among them, but mostly it was women's work.

At the head of each grave was a shrine with a lamp, a Pepsi or beer bottle of oil, a box of matches, a plastic bag of charcoal, incense in a screw of newspaper, a vase of plastic flowers and a photograph of the tenant. Many of the photos were old identification cards, wedding portraits or snaps taken at weddings and christenings long ago when the dead were young and handsome. It was not easy to match them up with the eighty- and ninety-year-olds you remember hobbling around the village. But that was how they still thought of themselves and how they expected to be again when they woke up on the day of resurrection we are promised.

The women filled the lamps with oil and ignited *kandili*. They lit crumbs of charcoal in censers and sprinkled them with a few grains of incense to fumigate the marble while they gabbled prayers. Then they sat on the graves to chat to the dead and each other until sunset drove them back home.

When they left the cemetery became an enchanted place. The lamps made a galaxy of stars against the blackness of the cypresses, the gentle west wind of nightfall whispered through the pomegranate trees, bats scribbled zigzags on the lucent sky and a little owl hooted from its perch. It was the moment when the souls of the dead came out to gossip and no living Greek would linger.

Bereavement counsellors nod and talk of the grieving process and say what a good thing this all is, but they miss the point. The real reason, as any Greek granny will tell you, is that the souls of the buried are still lurking around, especially between Easter and Ascension when they pop back to their old homes and go to parties. If you believe that the souls of the dead are uneasy in their graves and will walk among the living if they are not comforted by light and helped into paradise with prayers, it doesn't matter who does the job. Evidence that the grave rituals are more to do with the psychic health of the departed than the mourners is that if there is no family around to do the job, they will pay a professional. In our village I have already mentioned that this was Maria, the widow whose husband had been murdered by his friend the butcher.

There were no more than about thirty graves and I wondered how a village so large could have generated so few. One morning I found out. The bell in the little church in the middle of the cemetery was tolling and Papas Konstantinos stood by a grave with a large group of people, mainly women. Those closest to the grave were dressed all in black, while the degrees of mourning decreased the further back they stood until those at the edge wore ordinary dresses. I assumed that it was a funeral, although I hadn't heard of anyone dying. But they were not putting anyone under. They were digging someone up: Barba Christos, Eleni's uncle, the brother of Barba Vasilis the shepherd and Athina, my reed lady of the lake.

I sidled up and stood a couple of yards behind Vasilis and nobody seemed to mind. Eleni was opposite us, all in black, staring down at the grave. The marble cross and the shrine had been tossed aside and the musty smell of fresh, moist earth mingled with the incense from a censer perched on a neighbouring grave. Waxy-fingered Elpida was in charge and did the digging with the help of Athina, who had changed out of her flowery summer frock into black for the occasion. Mournful Maria was among the women, so I guessed we had a dirge to look forward to. The rest of us watched and chatted in low voices. When they got down to the coffin the moaning and sighing began and Maria let rip:

'Tell us Christos what did you find down there in Hades?
I found snakes plaited like a young girl's hair
One snake was bolder than the others
He sat upon my chest
He ate my eyes, which looked at you
He ate my tongue, which sang to you
He ate my hands, which caressed you
He ate my feet, which danced for you my love…'

I got a bit edgy. If you think funerals are not the best way to spend a sunny morning, you should try an exhumation. The worst part was not knowing what condition old Christos was going to be in. If he was a skeleton like the one in the science labs at school, I reckoned I could get through it without having to sit down. But if he was somewhere between the corpse and the skeleton stage, I might have to cover my eyes and peep through my fingers.

Elpida dropped her shovel and pulled the corner of the coffin. It was rotten and crumbling and came away easily. She crossed herself, bent down and rummaged around as casually as if she were sorting melons. Then with a flourish that would have done credit to Hamlet's grave digger, she held up the skull to moans of acclaim from Maria.

'Oh Christos! Haros has eaten your body and drunk from your eyes…'

With her hand Elpida brushed brown, scabby bits off the skull, which I told myself was dirt but might not have been. Christos's jaw and teeth were still attached and she looked hard at them as if she was wondering whether to give him a smacking kiss. But she was more practical. She put in her fingers, pulled out a gold tooth and dropped it into her pocket. Athina scowled and nudged her and held out her hand. After a histrionic gaze of non-comprehension, Elpida took out the tooth and handed it over. Then they carried on with their work as if nothing had happened.

Elpida wrapped the skull in a white cloth, which Eleni handed her, and tied it like a Christmas pudding before passing it to Athina. Athina wailed and clutched the skull to her breast, kissed it and unwrapped it and passed it to Vasilis, who was more manly with his low lament. He took a drachma note out of his pocket, licked it and slapped it on top of the crown like a stamp, before passing the skull to Eleni, who stuck on another drachma note. This was puzzling, as Christos should have paid his way across the Styx years ago. The skull was then passed round for hugs and kisses in the general congregation and I was grateful that the privilege was extended only to relatives.

Meanwhile Elpida was busy in the grave. Inevitably, as this was Greece, she got plenty of advice from the spectators: 'Don't break the ribs... hold the middle... hold the end... watch out for his gold ring.' She worked her way methodically down the upper limbs and the torso and passed bone after bone up to Athina and Eleni and two other women, who were now in a huddle round a bucket of water, a packet of Persil and a couple of towels. They washed and dried the grey-white bones as they came up and put them in a black metal box with a hinged lid, layering them between sprigs of rosemary and flowers. The *papas* waved the censer around, but whether out of ritual or to mask the smell of decomposition I wasn't sure. I started to relax. Like all Orthodox services it had the homely feel of household chores, very matter of fact and lacking the exaggerated piety I was used to in England.

> 'Ah, Christos, you were an eagle and Haros shot you with
>   his bow
> Where are you now, in the sky or on the mountain top?
> No, you are here in a little pile of bones…'

When the box was full and Athina had checked Elpida's work by grubbing around in the compost for the last little toe bone, she stuffed fresh rosemary and thyme on top of the remains. Someone handed a small brass urn to the *papas* and he seasoned the bouquet garni with a sprinkle of holy water. Athina tried to shut the box, but even when Vasilis thumped and pushed the lid it wouldn't close properly. The top of the skull peeped up like a jack-in-the-box for a last glimpse of the sun.

Barba Christos cleared up for me one of the mysteries of Greek cemeteries, the open grave. Bits of broken marble and trampled earth lie around the gaping trench. An empty packet of detergent, an old shoe, a scrap of cloth litter the bottom, a promise of resurrection or a reminder of the end of all things, depending on your conviction.

Another mystery was the little windowless building in the corner of the cemetery. I always assumed that it was for bits of marble, barrows and spades and other tools of the gravedigger's trade. In our cemetery it was a shack built of crudely mortared and skimpily rendered cement blocks topped with Ellenit. In fact this was the bone-house, to which we made a procession with Christos.

It was like a left-luggage office, with wooden shelves floor to ceiling all round the walls. Stacked on the shelves and heaped on the floor were boxes of wood or metal, each about a femur wide, half a pelvis deep and a skull high. Their owners were identified by numbers stencilled on the shelves. Many bore the faded grave photograph of the occupant when they had more meat on them. Most of the boxes were painted black, but others were brightly coloured and decorated with gold crosses and initials made of gold paper. Some, like Barba Christos's, were too small for the job and the skulls peeped out. Others were not up to the job at all and were broken, their contents scattered on the shelves and the floor. The bones were packed with dry and brittle flowers and herbs and yellowing white cloths with unpleasant brown stains. With lamentation and incense we found a space for old Christos, lit a few candles and left him.

In the middle of the concrete floor was a square wooden table carrying a metal baker's tray full of sand and bristling with nub ends of slender honey-coloured candles. Underneath was a brown beer bottle containing an inch or so of oil. More candle ends, *kandili* wicks, withered flowers, bottles and other rubbish littered the floor.

Once the dead-and-buried are unburied and put in the bone-house, active mourning ceases. Their souls are with God at last. On Good Friday, or the feast of the saint who guards the graveyard, they may get a candle in the sand tray for old time's sake, but it is generally accepted that they have left this world for good. Meanwhile their mortal remains moulder gently on the shelves, each one witness to the short story that was someone's life. They even have the musty smell of the stacks in the London Library.

That night at dinner Elpida was in a bad mood. She muttered to herself, glowered and banged the pans around. Barba Mitsos winked at me, man to man, and puckered his lips to signal that we should stay quiet and wait for the squall to blow itself out and not whistle up any more trouble. Some hope.

'Johnny was there. He saw,' she said, plonking a dish of sweetbreads in egg and lemon sauce on the table.

'What did I see?' I asked.

'The toilet bowl.'

With or without Mitsos's nudges and winks, I had nothing to say to this. I was sure she said toilet bowl. She rabbited on a bit more about the offending sanitary ware and the disgrace to the family and how they should be grateful to her. I whipped out the dictionary and discovered that the word for toilet bowl also means pelvis. But I wasn't much further forward. I defied Mitsos again.

'What was the problem with the toilet bowl/pelvis?'

'Problem? It was black.'

'Bah. It wasn't black,' said Mitsos.

'Were you there? Johnny, was it black?'

'I didn't see it.'

'Bah. I did that family a big favour. If I had said anything…'

'But what?' I blurted.

'Lust,' she hissed. This word I did know from the magazine shelf of Kyria Anna's kiosk.

Elpida put down plates of spinach pie, Greek salad, fried potatoes and wild greens. Mitsos poured wine. We crossed ourselves and muttered grace, clinked our glasses for good health, passed round the bread and tucked in. It was delicious and distracted us from talk of lust. Elpida was in no mood for further explanations, so I waited until after the meal and she went out to feed the scraps to the goats and chickens before I asked Mitsos what it was all about.

'We Christians dig up the bones of the dead. If they are white, the blessed one is with God. If they are black, he is unforgiven and has to stay in the earth another five years.'

'Barba Christos had a black pelvis? That means lust?'

'Bah. Christos was always too drunk to chase women. His bones wouldn't turn black. He pickled them too much. He brought death on himself.'

'He killed himself?'

'Eh. He said he didn't want an old picture of himself on his grave, so on the Dormition he had Ajax the butcher take a picture with his Polaroid. He posed in his best clothes outside his front door.'

'So that's why he's waving. He was saying goodbye.'

'He said he didn't care about dying, which was lucky because he died five months later. Everyone said it was the evil eye.'

Lying in bed that night I tried to figure out what had happened. The best I could come up with was that Elpida had taken a gold tooth out of Christos's skull. She dropped it in her pocket as one of the exhumer's perks. Athina told her to hand it over. This made Elpida angry. In retaliation, she was starting a rumour that Christos should have been put back under because of his sins. One public slight deserves another. It was the sort of thing that village feuds are made of, but the next day it had blown over.

Weeks later I overheard a conversation in the baker's about another exhumation. Someone's granny was due for digging up and they wondered if Elpida now expected to be paid for her services, because Dimitra saw Barba Vasilis giving Elpida money when they were giving out *koliva* for Barba Christos outside the church. If my theory was right, this was to compensate for the gold tooth. Honour was satisfied and a feud averted.

I think this was what might have happened. I lived in such a fog of misunderstanding that I might have been totally mistaken. The real story may have been completely different. Or there may have been no story at all. When you are an outsider it is easy to live in a parallel universe unrecognisable to those who live on the inside.

'Why do they give out cod liver, Dad?' asked Kate, as we waited for Kyria Sofia to bring the fried *kalamari*.

'Not cod liver. *Koliva*. It's food for the dead that they give out at funerals and after forty days and the other anniversaries. It's a mixture of boiled wheat and sugar and raisins and pomegranate seeds. It tastes like muesli past its sell-by date. When you're offered some you're supposed to say "May God forgive."'

'Do you think they believe in all this stuff, Haron and stained bones and the rest of it?' asked Arfa.

'No idea. But they act as though they do.'

Living in the past

We were close to moving in. Outside was a building site, but the house itself had a roof, floors, walls and plumbing. We wanted to keep it as simple as possible, like a real village house and not a folklore museum.

The back room was divided by big wooden cupboards cadged from English friends who were being posted back home. We bought cheap metal beds from Monastiraki, a flea market in the centre of Athens, and flock mattresses. The front room was divided by a half-height plastered wall into a sleeping area for the double bed and a living area. I stripped and sanded the lime green paint off a pair of sideboards from the Sacred Way and mounted a steel sink from Grecian-nosed Haralambos as well as the hob and the gas fridge.

As we had no electricity, we were obliged to have authentic lighting. I told the children we were going to use Ancient Greek technology, lights such as Homer might have had. In Monastiraki I bought half a dozen little oil lamps. They were terracotta globes with a flat spout at the side and a little chimney on top for refilling them. We filled them with oil and put a cotton wick in the spout. Every time I lit the wick the flame went out. So we put the wick in the chimney and I told them that the spout helped the air supply to the flame. Every time I lit the wick the flame went out. We tried different amounts of oil and different lengths of wick, with no success. I showed one to Barba Vasilis and asked him how it worked. He told me to half fill it with water and blow through the spout and it would trill like a canary.

'Eh, the old toys. These days the children have plastic things with batteries.'

Normally the children would have got tired of something like that in a few hours but in this case they played with them for weeks, bringing the 'lamps' out to whistle when I was showing them something at a museum or walking round an ancient site.

Arfa went back to Monastiraki for the real thing, flat terracotta bowls of oil with long trailing wicks, but they were as much use as glow worms. So we skipped forward a couple of millennia to oil lamps with mantles and glass chimneys. They gave a lovely amber glow and soft shadows, fine for doing nothing by but a strain on the eyes for reading or picking the bones out of a grilled fish. Camping gas lamps were safer to carry around and more practical, although they gave off a harsh light and a disapproving hiss. A good compromise was a big gas lantern made to hang from the trestle in the bows of a boat to lure fish into the nets.

Our landlady in Athens made us a treasured gift, a little table from the taverna that her father used to own. She said that Lawrence Durrell and Melina Mercouri ate there, although she had no recollection of their stabbing festive forks into the same dish. The table was too small to eat off and the top was hatched with knife cuts, so I doubt if it had been physically touched by celebrity. 'Look kids. You know Gerald Durrell's brother Larry? They cut up his cucumbers on this table.'

We needed chairs, so we trooped off to see Leonidas the chair maker, whose workshop was on the road to Kimi. It was an elegantly proportioned two-storey house with a pitched tile roof and a wrought-iron balcony. The ground floor had been knocked through for a workshop and the family lived above. His premises had no advertisement or signs, except for a large heap of old chairs in the yard and a three metre high hammer and sickle carefully painted on the wall facing the road.

Leonidas was a stocky man of about sixty. All of him, his clothes and skin and eyes and lips, was grey except for a shock of liquorice-dyed hair. He wheezed like a bellows from a lifetime of inhaling sawdust and tobacco. His wife had one characteristic so striking that it eclipsed everything else, an overshooting upper jaw with an overhanging pointed top lip like a tree-browsing mammal's. Their daughter had not inherited this feature. Instead she had one of her own, cross-eyes. She was in her thirties and apparently no longer considered herself marriageable. She wore long-sleeved denim dresses down to her calves and, by the look of her bob, had taken against professional hairdressing.

True to his convictions, Leonidas had Russian machines to saw and plane the silky wood into struts and dowels and gently curving legs. A taverna chair, like the yellow one that

Van Gogh painted, is made of nineteen separate pieces of wood. Only six are straight, the dowelling rods that connect the legs under the seat, handy for putting your feet on. The rest are curved, some of them in two planes, in other words front to back and side to side, like the legs. Leonidas spent the mornings turning planks into components and the afternoons assembling them. The scraps were fed into a pot-bellied stove lit winter and summer to warm a crusty brown saucepan of glue, homemade from bones. When he had mortised and glued the frames and whacked them tight with a mallet, he squinted at the legs and, without testing or measuring, sawed one leg to size in a couple of cuts of a handsaw and plonked the chair on the floor. It stood perfectly square.

The seat takes four metres of rush rope. In the mornings the women stripped the feathery outside off heaps of cream-coloured rushes and plaited them into rope on a horizontal spindle turned by a wheel with a handle. In the afternoons they sat and wove them round the frame into a seat. The last operation was to paint the wood with thick yellow varnish. While they worked they munched green chickpeas straight off the stalk and listened to music on the radio. I never heard them talking to each other. A miasma of depression hovered over them. It could have been caused by fumes from the glue, dyspepsia from raw chickpeas, the decline of the Soviets or cheap white plastic chairs hawked by gypsies from painted trucks.

Leonidas admitted that his main business, furnishing tavernas and cafés, was suffering. A giant press could whack resin into a mould in ten seconds. Lo and behold, a one-piece chair. With arms too. Leonidas's chairs didn't have arms. If you wanted to rest your arms in the café you pulled over another two chairs.

'Would it be better under Communism?' I asked.

'Bah. Who uses hammers and sickles these days? It's all plastic and typewriters.'

His chairs have done excellent service ever since. Ten years ago Leonidas, his wife and daughter, their house and piles of chairs outside all burned together in a fire allegedly started by the glue pot in the middle of the night. By then there was no demand for chairs made from nineteen pieces of wood and hand-plaited rushes.

Moving in was an anticlimax. There was still so much to do. It was like being billeted in a barn. We were disappointed, irritable and tired.

The weather had a lot to do with it. The end of the school term in Greece almost always coincides with the first great heatwave of summer. From sunrise to sunset the sun was livid, the sky gauzy blue, the air milky with heat haze and dust. In the morning you woke up soaked in sweat. You stepped outside and were bludgeoned by the heat. It was too hot to work, to walk, to eat. You tried putting clothes on, taking them off, wiping with wet towels, wiping with dry towels, showering, not showering, hot drinks, cold drinks, and it made no difference to your sticky, gritty skin and sweat-stung eyes. In the afternoon you lay down on sodden sheets with outstretched arms and legs like Leonardo's man in the circle and shrank from the touch of another fevered body. Telling each other how hot it was passed for conversation.

When the sun went down it was little better. Earth and stone radiated heat and concrete was worse. At night it was too hot to sleep until the cool hour before dawn. In the airless silence you heard the slightest sound, a black beetle inspecting the melons, a mouse creeping down the chimney, a gecko patrolling the wall. Dawn was the best time to get up. The heat crept up on you and was more tolerable. If you woke up when the sun was high you were already soaked in sweat. You stepped outside and were bludgeoned by the heat...

It was too hot for the beach. The children slumped on their beds with Asterix and Tintin and the Hardy Boys and Gerald Durrell until they were overwhelmed by desire for ice-cold water. They slouched to the little gas fridge and flung it open hoping for a miracle, jugs of frozen sherbet, lemony sorbets, crushed ice. But it could not cope. Powered by a little gas flame that forced coolant round the pipes at the back, it gave off more heat than cold. The ice tray with twelve tiny cubes never had so much as a glazing of frost. Bottles of water stayed resolutely *chambré*. The children crashed on our bed with tragic sighs and moans.

Arfa and I took to tepid Double-Os, ouzo and orange juice, a recreational beverage that we improvised out of desperation one evening when the wine ran out. The aniseed went well with the metallic tang of carton juice. Booze helped, but you paid for it in more sweat and lethargy.

In the morning the children lay quietly on their beds, hoping that their parents would think they were still asleep, knowing that if they got up they would have to do unpleasant things like wash their faces and lay the table.

They yearned to be young Durrell with an interesting family and cute animals and funny adventures. He didn't have insects chewing his mattress and rats running up the walls, wasn't chased by hornets and stung by wasps, never trod on thistles or sea urchins with spines that had to be dug out with a needle. He never had thirst or hunger or sunburn or fever or vomiting or squits. He didn't have to lug stones and mix cement, wash his clothes and sweep the floors. The Greeks he knew were funny and spoke English and didn't pinch his cheeks and pull his hair and spit on him. He wasn't annoyed by his brothers and shouted at by his parents. Life was never bo-ring. And he was never sent down to the village in the heat to buy breakfast.

Reality, in the lovely shape of their mother, banged open the door.

'Morning, sweeties.'

'Good morning, Mummy. Is it time to get up? Oh goodee. It looks a lovely day. Is there anything we can do to help? Shall I lay the table for breakfast?'

In your dreams, Mummy. She wasn't greeted with so much as a grunt. But revenge was sweet.

'We need bread for breakfast.'

She was rewarded with a collective groan. Sadistically, she took her time selecting the victim.

'Kate... I think it's your turn.'

The three boys punched the air and hissed 'Yessss!' Kate pulled the sheet over her head, willing herself to be spirited to Corfu where Gerald had no more to do than brush crumbs off the tablecloth and had a proper mother, not the wicked step variety. Resistance was pointless. She could string her parents along indefinitely but her brothers poked and prodded and needled and taunted, so that within minutes she was trudging down the path, squinting against the heat and clutching a limp and sodden drachma note in her sweaty little fist.

The simple act of going into the baker's and saying *dio kila parakolo*, two kilos please, was the least of the burdens of office of the breakfast fetcher. The big challenge was to avoid villagers by dodging into doorways and slipping round corners and scurrying down lanes and waiting until the shop was empty before sidling in. The smallest penalty for being caught was a barrage of Greek and, especially if it was an old lady, a cheek pinch.

Occasionally someone, often canny Barba Mitsos, would buy them an ice cream or a Coke, which they would brag about all day to the others. But mostly they dreaded generosity. Melons heavy as cannonballs, paper bags of eggs that halfway home made crunching noises and leaked yolk down their shorts, armfuls of spinach or beans crawling with caterpillars, soft fruit buzzing with wasps, cheeses dripping milky brine down their legs and onto their sandals. The gifts also meant that they could not carry the piping hot loaves at arm's length but had to tuck them under their arms like hot poultices for the long trudge home in the blazing sun.

Kate had a bad morning: hair bedraggled, cheeks aflame, T-shirt sodden, sweat rash under the arms, loaves dented in half, two enormous watermelons, one of which had split, dribbling juice and pips down her legs, just in case any wasp had trouble finding her.

She dumped her load in the kitchen and shuffled to the fridge for a cold pack. It was tepid, but it was better than nothing. Crook-backed, hands dangling histrionically round her knees, she shuffled back to bed to recover with Durrell in his Corfu idyll.

Bread was one of the few things we bought. We never had to buy the makings of a Greek salad or a potato omelette. We fried our neighbours' aubergines and courgettes in oil from olives they grew a hundred metres down the hill. We dressed their spinach and greens in lemon and garlic or, better still, *skordalia*, garlic purée stiffened with breadcrumbs and oil. In their season there were apples, apricots, pears, pomegranates, peaches and figs for the fruit bowl. We had melons piled like cannonballs in the coolest corner of the kitchen. In the fridge we had the choice of wine from half a dozen different barrels.

Most of the time we had no idea who had given us these things. We opened the front door in the morning and fell over them. We rarely paid for coffee or ouzo in Yannis's café if any of our friends were in there. In her fish taverna in

Limanaki, Kyria Sofia often plonked down an unordered can of wine and jerked her thumb at another table. When we ate in the company of Greeks it was unheard of to split a bill and impossible for us to pick it up. Even if we made arrangements with the waiter before we sat down, one of the Greeks would gabble very fast and undo them. They expected none of this to be reciprocated or even acknowledged with more than a nod of the head or a raised glass. It was heart-warming and also embarrassing, but there was nothing we could do. It has been the rule in these parts for thousands of years. We were strangers and that was the end of it.

We tried to reciprocate. When we went abroad we brought back shortbread in tartan tins and Christmas puddings in basins and toffees in double-decker buses. Arfa drew the line at haggis as bringing Britain into disrepute. For a time, when whisky in the duty-free was cheaper than in Yannis's café, we arrived like bootleggers. But it felt more like payback than true generosity.

There were three levels of catering we could be invited to. The first was when you weren't invited at all but happened to be around at a mealtime. This was pot luck and could be as few as half a dozen dishes. Something fishy like octopus or anchovies in brine, a couple of meat stews, a vegetable or two, feta and salad.

The next level was to be invited to *meze*. Although this means appetiser or snack, you were ill-advised to make dinner plans for afterwards. It consisted of the above plus two or three specially prepared dishes, perhaps a spinach and cheese pie, chunks of roast lamb, spicy sausage, stuffed tomatoes and peppers. 'Ah, tapas,' sophisticated readers may say and they would be right about the variety but misled about the size of the portions. A better comparison is an all-you-can-eat buffet.

Finally you might be invited to a *trapezi*, a table. This was like a *meze* but with even more elaborate dishes. It was where you got delicacies that took hours to prepare like *papoutsakia*, little shoes, courgettes halved lengthways with a lemony béchamel filling, or *imam bayaldi*, whose prosaic translation in Zorba's cookbook as 'baked stuffed aubergine' evoked nothing like its literal sense, the imam swooned. You were well advised not to make dinner plans for a day either side of a *trapezi*, an all-you-can-eat-and-half-as-much-again buffet with someone else heaping your plate.

Those who believe that first courses are hurdles in the race to dessert will be disappointed by a Greek meal. In summer there will be seasonal fruit, but generally there are no puddings or coffee or After Eights. These come first. The traditional welcome when you go into a house at any time is a glass of water and a spoonful of jam followed by a sugary coffee. (Arfa reversed the order to take the taste away.) A variation on the jam was *vanillia*, Kate's favourite, a lurid white sticky sugary putty tasting of face cream. She kept a big pot of it under her bed.

For more mature palates ouzo was on offer – but only to the men. It was immodest for women to drink in public. Arfa was prepared to respect most norms of decency, for example by always wearing skirts and not trousers in the village, but here she drew the line. She chipped in with 'Yes please and John will have one too.' They didn't seem to mind. Foreign women were assumed to be hussies.

Greeks bearing gifts

'**M**aam, Daad, they're coming they're coming…'
'Who? Who?' shouted Arfa, sitting bolt upright in bed, jerked out of deep early morning sleep.

'Hoo Hoo… Hoo Hoo,' yelled Harry and chuff-chuffed around the bed pulling an imaginary whistle.

'Hoo Hoo Hoooo,' hooted Kate, who wanted to be an owl when she grew up and practised swivelling her head over meals.

'Hoooo Hoooo,' howled Jim, who tried to frighten the little ones with werewolf stories and gave himself nightmares.

'Hoo Hoo, Hoo Hoo, Hoo Hoo,' grunted Jack, sticking his tongue under his lower lip, scratching himself under the arms and doing bow-legged two-footed jumps round the room.

'Who?' I grumbled.

'Don't you start,' she said and went bleary-eyed to the door to see what had stirred up the menagerie.

The doors of our little church were wide open. Out of them came Roula's shriek, audible three fields away, and Elpida's laugh and other voices I could not identify. A cloud of dust billowed on the threshold, chased out by a yellow straw broom. Up the path from the spring came Antigone and two other women carrying armfuls of flowers. They filled vases on the iconostasis and made a wreath for Ioannes's icon.

Other villagers came up the path on foot, on donkeys and in vehicles. The Greek flag was run up the olive tree. The air was blue with exhaust and white with dust. Haralambos ran a cable from the battery in his pick-up to power a busker's amplifier for the PA system. Squeals of feedback and the Greek equivalent of 'wanoofree wanoofree' echoed around the old village.

Papas Konstantinos arrived with Ajax the butcher in the red Mercedes. Eleni carried a carpet bag with his vestments, which he put on in the privacy of the sanctuary behind the iconostasis.

From a table beside the door, Elpida sold dog-eared black and white postcards of Aghios Ioannes and candles for the icon inside. The church quickly filled up, so most of us milled outside, the keen ones crowding to the door to see and the rest chatting and smoking on the fringes like Irishmen outside Sunday mass. Ajax worked the crowd like a cocktail party, gleaning information and doing deals. Haralambos achieved the same result by sitting on a wall and letting people come to him.

The liturgy dragged on, with incense and chanting and signs of the cross and lighting of candles and kissing of icons, punctuated by the deafening thumps of Konstantinos slapping his microphone. When we westerners pray we join our hands, close our eyes, kneel, hunch up and put our hands over our faces to close up our bodies. Our God is inside us, his universe inside our heads. When Orthodox Christians pray they keep their eyes open. They hold their heads up and open up their senses to the universe. Their God is outside in a real world. The liturgy and the music, the no-nonsense ceremony, the annual resanctification of a place where once a goat-god lived and was embodied still in the form of shape-changing Aghios Ioannes was a living timeline to ancient times. At last two old women came out with round, flat loaves that the *papas* had blessed. We all scrummed in to grab a piece, although there was plenty for everyone. It was flavoured with sesame and cinnamon.

Our house was as much an attraction as the church. We invited the *papas* up for coffee and left the front door open for people to wander in and out and comment and criticise and wish us *kalo risiko*. Arfa fussed round them with coffee and Coke and a tin of duty-free shortbread, while I did the manly thing with worry beads beside the *papas*. The children disappeared up the hillside to avoid spits, pinches and speaking Greek.

Elpida took it upon herself to give our visitors the tour, praising the view and the quiet and the fresh air up here on the hillside and pointing out the lack of electricity and the holes for the rats and how impossible it was to keep clean. Leaving their coffee undrunk, for it was foreign filter and not proper Greek coffee, they went back to the chores in their own houses leaving behind, without any fuss or expectation of thanks, bags of tomatoes and peppers and cucumbers and aubergines and cheese and eggs, so that our kitchen looked like a harvest festival.

That evening, after he had finished replenishing the water and grain for his birds in the house opposite, Spiros came to admire his carpentry and congratulate us on moving in. He brought us a plastic water bottle full of wine out of his best barrel. In return, I offered him a glass of Single McSozzle out of my own *grande réserve*. We carried drinks and bits to the table under the olive tree. The day's heat lurked in the earth and the stones and the trunks of trees, while the hesitant cool of evening rustled leaves and brassy grass.

The sun was low over the horizon, turning from unbearable incandescence to a ruddy bronze that the eye can stand. The Greek for set is *vasilevi*, which also means to reign, like a king. Read it in a dictionary and it seems an odd word for decline and dissolution, but in the majesty of reds and purples and golds it makes sense. The beauty even overawed the children, seen but unheard except for the gentle burping of cola and the crackly mastication of crisps.

As the western horizon caught fire, Spiros pointed with his hand and conjured his doves out of the translucent porcelain blue of heaven. They circled and dipped and the sunset turned them into crimson firebirds.

'So beautiful,' breathed Arfa as they made a final pass above us before fluttering down into their own house.

'You like doves?' he asked. I thought of how they cooed and rustled during the day and wheeled over the house in the evening.

'Of course,' we said.

'Come with me then,' he said, sucking the last of the whisky from his moustache.

While the children fought over the last crumbs of crisp, Arfa and I followed Spiros to his house. He opened the wire gate into the yard. It was overgrown with thistles and buddleia and littered with old plastic bags, rusted jerry cans and heaps of pigeon manure. He picked up a plastic bag, shook out a few grains of yellow corn and told us to wait while he went up the stone staircase into the house. There were scufflings and flutterings inside.

'Oh no, he's giving us pigeons for the house,' whispered Arfa.

'Where will we put them?'

'They'll have to go in the cellar.'

'They'll attract rats.'

'We'll have to build a pigeon house like on Mykonos.'

'As if we didn't have enough to do.'

'We can't refuse them.'

Spiros came out of the house and down the steps and handed Arfa the bulging plastic bag. She peeked inside. It was full of feathers and little pink claws. A beady eye looked up at us. On the end of a little yellow beak was a tiny drop of blood like a ruby. Suddenly the bag jumped. She yelped and dropped it. Spiros cackled, picked it up and banged it hard against the side of his knee. He handed it to me.

'On the spit if you like. But try stuffing them with hard cheese and roasting them in a pot in the oven.' He kissed the tips of his fingers. I held the bag away from my body so that

I couldn't feel the warmth of the soft little bodies.

'Don't let the children see,' warned Arfa. But it was too late.

'Cor.'

'Can I have the feathers? Can I? Can I?' insisted Harry.

That night in bed I got the blame for the animal cruelty of Greeks and the callousness of our children and the general malevolence of the universe, but for the time being we went back to the table, refilled the glasses and opened another packet of crisps.

'My wife's old grandmother told us stories when we came here in the summer. She sat on the step over there. The garden was different then. It was full of vegetables and flowers,' mused Spiros.

'Tell us one.'

'Eh. It's so long ago.'

'Tell us one for the children.'

'Eh. There's one I remember.'

Arfa's Greek was much better than mine, so she did the consecutive translation into English while I frowned and tutted to keep the audience in order. They would rather have had a Fingers Bumcrusty, but learning to listen politely to a bo-ring folk tale would do them good.

'On his travels, Aghios Ioannes came to an island where they only ate doves. The sea was too rough for fishing and the grass too poor for animals and the soil too thin for good crops. Oil and stones were all they had. The doves were the only plump things in sight. They lived in special stone houses that were bigger and finer than the hovels the people lived in. They were tall and square with battlements round the top and narrow windows in the walls like arrow slits for the birds to fly in and out. The island looked ready for a war of midgets, dotted with tiny castles. On Sunday every person on the island ate a dove in a pie or on the spit or in a stew. For the rest of the week they scratched what they could from the dirt.

'Aghios Ioannes preached to the people, but they wouldn't listen. They were too busy in the fields. The only thing that attracted their attention was the gold cross he wore round his neck, which was given him by our Patriarch in Constantinople. It was made for blessed Queen Eleni out of the gold that the three wise men brought for Our Lord. One day, in the middle of his preaching, he took it off his neck and held it above his head. A large black crow swooped out of nowhere and carried it off towards the mountain at the end of the island. The people were frightened and spat at the saint and went back to their labour. But Aghios Ioannes went after the crow. He followed it for forty days and forty nights across salt lakes and through thorn forest and up into the bare mountain, swimming like a fish and running like a hare and climbing like a mountain goat and living off berries and locusts.

'At last he came to a cave at the top of the island where the queen of the island lived. She was a witch who kept the whole island under an evil spell. In the middle of the cave was a pile of gold and jewels she had stolen from her people and the saint saw his holy cross on top of them.

'Now, Aghios Ioannes noticed that the witch kept a flock of goats in a field next to the cave. And hanging on a tree to dry were the skins of animals she had slaughtered. So he put one of the skins on his back and joined the flock so that she wouldn't see him. When she came out of the cave in the evening to milk them, he grabbed her by the throat. Oh what a fight they had! She turned into a pecking crow, but he hung on. She changed into a spitting cat, but he hung on. She changed into a writhing weasel, a roaring lion, a clinging octopus, but he hung on. Finally she changed into a pure white dove, but he was not deceived and wrung her neck and she changed into nothing else. The tyrant was dead and the spell on the wretched people of the island was broken. No longer slaves for the profit of the witch, no longer forced to toil in the stony fields to feed her, they changed back into their rightful shapes, white doves, and spent the rest of their days swooping and wheeling over the island in freedom.'

There were six in the bag, one each. First I boiled a pan of water and poured it over them so that they were easier to pluck. I started at the tail feathers and worked my way up each soft little body to the dislocated neck. The worst part was the smell of warm pigeon shit and damp feathers. When they were naked, I cut off their pretty heads and their wizened little feet. Through the anus I tore out the intestines. From the neck I emptied the crop, which was lumpy with gravel and undigested grains of yellow corn. I stuffed the insides with hard cheese and took them down to Dimitra's to put in the oven.

The rest of the family didn't want theirs and watched in silence as I ate all six. There wasn't much meat on them, but they were very tasty.

While Arfa and I laboured on the house, the children played in the yard and in the fields above. What they got up to we could only guess. Their *omerta* was impervious to our wheedling and trickery and not even the youngest would grass.

We had occasional glimpses of the world they lived in: Kate stark naked and painted blue, running for her life with reed arrows whistling round her; rope burns on Harry's wrists and ankles; a barricade of thorn bushes between two mulberry trees across a rocky path; requests for tools and supplies, of whose purpose we suspected the worst; Jim's pockets full of feathery snake skins; a massive warty toad hidden under the T-shirts in their bedroom cupboard; a scorpion and a stag beetle fighting it out in a Tupperware box under Jack's bed; a stash of swords and spears, snake pokers and lizard teasers, fashioned from laths and reeds. They brought bruises, stings and bloody knees for medical attention, tight-lipped about the causes, like criminals in Accident and Emergency.

Their favourite place was an ancient olive tree in a small field above our house. It was at least five hundred years old, a living monument, a golden thread leading us back as surely as a fresco or a carving to the Venetians or the crusaders, perhaps even the Byzantines. Olive trees reach their peak in about two hundred years and then the main trunk dies away. It is replaced by shoots from the base that over the decades grow thick as trunks themselves and twine round each other to make a knotted mass like the drum of a colossal pillar, with a hollow core where the original trunk was. In a forest fire the air inside the hollow explodes, ripping the drum apart and leaving the core exposed. This had happened to the ancient olive tree near us, leaving a gnarled, woody semicircle like a spoon-back chair looking downhill over our new roof to the valley. Old age, disease and the harvesting of generations had left it with a spiky crown of spindly branches, out of scale with the massive base but enough to shade the hollow. It was their camp, their hideout, their tepee, their fort, their den.

One morning, after shouting at them to stop making a noise and get out from under our feet, we were unnerved by their silence and absence and went to look for them. We found them sitting in the embrace of the ancient tree, telling each other a tale of chivalry concocted out of Achilles and Lancelot, Maid Marian and Helen, Alexander and William Tell, something out of a mediaeval romance or a Disney animation. We crept back to the house feeling envious and smug.

The tree belonged to Barba Fedon, the old man with the chestnut comb-over, whose life's course had been changed by spying on the ladies-only bacchanalia. He came past the house on his donkey a couple of times a week. I couldn't work out what he did except scavenge for rubbish on the hillside. He had a keen eye for what he might find useful: a piece of plywood, an old bed frame, an empty cheese tin. He was especially fond of the bent nails that lay in profusion round our house – I was getting better, but I still bent a couple before I managed to hammer one in straight. He reminded me of an ant, the kind who will carry a piece of straw fifty times bigger than itself.

I was going for a walk up the hill when I saw him standing in front of the ancient olive and looking up into the branches. I took the opportunity to get his permission to use it as a playhouse.

'Beautiful tree,' I said, hopping down from the stone wall.

'Bah,' he said, whacking the wood with his stick, 'it's finished. Five years now it hasn't made fruit. It's only good for firewood.'

'What? You can't cut it down.' My voice sounded like a stranger's to me, I was so shocked.

'You're right. It's too big. I don't know where I'd find a chainsaw big enough.'

'Please, Barba Fedon, tell me if you decide to cut it down.'

'It's OK, thanks. My two great-nephews will help me.'

I scooted back home and told Arfa the news.

'It's like everything, animals, friends, relations, people, things, the relationship lasts only as long as they are useful. It's a crime,' I said, with a suitably Hellenic gesture.

'Don't get excited, Toad. We'll do something.'

'What? Go the council for a preservation order?'

'Why don't we buy his field? He's got no use for it.'

'Light of my life, you are a genius.'

And so began the courtship of Barba Fedon. We had to show that we were serious about buying, but not so keen that he could ask a ridiculous price. We had to give him a reason for buying that he could understand, but not the impression that we had found some hidden treasure. There was no point in telling him it was for love of a beautiful tree – he would simply not understand and assume that it was a smoke screen for something else. We had to think of something that fitted in with his view of the world.

The next time he passed the house on his donkey we invited him in for coffee, which he refused, saying he had drunk one already that day, and for a drop of The Glugmore, which he accepted. He sat down, took off his big straw hat and smoothed the chestnut comb-over down on his chalky skull, missing a bit, which dangled down onto his collar. The industrial tang of cologne and liniment filled the room. While we futtered around with glasses and ice, he appraised our belongings like an auctioneer. We followed the social niceties of clinking glasses and wishing for health and answering questions that in Britain you only expect from your financial adviser. At last we could get to the point.

'Barba Fedon, if you ever want to sell your field with the big olive tree, please let us know.'

His bright black eyes bored into mine. 'Why do you want that field?'

'We want to buy a donkey, but we don't want it in our yard. We need the space for vegetables.'

'Why do you want a donkey?'

'For the children.'

'Eh. I need that field for my own donkey. And in the autumn I grow beans…'

It was hard to keep a straight face, to avoid Arfa's eye, to stop punching the air with a triumphant 'yesss'. He had taken the bait. He had started to list all the reasons he did not want to sell his field, which meant he was going to. If he had said OK, let's talk about it later, it would have meant we didn't have a hope. We had started on the arduous process of negotiation, which would culminate in our being the owners of the little field with the ancient olive tree.

And so it turned out. For the price of a meal in a decent restaurant, we owned a living timeline to Byzantium.

Ambrosia and shepherd's pie

'*D*aad, what's ambrosia?' asked Kate, tucking in to her favourite breakfast of mashed-up feta and olive oil, the savoury version of yoghurt and honey.

'Tinned rice pudding, sweetheart. It's not bad but it doesn't have any skin. The skin's the best part. It sticks to the roof of your mouth and you suck it.'

'I like the skin on the top of cocoa. Trouble is you don't get enough with Greek milk.'

'When I was a monitor in a *colonie de vacances* in France, our breakfast treat was the skin off the boiled milk for the kids' hot chocolate. You heaped it on your bread all warm and slimy. *Délicieux.*'

'Sounds luvverly,' said Kate. 'Can we have that, Mummy?'

'Beugh. If you two don't stop I'll be sick,' said the Guardian of Taste.

'Dad was only telling me about ambrosia.'

'Ambrosia was what the gods ate. It has nothing to do with rice pudding skin.'

'What was it then?' asked Kate.

'Dunno,' she said. 'Whatever they liked best, I suppose.'

'Tapioca pudding with condensed milk? Stewed tripe with parsnips? Poached calf's brain on toast?' I suggested.

Arfa tried to change the subject with a rambling description of how the twelve most important gods lived on Olympus, even Hades, the god of the underworld, and were served ambrosia and nectar by Ganymede, a pretty young Trojan boy snatched away for the job by Zeus's eagle. The real purpose of this epicurean discussion was to decide on a menu for our first dinner party. It was the only way we could think of to reciprocate our neighbours' hospitality.

'What shall we have? We can't give them back what they've just given us,' said Arfa.

'When we've finished they won't recognise it as food.'

'What do you mean by that?'

'Don't get touchy, darling. I mean we'll cook it differently from them. It will still be food for the gods.' Phew, I got out of that one.

'It'll just be a sub-standard version of what they give us.'

'Nooo. They've never had anything like The Dish and Biscuit.'

This had been our regular dinner party offering in London. In its original form it might have been *boeuf bourgignon* or *coq au vin*, but it was now any kind of chopped-up supermarket meat stewed in a tin of tomatoes and graced with roundels of what purported to be puff pastry. This was the biscuit, in the potter's sense of porcelain, which has been fired but not glazed.

'We've only got two gas rings.'

'I'll dig out *Cooking in a Bedsitter*,' I said.

'We'll have to use the *fourno*.'

We didn't use the bakery oven very often, as we felt embarrassed when Dimitra peered into our dishes with disdain. Eventually we noticed that she looked like that at everyone's, as she worked out in which part of the oven to put it and how much extra water to add.

'How about shepherd's pie? We'll tell them it's our national dish.'

'It's not very exciting.'

'Here it's exotic. And if it goes wrong they'll think that's what it's meant to taste like.'

'I suppose I can't go wrong with shepherd's pie,' Arfa said and I kept a diplomatic silence.

'Can we have rhubarb crumble for pudding?' asked Kate.

'Where do we get rhubarb in Greece in August?' I said, always ready to pour cold water on ideas that weren't mine.

Although we should have invited the whole village, we only had a limited number of chairs. We started with Ajax the butcher and Eleni, Haralambos the builder's merchant and his young bride Antigone. Antigone's father Spiros the carpenter would come alone, as his wife was in Athens looking after the grandchildren. Barba Vasilis accepted for himself and his wife, but we knew she wouldn't come as she had agoraphobia and never left the house. Elpida and Barba Mitsos made up the guest list.

We decided to treat them to traditional English cuisine. We plumped for Hawaiian prawn cocktail followed by shepherd's pie followed by nectarine crumble and ice cream. We searched Aliveri for Bird's custard powder, because what is a pudding without custard lumps to squidge between the teeth? But it hadn't caught on yet, along with Bisto gravy powder, Daddy's brown sauce, Heinz salad cream and other Great British delicacies. All the other ingredients were easy to come by, including a tin of pine-apple chunks for the cocktail sauce.

Some parties go off better than you hoped. The food turns out like the recipes promised. The drink is just right and doesn't run out. The guests are on form and play off each other like a chamber orchestra. Everyone enjoys themselves. You don't mind clearing up the mess afterwards because you have been wonderful hosts.

That rarely happened to us and this evening was no exception. In every way it was the opposite of the above. Food for the gods? It was the dinner party from Hades.

'Everyone looked like corpses under that camping gas. You should have hung up oil lamps,' said Arfa, as we lay in bed later, unable to sleep for chagrin and embarrassment.

'We'd have set fire to the tree.'

'Is that why you didn't put out mosquito coils? It was like the Bavarian slapping dance out there.'

'The smell puts you off your food. It's worse than a Body Shop.'

'Poor Antigone. Her thighs must be raw.'

'Serves her right for wearing that outfit. She looked like the strippergram.'

It started off all right. Arfa had invited some for eight and I had invited the rest for nine, but it didn't matter because they all arrived at sunset, as they would have whatever time we'd said. They came dressed up and with gifts of embroidery and brightly coloured liqueurs, sowing seeds of apprehension that they might be expecting a grander occasion than we had prepared. They toured the house and talked about the old days and pointed out what the builders had done wrong.

We men then went outside to the table under the mulberry. Arfa let me play the Greek male and be waited on. It wasn't for my honour but hers. In Greece women control the home and letting a man interfere means that he is not under the thumb as he should be. I had put on dark trousers and the shirt I saved for weddings, a short-sleeve white polyester *plissé*. The others wore similar, so we sat round one end of the table like a waiters' convention, sizing up each other's pot bellies. We were all slicked back and scented with the same pungent cologne that Aussie Alekos the barber pushed on all his customers.

Ajax won the moustache competition, with handlebars so preposterously sculpted that they looked stuck on. Spiros the carpenter was runner-up, with his festive yard brush embellished with blue pencil and the relics of meals and spangled with golden sawdust. Barba Mitsos's was pure white in the gaslight and looked as if he had been quaffing cream. Barba Vasilis favoured the dyed brown hairy caterpillar. These days my own contribution would be called designer stubble. It was designed by mosquito bites that made shaving a torment.

'Ruddy Pimm's,' I said.

'It was your idea. A taste of England, you said.'

The bottle had been lurking at the back of the cupboard for years, a relic of duty-free delusion along with other failed attempts at stylishness, like my panama hat and Arfa's parasol. Biting his lip in concentration, Jack carried out the tray of glasses and gingerly set it down like Ganymede on his first day at work.

'We drink this in England in the summer,' I said. 'It's very traditional.'

'Is it warming?' asked Ajax, who had heard about our weather.

'It's gin with quinine and herbs. The mixture is a secret. Only six people in the world know it.'

'Why is it a secret?' asked Haralambos, sniffing his glass. 'Who else would want it?'

'Then you add Sprite and the other things.'

They picked up their glasses and peered and sniffed and poked at bobbing cucumber and fished out bedraggled mint.

'Our health,' I said and took a swig. They took the tiniest sips.

'Shall we have a whisky?' I ventured.

With synchronised twists of the head, the vote was unanimous. In the kitchen Arfa had a similar experience offering Pimm's to the women. They asked for coffee instead. Elpida made it, in case they were given foreign filter stuff.

They came out to join us. For our taste of England Arfa had put on Laura Ashley, but without the complementary white cardy, *de rigueur* in its native habitat. If she was an English rose, Eleni was a Greek lily, tall and graceful in a cream dress falling in loose folds from a flounce under her bosom. Her blue-black hair was carelessly swept up in a chignon. Antigone glittered in lamé, sequins and silver-flecked gauze. Elpida wore black except for a yellow Evia scarf to cover her bald patch. Her moustache scored higher than mine.

'So quiet up here,' said Eleni. 'You can't hear anything.' This was true, since the hiss and pop of the gas lamps drowned out everything else.

'Aren't you afraid to be so near the cemetery?' asked Antigone.

'There are no vampires in our village,' said Elpida. 'We are good people.'

'Eh, don't you believe it,' said Vasilis, 'there are still some who'd eat your liver. Dead or alive.'

'Bah,' said Mitsos.

Your Greek vampire, the *vrikolokas*, is a different breed from Bram Stoker's variety. They are partial to human liver, which they cook with their hot breath. The remedy is to dig up the body, if exorcism fails cut it into small pieces, and if that doesn't work burn it. Anybody born on Christmas Day or not properly baptised or excommunicated or dying a violent death runs the risk of becoming a *vrikolokas*.

'Or if a black cat jumps over your corpse,' said Spiros.

'Or if you marry a *koumbaros*, Granny used to say,' said Antigone and giggled and glanced at Ajax. As small talk went it was a change from the weather.

For special occasions such as this, Arfa had invested in a jar of deluxe loganberry conserve from Harrods. (How much? For a pot of jam!) She scooped out spoonfuls and passed them on saucers to the coffee drinkers, who took little tastes for politeness and pushed them aside.

'It needs sugar,' said Elpida, 'you should put more in next time.'

'I didn't make it,' said Arfa. 'It's from Harrods.' But brand recognition was not a consumption influencer in Elpida's consumer profile.

'Eh,' she said with a twitch of her moustache, 'I thought so. Shop-bought.'

They didn't think much of our other delicacies either. Our great innovation was to fry almonds in olive oil with salt. Our neighbours thought of them as sweet not savoury and put them in honey cakes or coated them in hard white sugar to be given out in little net bags at weddings and baptisms. Although those who tried them liked them fried, we ran up against the ultimate sanction: 'Eh, we Greeks don't do it like that.' They had a religious attitude to food and drink. Anything other than strict Orthodoxy was heretical.

They were baffled by thin strips of ham wrapped round cubes of melon and impaled on toothpicks. They carefully unpicked them and threw the melon away. No one even tried the last of our stash of smoked oysters. As for the little round cantaloupe stuck all over with feta and pineapple cubes, it might have been voodoo for all they found it appetising. They ate only the crisps and the olives.

'Barba Vasilis, how's your wife?' I asked.

It was a standard question when he came past the house with his flock and the standard reply was 'Well, thank you'. This time I might have asked if his bowels had moved today. He flushed. Barba Mitsos scowled and discovered a fascinating knobble in the mulberry branch above his head. Eleni's lovely eyes blazed at me, Elpida rearranged her bosom with folded arms and Ajax and Haralambos seemed amused, like boys seeing a classmate getting into trouble.

'She's fine,' said Vasilis and turned his attention to the bats flitting in the half-light.

What had I said? I had put my foot in something, but I had no idea what. As the evening wore on I noticed that Vasilis and Mitsos never looked at each other. When one spoke the other frowned and sighed and looked away. I felt the creeping chill in the stomach familiar to hosts who unknowingly invite sworn enemies to their party.

There were other dynamics. Antigone made a display of doting on her new husband Haralambos. She served him the hors d'oeuvres first, although this could have been interpreted as malice. She refilled his glass and his plate after every sip and forkful. Every so often she stood up, went round behind him, draped herself over him, nuzzled the back of his neck and fed him choice morsels. He reacted with quiet gratification, so quiet that it was hardly noticeable. He sat upright and dignified and carried on with the conversation as if she were just a breath of breeze round his shoulders. Ajax the butcher paid her more attention, smiling and glancing up at her as she played the infatuated young bride. Meanwhile he ignored his own wife, Eleni. She talked babies with Arfa and helped her with dishes and condiments. Elpida talked to everyone and as she had grey hair was ignored.

'Time for the first course, darling.'

'Good idea, darling.'

'Shall I carry it out for you, darling?'

'You sit there, darling.'

'Don't drop it, darling.'

'I won't, darling.'

I heard the crash over the hiss of the lamps and ran to help. It wasn't really serious because she'd washed the kitchen floor that morning and prawns have gritty bits in them anyway. They were giant specimens complete with heads and feelers and little hairy legs on a bed of chopped lettuce and smothered in bright pink cocktail sauce with a garni of shredded pineapple. I was proud of the sauce, which I had improvised out of yoghurt, a precious bottle of Heinz ketchup and a dash of Worcestershire sauce I hoarded for Bloody Marys. It tasted just like Sainsbury's. Lacking this benchmark of excellence, our guests carefully wiped it off with paper napkins. They threw the shells to the family of feral cats gathering in the dark outside the pool of gas light. Their yellow and green eyes in the blackness reminded me of reflector studs on English roads – as they are called Catseyes it wasn't a great imaginative leap.

In Greece all dishes are served at once, so we immediately served the main course before they panicked that there was nothing else to eat. I insisted on bringing out the big round earthenware pot, as I was less likely to drop it. If only I had. Arfa and Kate had laboured all morning, peeling potatoes and mashing them with Neo Vitam margarine and rendering the fat off Ajax's frozen lamb mince and dicing onions and carrots and opening tins of peas and mushroom soup and dissolving stock cubes and grating Greek gruyère for the topping. It had spent the rest of the day at the baker's.

Arfa hammered the golden crust with a serving spoon. It sounded as if she were calling us to order. She smashed through the carapace and discovered with relief two layers of different consistencies of mush. She dolloped it out for the children to hand round while I spoke about its culinary heritage, including such subtleties as the difference between shepherd's pie and cottage pie, which hinges on the inclusion of carrots. In spite of its cultural credentials, our guests looked on their dinner with dismay. I thought of the old story of a Frenchman in Scotland faced with his first plate of porridge. 'Am I to eat this', he asked, 'or have I eaten it already?' They picked and poked and threw choice morsels to the cats' eyes while the family scoffed it and had second helpings.

'So how is life in England?' asked Haralambos, warming at last to the theme of the evening. 'How much do you pay for rent?'

In England our dinner-party conversations were dominated by London house prices. In Greece they were dominated by London house prices plus the price of everything else from Pampers to petrol. Our friends were fascinated by the retail price index. Arfa and I took little interest in this sort of thing – hence regular crises in the household budget – so we made up the answers. Our guesses were even more distorted by having to convert in our heads pounds into drachmas, gallons into litres, pounds into kilos.

'Po-po-po,' they said at each new piece of misinformation.

'Johnny, your life over there is very different,' said Haralambos and they all tutted and shook their heads, whether out of pity or envy I could not say.

To lighten the mood we brought out dessert. I insisted on bringing out the big round earthenware pot, as I was less likely to drop it. If only I had. Arfa and Kate had laboured all morning over flour and Neo Vitam margarine and sugar and various soft fruits. It had spent the rest of the day at the baker's.

Arfa hammered the golden crust with a serving spoon. It sounded as if she were calling us to order. She smashed through the carapace and discovered with relief two layers of different consistencies of mush. She dolloped it out for the children to hand round. The crumble had the same consistency as the mashed potato and the fruit had coalesced into a brownish, minced-meaty colour with carroty-looking lumps. Our guests looked at their plates with dismay.

'Don't worry,' I said, in case they thought they were in the grip of a horrible déjà vu, 'it's not the same. It's sweet.' But not sweet enough for a Greek tooth. They picked and poked and threw choice morsels to the cats' eyes while the family scoffed it and had second helpings.

'English cuisine was a great success,' said Arfa with a shudder. 'Did they eat anything?'

'Bread. Their own cheese and tomatoes. Thank God we made a Greek salad.'

'I should have done something different for pudding.'

'Noo, darling.'

'Pity we had no custard. They'd have been really impressed.'

'What was with Barba Mitsos and Barba Vasilis?'

'I asked Eleni in the kitchen. She said that before he met Elpida, Mitsos was nearly engaged to a girl called Despina. All they had to agree was the dowry.'

At that time engagements in Greece were far more significant than in the West. It was often the engagement that was consummated rather than the marriage and to walk up the aisle in a dress that billowed over the front was no disgrace. On the contrary: it showed that the marriage would fulfil its primary purpose.

'So then he met Elpida in Aliveri when her ship broke down. They got married in a rush and left Despina in the lurch. Big dishonour. There was talk of her becoming a nun. They even doubled the dowry. Then the Italians invaded and Vasilis married her just before he went off to the war.'

'Didn't want to get killed before he...'

'Whatever. Anyway, Mitsos broke a leg or something and came back early. Despina had to stay out of his sight for

Vasilis's sake. She's been a bit funny ever since. Now she never comes out of the house.'

'And Vasilis blames it all on Mitsos. But that was forty years ago.'

'In Crete they'd have been murdered by now.'

'Then cack-handed foreigners invite them to the same dinner table. They'll never speak to us again.'

And so we dissected the corpse of our evening. I didn't mention how lovely Eleni looked and how Haralambos couldn't keep his eyes off her either, as we had had enough ego bruising for one night. Lying in bed, dropping off to sleep, I thought of our little bubble of light and Englishness under the mulberry tree and great emotions swirling round in the dark outside, looking in at us with the cats' eyes of Furies.

Off to Turkey

~~~~~~~~

August is a gentler month. The Greek holiday season traditionally finishes on the fifteenth of August, the Orthodox Feast of the Dormition, when the All Holy One fell asleep. Catholics call it the Assumption, when Our Blessed Lady was taken bodily into heaven. After Easter and Christmas, it is the most important feast of the calendar and like them marks a change in the seasons. Around this time the first grey clouds since April appear in the sky, with rain showers and perhaps a storm. Other signs are trees by the roadside hung with goggle-eyed carcasses and bloodstained fleeces. Pious Greeks fast and abstain from meat for fifteen days beforehand. The Dormition is the name day of anyone named after Our Lady – Mary and Panayotis, Despina (which means Virgin) – and anyone who doesn't have a proper saint's day, like Aristotle and Pericles and Ajax. Name days are more important than birthdays, a reason to feel special and eat cake.

We still went to the beach every day, if only to wash off the building grime. Usually we didn't go as far as Limanaki harbour but turned off down a steep rutted dirt track to the lovely bay of Klimaki, which means little vine. It was a perfect crescent of white sand between two rocky horns with a gently shelving beach, clear water and a few jujubes for shade. It faced east, so that early in the morning the sea was molten silver flowing straight from the sun and in the evening a sheet of lapis lazuli stretching to the Anatolian horizon.

For foreigners and Athenians, Klimaki was hard to find along the potholed dirt road from the village. Locals used to come occasionally to bathe, but now most of them had showers at home. Being fishermen, few of them were interested in swimming. In spring you would sometimes see a fellow pottering round the rocks on the horns of the bay with a trident on the end of a long pole baited with a bit of white rag. The trick was to flutter the rag in front of holes in the rocks and when a squid came out to play, stab it. But in summer the water was too warm for squid and they went deeper out to sea, so we usually had the beach to ourselves. The children racketed around and screamed and fought in the water without embarrassing their parents.

So we were disturbed one morning to see a procession of donkeys and a cart towed by a tractor coming down the steep track and onto the beach. A dozen riders and passengers got down and hobbled over to the water's edge, each one carrying a shovel or a back hoe. They were old, bent and lame. The women were all in black with yellow scarves round their heads and faces. The men wore white shirts buttoned to the neck, baggy jackets and wide-brimmed straw hats. They lined up in a row, parallel with the water's edge and far enough away from it that they were on dry sand. With their tools they dug shallow pits like an execution party digging their own graves – and there were some among them who would remember such incidents in their lifetimes. They took off only their shoes, sat down in their pits and buried themselves up to the waist, looking out to sea.

Nervous in case we were disturbing some ancient ritual, we went over to see what they were doing. I recognised some faces from the back of the church or dark corners in village houses where the old lurked and fiddled at strange chores.

'The doctor sent us,' said a toothless old biddy whom I usually saw in a nook by the baker's oven, keeping warm. 'It's for the rheumatism.'

'Doctor Solomos?'

'Him. He knows things.'

He gets them out of books, I wanted to say. Our village doctor was fair-haired and gangly and wore round black-rimmed glasses with bottle-bottom lenses. He suffered the professional disadvantage of looking about seventeen years old. Youthful qualities included acne and awkwardness and an adolescent vagueness that made you wonder if he was really paying attention and, if so, what was getting through. He was unusual for a Greek in that he was often seen carrying a book and even reading one on his own in a corner of the café. This was unusual. For many of our Greek friends a book is a final desperate attempt to fill the existential void when there is no one to talk to, nothing to do, no television to view, nothing in the street to watch and even the middle distance holds nothing to stare at. To be seen carrying a book in public, let alone reading one, is a mark of eccentricity or foreignness.

Like his medical expertise, Doctor Solomos learned his English off by heart from textbooks. He often took both parts of the dialogue. 'Good morning. Good morning. How are you? I am well, thank you. How are you? Fine, thanks. The weather is very good. Perhaps it will rain later...'

One of the diseases endemic among the elderly was rheumatism, brought on by hard work and the damp and chill of stone houses before insulated concrete and electric radiators and anti-inflammatory painkillers. Whenever I went to Athens or London, I took orders for the latest pills and lotions that my friends read about but were unable to find on Evia. Youthful Doctor Solomos had evidently read about a burial-in-sand cure. He prescribed five hours every day. His patients sat bolt upright from mid-morning to mid-afternoon under the blazing sun, making conversation, from time to time passing a bottle of water or slices of watermelon down the line. When you swam back to shore after a dip, they looked like ancient statues waiting for some promised god.

We had to forbid the children to treat them as goal posts or to slalom around them making motorbike noises. After three days, two of the patients took to their beds with sunstroke and the good doctor discontinued the treatment. We had the beach to ourselves again to pollute with rowdiness.

From time to time, when her mother or his sister could mind the butcher's, Ajax and Eleni brought the twins to the beach. They came with the two essentials of any Greek expedition: food and *parea*, company, as many aunts, uncles and cousins as could fit in their two vehicles. They set up camp with parasols, rugs and coolboxes. Ajax anchored melons and bottles of water in the shallows. He blew up an inflatable desert island complete with bright green palm tree and anchored it a few metres offshore. Eleni kept the toddlers out of the water and the sun and chased them around with spoonfuls of food. The relatives huddled under the shade to eat pita and chain smoke. Ajax stood waist deep in water with his hands on his hips.

We joined them, feeling underdressed as only Ajax was in swimming trunks. Eleni wore a disappointingly unrevealing black swimsuit under a Hawaiian-pattern beach robe, which she only took off when she went in for her dip. She paddled around up to her neck, in the unconvincing manner of swimmers who don't take their feet off the bottom. You got the feeling that they knew it was European to go to the beach but hadn't yet cottoned on to what you were supposed to do there.

Ajax did excel at one aspect of beach life, paddle ball. He had learned to play in Düsseldorf and said it was his favourite sport. It's not really a game, because there are no rules and no scoring and nobody wins. The principle is to bat a tennis ball to each other without it touching the ground using large wooden bats. The idea is to keep the rally going for as long as possible. If you volley or smash past your opponent, you have both lost. At the same time you test each other with more and more difficult shots to win mutual recognition of one player's superiority. The combination of having to cooperate, the pleasure of keeping it going and the demonstration of superiority are at the heart of Greek life. You collaborate and compete at the same time. Thanks to badminton I did OK. He was very good. When I told him it was like playing against a wall, he glowed.

Paddle ball was the only thing I ever saw Ajax or any of the villagers do that didn't have a practical purpose. Like the fishermen of Limanaki, he was puzzled by the dinghy.

'Johnny, where do you fix the fishing light?'

'It's not for fishing.'

'Ah. Where's the motor?'

'There's no motor. It has sails.'

'Ah, *vairy chip*. But it takes a long time to get where you're going.'

'We don't go anywhere. We sail round and round the bay.'

'Why do you do that?'

Apart from paddle ball they couldn't see the point of doing something for its own sake, especially if there was no food involved. Boating without a net, swimming without a spear, hiking without a gun were crazy or foreign, which meant the same thing. In the end we gave in and said that the boat was for fishing and the sails were so you could sneak up on the fish without being heard. They didn't buy the explanation – we Greeks don't do it like that – but at least it was within their frame of reference.

We were not strangers to fishing. Carelessly put your hand into a cupboard and you ran the risk of taking it out with a hook stuck in your finger. If you wanted a pot scourer there was no shortage of matted skeins of fishing line. Bait was a constant topic of conversation. Jim favoured worms, which he could also drop down his sister's T-shirt. She went for a paste of bread and feta because she liked the taste, so by the time we reached the fishing grounds there wasn't much left for the fish. Jack went for raw fish guts despite his antipathy to wasps. Harry favoured fish too, but thought that leftovers from his plate, fried with a lemon dressing, would attract the finer piscatorial palate. As usual, Arfa gave advice but would have nothing to do with implementation as she hated seeing the hooks in their mouths. She needn't have worried. In our whole time in Greece I think we have caught three. My personal tally is a two-inch bottom feeder that had the misfortune to swim over my hook as I pulled it up. It snagged him on the belly.

Anglers are optimists as well as liars. The time you felt a tiddler wriggling on the end of the line fuels hours and hours of hopeful boredom, treating fish to a free meal. Now we had a boat we could move up a league. On calm days we paddled out to the cliffs or the middle of the bay, dropped anchor, oh so very carefully, and set out the lines. With the same result as on land.

'OK, we're going to do this properly,' I said as we tucked into Kyria Sofia's horse mackerel, grilled and dressed with oil and lemon. 'You never see Greeks fishing by day. They do it at night with a light in the bow. They don't catch fish, fish catch them. Don't worry. This is the last fish we'll pay for.'

I still shudder when I remember these words.

*W*e made careful plans. *Blister* was too small for all of us and a proper fishing lamp with its gas canister, so I skilfully improvised a pencil torch inside a plastic bottle. In the dead calm of dusk we would paddle out to the middle of the bay. At nightfall we would put the torch in the water, tethered with a length of line. When our creel was full we would hoist the foresail, heave-ho the anchor and hitch a ride on the breeze, which, as any experienced sailor will tell you, blows in every evening from the sea to the land. It's something to do with differences in temperature as things cool down.

As it was calm and we were not taking the mainsail, Arfa came along. So she couldn't get in the way of serious fishing we made her sit in the landlubber's seat on the little fore-deck, facing backwards with her legs astride the mast and her feet dangling in the minestrone of soggy bait and old seaweed that washed around the bilges. Everything started according to plan. We paddled out into the middle of the bay, halfway between the shore and Camel Island. It was too deep for the anchor. We baited up and resolved the usual crises and tiffs that this produced: tangled lines, hooks in fingers, worm overboard and so on. Arfa gave advice but did not participate, as this would have meant slackening her grip on the mast.

By now it was dark. I switched on the torch, sealed it in the bottle, tied the string and threw it overboard. It looked pretty but disappointingly feeble. At eye level it looked bright enough, but when you looked down on it... eye level? EYE LEVEL? I felt the all-over tingly feeling that is nice under a duvet with the right company but in other circumstances means only terror. This particular circumstance was a two-metre ocean swell. Arfa telepathically voiced my thoughts.

'Where are we?'

It's never dark at sea, as we sailors say, but it can get close. On the crest of the next roller I just made out the reassuring shape of Camel Island. Unreassuringly, it was between us and the scattering of lights on the shore. We were on our way to Turkey.

Earlier on you may have spotted the deliberate mistake. An experienced sailor will not tell you that the breeze blows from sea to shore in the evening – exactly the opposite. At the time the error was not deliberate but entirely unforced. You may wonder how we hadn't noticed we were scudding out to sea. It was the same as when you ride a bicycle, the wind is always against you – you never feel it when it's at your back. I did my best to speak slowly and keep panic out of my voice.

'Hey kids, let's row back a bit. There'll be more fish closer in.'

'Daad, why are you talking like a Dalek?'

I stationed Jack on the tiller and took the oars. I pointed to a light I reckoned would guide us into the bay and not onto the cliffs on either side.

'Just steer us in but give Camel Island a wide berth – there's an underwater reef sticks out.'

As I turned my back on Arfa, she gave me the long reproachful look of a calf that knows what a stun gun is. Her knuckles glowed in the dark as she clung to the mast. I gave her a reassuring smile that fooled nobody, least of all me. I put the oars in the rowlocks and pulled.

The minute we turned into the wind we were in its teeth like a gob of spinach. I summoned up every scrap of expertise acquired on the Avon and the Cherwell and the Serpentine. Never before had bank holidays seemed so well spent. But there were other things from Stratford running through my head as my joints cracked and my lungs burned. 'Full fathom five thy father lies/Of his bones are coral made…'

The crew was magnificent. They knew what had happened and what we had to do. Jack gripped the tiller and set a determined face to land. He told Harry to keep an eye on the wake phosphorescing behind us and shout if it deviated from a straight line. Jim leaned out to starboard and Kate to port and with unflinching gaze looked out for rocks and landmarks. Arfa played her part. With her eyes closed and her forehead pressed to the mast behind me, she whispered prayers.

We ploughed on through the gathering seas. The offshore breeze gave way to the Melteme gusting from the north. Rollers began to crest and break. Water sluiced over the foredeck. The prayers behind me turned to throaty, lip-clenched moans. Harry was switched to bailing duties with a bait box. The rowlocks, the oars, my back all protested. I prayed that the gear would hold out and tried not to think of Barry Bucknell and his collapsing wardrobes. My glasses salted up so I couldn't see with or without them. I was disoriented and exhausted. Every oar stroke was agony.

I drew strength from the children's calm until it occurred to me that it was founded on trust in their father.

He would not let them drown. Little did they know. As the wind dropped and the waves subsided, I dared not tempt fate with hope until the sweet crunch of the hull on sand beneath us. Arfa was first off. She fell out of the boat and threw up on the sand.

'Cor, that was good fun, Dad, can we do it every night?'

'Ask your mother,' I said weakly.

Arfa didn't say a word about our adventure. Nor has she ever set foot in a dinghy again. Leaving sleeping lies doggo, I have never asked about her stories of the Spanish trapeze. It was before we were married, after all, and I told much worse fibs.

The children were soon sailing on their own. They went out in all weathers, the rougher the better, skipping and planing round Camel Island. When they took me out I was relegated to the foredeck, facing backwards with my legs astride the mast where I couldn't get in the way. Mostly I was set to painting and varnishing and mending the tackle. It was satisfyingly nautical without the danger and inconvenience of putting out to sea.

Traditional recipes

~~~~~~

*C*oming home from our fishing expedition, I was bent double with dangly arms and there were cheeky offers of bananas. When I woke up the next day, I couldn't move my legs or roll over without agonising pain in the small of the back and down the sciatic nerves through the buttocks. Getting out of bed or sitting up was out of the question. Aspirin and hot flannels throughout the day made no difference. I lay on my back without a pillow and mentally designed a wheelchair ramp up to the front door. With Arfa helping me I could roll on my side to pee over the edge of the bed into the bucket I used to mix whitewash. In preparation for weightier deeds, Arfa washed out the old roasting tin I used for knocking up bits of mortar.

For some reason she took exception to my helpful comments on her nursing and after siesta, with wholly unwarranted remarks about not being able to stand my snapping and moaning any more, she said she was going down to the village to fetch Doctor Solomos. I sped her on her way with a categorical refusal to let any barefoot doctor, Balkan quack or spotty Hippocrat near my person and promised that by the time she got back I would be dancing the Hokey Cokey.

I summoned the children and told them to push this limb and pull that foot while I puffed and blowed according to the natural childbirth methods I had picked up from their mother when they were born. I managed to half sit up on the edge of the bed, but the pain was too much and we were all in tears. I collapsed back on the sweaty mattress.

Arfa was back within the hour. Youthful Doctor Solomos sidled in after her, lugging a shiny new black bag with hardly a scuff on it, probably a graduation present. He sat down nervously on the bed, goggled at me through bottle-bottom lenses and took my pulse while Arfa described my symptoms. He gazed into my eyes and tickled my feet. Together we rolled me on my stomach and he poked gingerly at the affected part. He sat with his arms folded, picking at a spot on his chin.

'High do not thingit meningheetis,' he said in English. 'High do not thingit teetanos. High do not thingit poliomeealeetis.'

'That's good news. What is it?'

'High thingit bad back.'

'You don't say.'

'High 'ave medicine for this.'

He bent down and struggled with the stiff new locks on his black bag. He rummaged inside and pulled out a syringe like a cake icer. The needle! My earliest memory of primary school was the rumour that fired wildly round the class at the first glimpse of the school nurse's white coat – it's the needle, it's the needle – and girls screamed and boys peed down their legs (their own, not the girls'). Usually we queued up and they did no more than look at our tongues and rummage in our hair for lice.

Once it really was the needle and the mothers of cissies like me stayed at school instead of dropping us off at the gate, while tough little Irish kids faced the ordeal on their own. One of them, a freckle-faced, red-haired hooligan called Rory, forfeited forever his post of school bully by fainting in front of me.

Since then I turn my head away from the needle as soon as it comes out of the packet and wait to feel dizzy afterwards. If anyone was going to jab a needle into my spine, it was not going to be a recent graduate doing a rural stint before continuing his training.

'I'm allergic.'

'Oh no you're not,' said Arfa, happy to be getting her own back for the day's abuse.

'Oh yes I am!'

'Oh no you're not!'

'I'm a rare blood group.'

'Oh no you're not!'

'I'm a Jehovah's witness.'

'What do you want? An injection or a suppository?'

I was saved from this terrible dilemma by the slamming of car doors and the kerfuffle of visitors outside. News had spread fast. First up the steps was Elpida, carrying a dish of meatballs and a stone hot water bottle. Behind hovered Ajax, who had brought her up, clicking his car keys like worry beads. Elpida put down her dish, threw her arms wide and began a lament.

'O Blessed Virgin. What have they done to you? Why are you laid low? What evil eye has struck you down?'

'*See. About time I got some sympathy.*'

'Poor child. Show me. Where does it hurt?'

Doctor Solomos meekly moved out of the way to let Elpida stand over me. She pulled the sheet down to the top of my buttocks. With strong, waxy fingers she poked and prodded. Everyone crowded round the bed to see the fun. It felt like a ward round and Elpida was the consultant. Somewhere to the right of my spine she touched a spot that sent a shooting pain from my toes to my skull and a scream from my cracked lips.

'There we are,' she said to Doctor Solomos, one professional to another. 'Please give me an egg,' she said to Arfa.

'A what? What for?'

'*GIVE HER AN EGG!*' I shouted.

Arfa went to the fridge and came back with the smallest egg she could find. Elpida cracked it onto the small of my back and handed the shell to Arfa. Muttering under her breath, she rocked my back from side to side and up and down so that the egg white was spread all over the area. I bit my lip with the pain. She finished her incantation and asked Doctor Solomos for a bandage out of his case. She tied it round me, the egg still in the small of my back. I felt the yolk burst. It was slippery and wet and warm against my skin. She wound the bandage tightly round me several times, pushing the roll under my stomach and making me wince.

'Take the bandage off tomorrow. The bad will go with the good,' she said and pinched the children's cheeks.

Ajax wished me a speedy recovery and offered Doctor Solomos a lift back. Solomos looked awkward and embarrassed as he closed his bag.

'Doctor, if it's no better tomorrow, I promise I'll take the needle,' I said, with my fingers crossed.

The pain kept me awake most of the night. In the morning it was no better. I pretended to be asleep until the children came in, anxious to see the result of Elpida's magic.

'How is the fat toad this morning?' asked Arfa, with a smug little smile.

'Let's see, shall we?' I said.

With a struggle I could just about get my legs over the edge of the bed. The pain shot down to my toes. It was as bad as yesterday.

'Ooh, that's much better,' I said. 'Could somebody untie the bandage?'

Arfa untied the knot and unwound the cummerbund. The egg had turned pitch black.

'Look,' said Kate, 'all the badness has come out of Daddy.'

'There's plenty more where that came from,' said Arfa.

'I'm cured,' I said, flinging my arms out wide and standing up like the picture of Lazarus in the *Children's Bible*. 'See, Elpida did the trick.'

Walking up straight, I strode over to the sink and put the kettle on. 'What's for breakfast?' The five of them were goggle-eyed, open-mouthed.

'It couldn't have been very serious,' was Arfa's explanation.

'Elpida's a witch,' was Jack's.

'Does she eat girls?' said Jim, for his sister's benefit.

For the rest of the morning I was almost my normal self. I said it was prudent to take things easy and avoid whitewashing and other manual labour. Arfa accepted my recovery with bad grace. I caught her unawares inspecting the blackened bandage. She tossed it guiltily on the bed and pretended that she was clearing up. Young Doctor Solomos came up at noon and prodded and poked, diagnosed some swelling and inflammation and rabbited on about combining the old medicine and the new.

In fact, I have never before or since been in such agony. It was made worse by the effort of will to conceal it. I took double doses of aspirin. Every half an hour when no one was looking I took a large slug of ouzo straight from the bottle. I would have preferred whisky, but they would have smelt it on my breath. From my head to my fingers to my toes I was being dissected bone from bone with a hot, blunt knife.

Why did I do this? Dread of the needle? To pay back the mockery of my family? To rub in the innocent incompetence of Doctor Solomos? I prefer to think that it was for my friend Elpida, so she would not be made a fool of.

After lunch I collapsed on the bed face down to hide tears of pain in the pillow. I fell asleep with my head reeling with heat and exhaustion and ouzo and pain and promising myself to stay in bed until it was better.

When I woke up at five, I had a headache and a hangover but the pain in my back was truly gone. The twinges when I bent down were no worse than usual. It was a miracle.

'Rise from your beds and walk,' I shouted to the others, 'we're going to the beach.'

I swam and threw skimmers and chased beach balls with the brio of a father on his access day. On the way back we stopped in the square and I saw Elpida, sitting as usual outside her house with her crones and cronies. I walked up to her with arms outstretched and gave her hairy cheeks the most public of kisses. It was all the reward she wanted, although I bought her cakes and flowers the next time we were in Aliveri.

So there were more questions to ask myself. Did it go by itself? Was it Elpida's magic? Was it her manipulation of my back to spread the egg? Was it the loosening of the muscles from forcing myself to move? Was it the ouzo? Probably a bit of everything. Whatever it was, I had avoided the needle and struck a blow for the folk wisdom of centuries.

Youthful Doctor Solomos had no hard feelings. He may have been secretly relieved that Elpida saved him from a difficult patient. He moved on soon after to a houseman's job at Dudley Road Hospital in Birmingham. I told him that was where I was born and we struggled to find this meaningful, but it was not so much a coincidence as one of life's so-whats.

The fillip to Elpida's reputation increased demand for her folk remedies. She was often to be seen on the hillsides in the early morning, bottom in the air, digging for roots and herbs with an old kitchen knife.

One evening, smitten by nostalgia for the English countryside, we took the children to pick blackberries by the side of the cemetery road. Because it's hot and doesn't rain, Greek blackberries are not luscious fruits of the autumn hedgerow but little nutty things ripe in August. Elpida spotted us on the way to her graveside duties.

'Who's got a cough?' she asked accusingly, as if she had caught us raiding the medicine cabinet.

'Nobody. We don't have anything wrong,' Arfa said. Elpida didn't believe her. She tutted and tried again.

'Who's got diarrhoea?'

'Nobody. We just like to eat them.'

'How?'

'We boil them for a bit with sugar to make jam for yoghurt instead of honey.'

'Eh. We Greeks don't do it like that,' and that was the end of the conversation.

I've never been one for herbalism. The mother of a friend of ours grew medicinal plants in the garden. She had what looked like ordinary flower beds, except that the plants were labelled with the diseases they treated and not their proper names. Here was a bed of emphysema coming into bloom, there she was pricking out the angina, and doesn't the anaemia have a lovely scent? For hypochondriacs like me it diluted the charm of the country garden.

Arfa was more intrigued. On her next visit to Athens she bought *Medicinal Plants of Greece* by George Sfikas. Elpida was right about blackberries. Allegedly they are a cure for diarrhoea and not a cause, as the layman might assume.

Indeed, the main function of most natural remedies seems to be the loosening or constricting of the bowels. Many are recommended for 'general lassitude of the organism'. More specific specifics are artichokes for tonsillitis, basil for stomach ache and celery for fever and diabetes. Mistletoe berries can be popped like pills for indigestion. Arfa promised me the nettle cure if my back gave out again. The practitioner puts on gloves and whips the affected area with fresh nettle stems. This causes burning and swelling, but is alleged to be a very effective remedy and doubtless takes your mind off what's really wrong with you. It's enjoyable for the practitioner too.

My favourite was the common-or-kitchen-garden onion. It was the most frequently depicted plant in the tombs of the Pharaohs and for good reason. It is a pharmacopoeia in your vegetable rack. Rub neat juice into stings and burns. Mix the juice with potassium carbonate and rub into the scalp for baldness. Eat a raw onion for lassitude, hypertension, arteriosclerosis, cirrhosis of the liver, stings and burns. Best of all, for haemorrhoids, fry an onion in pork fat and leave as long as possible in the affected place. Sfikas is silent about the size, but presumably you should take measurements. He advises letting it cool down first – you wouldn't want to burn your fingers.

We were intrigued not so much by the efficacy, but by how they found out. Did they try it raw first, or boiled or baked in the oven? Did they try other vegetables on a testing panel? Was it pure coincidence that someone's piles got better the day after a fried onion suppository? If so, what were they doing sticking fried onions up their bottom in the first place? Was it a dare, a cult, a whim? And how many people, having read Sfikas, have tried it for themselves? So many unanswered questions.

'Hey kids, listen to this.'

'Why? We're busy.' They were engrossed in harassing a column of ants. I caught Arfa's Gorgon glare over her wine glass.

'Oh, nothing.'

I t was late August and the almond harvest was in full swing. The hillside echoed with the whack whack whack of long poles on the trees and the patter of nuts and twigs on sheets laid underneath. We collected our own almonds, peeled off the green husks and spread the nuts in their pockmarked shells on the terrace to dry.

Genial Spiros capped his generosity with the doves by presenting us with a hen. He carried her over by the ankles, spread-eagled, or rather spread-chickened, more stupefied than frightened at her unaccustomed view of the world. He sat down on the terrace and let her go to peck under the table for breakfast droppings.

'Oh lovely, our own eggs,' said Arfa, but I could tell she'd rather be given them in a paper bag.

'Bah, she's too old for eggs. That's why I'm giving her to you. Simmered slowly with onions and tomato is best for the old ones. Isn't that right?' he said to his gift, who had found rich pickings under Harry's chair.

The children, who had been hiding from clearing the table, emerged.

'Maam, is that for us?' said Harry.

'Is it a girl chicken?' said Kate.

'What shall we call her?' said Harry.

'How about Pecky?' said Kate.

'Pecky's not a name,' said Jim.

'Becky is,' said Jack.

'Pecky-Becky,' said Kate.

'Can she live in my bedroom? Can she?' said Harry.

They chased her round the terrace while I got Spiros a whisky. When he had gone we had a family discussion.

'Darlings, Spiros didn't give us Pecky-Becky for a pet. He gave her to us for dinner,' said Arfa.

'What? Alive? Is Dad going to kill her?' said Jim.

'Why not Mum?' I retorted.

'Chickens don't make very good pets. Especially old chickens. She's probably got lice. You can't cuddle a chicken.'

'Yes you can, yes you can,' squawked Harry and ran over to where she was grubbing in a geranium pot.

Had she known what was at stake, Pecky-Becky wouldn't have pecked his finger. Despite Harry's thumbs down, the majority vote was to save Pecky-Becky from the pot and welcome her into the bosom of the family.

A veteran of the free range was not to be so easily domesticated. First of all, she was not naturally endearing. She had lost an eye to a rat or a cat or a rival, she was bald under the wings and on the neck, the feathers that remained were crusted with dirt and droppings, she walked with a limp. A filthy, balding, one-eyed, limping chicken is not an ornament to the home. She refused to sit in a bed lovingly crafted out of cardboard with a dry grass mattress and a quilt of tattered blanket. Offered food, she pecked the hand that fed her. Lassoed with a piece of string and taken for walks, she either strangled herself to escape or ran full tilt at the legs of her leader. She was distasteful to cuddle. There was nothing nice to stroke. The tattered comb, like Grandpa's earlobes, was unpleasant to fondle. It was a relief when night fell and she could be shut in the basement.

When the children were in bed, I delicately raised the subject of what to do with her.

'What are we going to do about that effing chicken?'

'Don't swear at me. I'm not responsible.'

'It wasn't my idea…'

'It's too late now…'

Spiros took the decision out of our hands. The next morning he came over for a tot and saw Pecky-Becky gleaning the harvest under the table.

'She won't fatten up you know, she's too old.' I looked round. Arfa was in the kitchen fetching glasses. The children were in their olive tree.

'I don't know how to kill it. Can you do it for me?'

'It's easy,' he said and it was. He dived for her and grabbed her by the leg. A quick flick of the wrist and he tossed her back down again, where she proved that the popular saying about a headless chicken is well grounded in fact. I can also tell you that it draws a veil over the prodigious amount of shit that is released. She scurried round with her head dangling until she ran into a wall and collapsed in a quivering heap of feathers.

While no one would admit that her passing was a relief, she went unmourned. Arfa did not ask what had moved Spiros to do the deed, so I did not have to tell lies. My expiation was to prepare her for the pot. The worst was plunging her into hot water to make her easier to pluck. I had the dreadful henhouse stench of hot, wet feathers in my nose, on my beard, my hair, my skin, my clothes all day.

After my initiation on the doves, I was used to the subsequent intimacies. Pecky-Becky looked up at me with her beady black eye and made little squeaks and grunts as I rummaged in her intestines. A lady of mature years, she had shrunken breasts, massive thighs and a wrinkled yellow skin. But when I chopped her up and covered her in cling film she looked like a proper chicken from Tesco's, not the beady-eyed, strutting, limping, pecking harridan that crapped round our terrace.

Arfa adapted her favourite recipe to the local ingredients. Her *coq au retsina* was tough but tasty, despite the turpentine tang.

Exploding myths

~~~~~~

*A*rfa was reading Proust under the mulberry in the way one reads Proust; that is, not reading more than a page or so before the world outside suddenly seems so much more interesting, an ant crawling up a twig perhaps or a beetle sitting on a stone. I rescued her with a glass of Spiros's best. For most people, if the name of the great French novelist Marcel Proust means anything at all, it is for the description of how sponge cake and lime-blossom tea transported his hero, also called Marcel, back to his childhood. For the Marcels this was a blinding revelation. To the rest of us it happens all the time. My first sip of Château Yard-Brush brought to life one of my earliest memories.

Grandad was in bed with his kidneys. They had moved him into the front room of the prefab. He kept the curtains shut so that nobody could see in. The room was gloomy, full of shadows lit only by his feeble bedside light. I played on the red floral carpet with a little gypsy caravan and he looked down at me with a smile on his puffy yellow face. I pushed the caravan too hard and it went under his bed. I crawled after it. The chamber pot was in the way. I put my little hand on the rim, jerked it towards me and the contents lapped up against my fingers. It was thick and yellow and spicy and foul and acid. I sipped Spiros's wine again and heard the bedsprings creak as Grandad rolled over to see what I was up to.

Greeks took the word for wine from the Phoenicians, passed it onto the rest of the world as *oinos*, or *winum* in Latin, and then abandoned it in favour of *krasi*, pronounced krasee. With the accent on the *a* it means temperament or constitution. Many's the time I have asked for half a kilo of temperament with my dinner. *Krasi* is a different drink from the beverage that the rest of us call *vinum*, *vin*, *vino*, *vinho*, *Wein*. The word comes from the Ancient Greek for mixture. Ancient Greeks liked their wine thick, sweet, oxidised and mixed with sea water, honey and spices, like punch or liqueur. These days you mix your *krasi* with soda water or cola or lemonade; old Barba Lekos cuts his with Heineken. Most Greeks still prefer their white wine dark and tangy and their red wine thick and sweet. In our village the only red wine you could buy until recently was Mavrodaphne, which is like alcoholic Ribena. Some of the islands produce western-style wines, but these are relics from the Franks and Latins who colonised them.

Krasi is not really drink. It is food. You don't buy it by the litre but by the kilo. Giving a Greek a glass of wine on its own is like giving someone a glass of gravy. A glass is inseparable from a fork. Only foreign drinks like whisky or beer are drunk without food. *Krasi* isn't even drunk like wine. You don't pick a glass up by the base and swill the wine around the bowl and sip it and let it trickle over your tongue. Only in the posh suburbs of Athens do you find wine glasses with stems. A proper Greek wine glass is between a tumbler and a shot glass. You pick it up by the rim, clink it against everyone else's, slug it down, slam it back down on the table and reach for a fork.

There is a kind of cultural materialism that tries to explain away the odd things that foreigners do in terms of home economics. For example, they dig up the dead because village land is scarce or they eat male lambs at Easter because the new grass is better saved for milk-producing females. It is said that retsina originated from the use of resin to seal the amphora it was made in, a large clay pitcher with a narrow neck and pointed bottom. The resin produced a thin film on the surface of the wine, which reduced oxidisation and masked any faults found in the wine.

This assumes that Ancient Greeks really wanted to drink our kind of wine and that the retsina was an accident. Or that, even if they liked the taste, it was an afterthought, an additive, a preservative, something thrown in afterwards to make the wine last longer. If this were the case, you would mix it in after the fermentation. But you put it in right at the beginning, as soon as the first fermentation starts. It has its own sugars and oils and is as much an essential ingredient of the drink as grapes. It's pine wine as much as grape wine. The wine god Dionysos is often pictured with a staff tipped with a pine cone. Chances are that ancient Greeks and Romans would think the same about the thin, bland, grapey brew we call wine as Europeans think about pissy American beer.

'Such a shame about Proust,' I said as I refilled Arfa's glass. 'He shut himself away in a room lined with cork for over ten years because of asthma and nervous debility. He only discovered on his deathbed that it was cork he was allergic to.'

'Toad,' she said, 'you don't half talk rubbish.'

In September tell-tale signs appear that the grapes are ripening: plastic barrels outside every other shop and hand-made advertisements for oenologists. Albanians, gypsies and village women invade the vineyards with sharp, curved knives. They load skips and trailers and pick-ups that queue up in the sun outside the shiny steel tanks of the winery. Wasps are first to get pissed on the harvest. They swarm and crawl and fall down and lie on their backs wriggling their legs, out of their little skulls with the alcohol that already ferments under the sticky skins of the fruit. Very soon they will be closer to the fermentation than nature intended, along with the flies and bugs and bird shit that enrich the juice.

In our part of the world they grow Savatiano grapes, which are said to have originated in Greece. They are resist-ant to disease and drought and have an adequate yield on poor soil but, like the innocuous Chardonnay grapes before the wine makers muck about with burnt oak chips, don't have much flavour. The growers have only one quality stan-dard and that is how many kilos they can produce. They fer-tilise and water the fruit so that they are big and fat and juicy as table grapes. Unfortunately, this is not what you need for wine. Fat, juicy grapes in a hot climate make thin wine with high alcohol and low acidity, what tasters call flabby, flaccid, mousy, lacking in nerve and all the other things they used to say about me when I was in the school cadet force.

Around this time every housewife treats you to a dish of *moustalevria*. Fill a saucepan with fermenting grape juice and bring it to the boil. Throw in a handful of wood ash tied in a cloth to take away the bitterness. After boiling for ten minutes take out the ash, let it sit for half an hour and then strain through muslin. Boil for another half an hour, let it cool and beat in a handful or so of semolina. Pour into little dishes and let it set like blancmange. Garnish with chopped nuts and sesame and cinnamon. Taste a spoonful and leave the rest. Ah, Proust again – memories of baby sick come flooding back.

Instead of waiting for the winery to finish the job, you can make your own retsina. You buy a plastic barrel, say a hundred kilos. It lies on its side and has a hatch on the top so it looks like a fat little one-man submarine. You take it to the factory and they fill it up with raw juice, in which all the wild bacteria and yeast have been killed off with one of the sulphur derivatives. You go to an oenologist, who gives you little packets of chemicals with instructions when to tip them in the juice. Who are these masters of the art of wine making? Chemistry students, science teachers, anyone who knows the difference between a sulphate and a sulphide. You park the barrel round the side of the house or in the garage or the shed. You leave the hatch open, covering it with muslin to keep out the insects, until the last dose of chemicals, after which you close it tight.

After a month or so, you draw off some of the liquid into a bottle. You have a sly swig, which you wish you hadn't because it tastes like fruity vinegar, and take the rest to the oenologist, unless he has gone back to school in Athens or been driven out of town because he mixed up his sulphides and his sulphates. He fiddles with litmus paper and little glass floats and gives you another packet of chemicals to tip into the mixture. Just before Christmas you draw off half a kilo to see if it is ready and it gives you colic for two days, so you lay in a couple of cases from the supermarket for the holidays.

At last, around February, everyone agrees that the wine is ready and you bring it triumphantly to the table. They all say it is the best anyone has ever tasted and you lose your temper if anyone in the family buys anything else to drink and you give it away to friends and relations, with the unavoidable result that they give you theirs. It is either better than yours, in which case you are in a bad mood, or not as good, in which case you get an even bigger headache than from your own. It's hard to know what gives Greek wine a worse name, the wineries or the jobbing oenologists.

The best meals I have ever eaten have been in Greece:

honey-sweet red mullet fried deep pink…

summer horse mackerel, self-basted on charcoal…

octopus dried in the sun, browned on the grill, weeping every taste of the sea…

spit-roast lamb marinated with wild herbs and mountain grass…

suckling pig roasted in a stone oven on ashes of olive wood…

wild greens blanched and dressed with olive oil and lemon…

or baked in a tissue-thin filo with sheep's cheese…

winter hare simmered with onions and spices on a bed of garlic purée…

pot-roasted kid wrapped in paper on a bed of hot mashed aubergine…

pork stewed in celery on rice dressed with garlic and sheep's butter…

onions sweet enough to scoff like apples…

tomatoes red and rich as a setting sun…

rigani, wild mountain oregano, heady as incense…

olive oil, thick and green to chew on or delicate and pale to anoint with…

cucumbers tasting of … of… of…. cucumber…

washed down with copper jugs of cheek-puckering, lip-curling, gum-shrivelling, tongue-gagging, tooth-aching, head-shuddering, throat-burning, stomach-churning, bowel-trembling, squit-shitting, arse-burning turpentine.

If it is so bad, why have we drunk so much of it over the years? Why do we always have a jerry can of the stuff in the basement and a bottle in the fridge and a copper jug on the table? A wooden barrel of the best retsina, properly made, light and clear and fresh and redolent of fragrant vines and shady pines, terracotta vineyards and marble mountains, is a world apart from anything that ever came out of a plastic barrel or a steel tank or a bottle with a fancy label. It reverberates with layer on layer of flavour and aroma, from springtime zephyr at the top of the register to a myrrhic *basso profundo*.

Nothing cuts better through the Mediterranean diet of olive oil and lamb grease and fish oil and pork fat. A slug between mouthfuls cleanses the palate and the tongue and the gums and the sinuses and gets them ready for the next delicious bite of unctuous, chin-glistening, cheek-buttering lipids.

So how do you find this nectar? By getting to know who makes it the traditional way from their own grapes. If it's for themselves, they go easy on the weedkiller and fertiliser. Compared with the fruit they sell to the winery, the grapes are small and thick skinned and brown speckled and full of taste. They let the bacteria that lives naturally just under the skin do the work for them rather than using commercial wine yeast. They crush it with their feet in a wooden barrel or a stone vat or they use an Italian hand crusher. Then they throw in a fistful of fresh resin.

Anyone who makes wine knows that the three most important elements are grapes, grapes, grapes. The quality of retsina also depends on the quality of the resin. The best does not come out of bottles or packets but straight from the sprawly, feathery Aleppo pine that perfumes the mountains of central Greece. Ours comes from Strapontes on Mount Dirfis in the middle of Evia. This pine juice is nothing like the harsh, astringent stuff that goes into turpentine, paint and glue. It belongs with the fragrant resins and gums that make frankincense and myrrh. It should be tapped in the year the wine is made, starting in spring when the sap rises and finishing in autumn's second spring. You don't need more than a few fistfuls. Two or three kilos of resin per thousand kilos of grape juice is enough.

Everyone has their own tips and tricks. Yannis lets the retsina oxydise enough to leave a hint of caramel on the back of the tongue, but not enough to make it flat and brown like tea that's been left too long in the pot. Vasilis tips a jug of olive oil into the barrel at the end of the second fermentation around the end of November. The oil floats to the top and seals the wine off from the air. The disadvantage is that it is harder to clean the barrels and if the wine lasts more than a year the oil can go rancid. Barba Nikos puts half the resin in at the first fermentation and half in at the second, because he likes the fresh resin taste. Aussie Alekos likes a deep yellow colour, so he leaves the skins in for the first fermentation. At Easter Dimitris racks his wine, tipping it into new barrels to stop the fermentation and get it off the lees.

These wines are different from each other and the taste changes throughout the year and from year to year. What they have in common is a Proustian extravaganza, compressing time and experience in a kaleidoscope of tastes. *Stin ya mas.* Our health.

A beautiful late summer's day. Hot sun, bright light, tender breeze. Chirring cicadas, zizzing flies, droning bees, snoring wife. I should have been mortaring the slates on the terrace, but instead I lay on the bed watching a long-tailed wood wasp, harmless and dozy, hover round the reeds in the ceiling looking for a nest or food or just passing the time of day. On my stomach was a book by a Swiss archaeologist about the temple to Isis in Eretria. Egyptian merchants probably founded the temple in about 300 BC. Who was Isis? An Egyptian goddess, who became very popular in Greece and Rome until the second century AD. She had a litany of names including Queen of Heaven, Mother of God, Mother of Mankind, Help of the Dying, Star of the Sea…

History and comparative religion lay too heavy on a day like this. Better see what the kids were up to instead. They were in the field at the back, huddled over an elaborate wasp trap that they were making out of plastic bottles and honey water. The wasps were more interested in the octopus hanging by its neck from the washing line. I had bought a frozen specimen in Aliveri and smuggled it to the beach in the hope of bolstering my street cred by bringing it out of the sea on the end of a spear, but I was rumbled by a tentacle dangling out of the crotch of my swimming trunks. The more water you dry out of octopuses the better they taste. I like them leathery as biltong. Put them on the grill and they twist and turn and bubble with oil, the essence of everything that lives in the sea.

The blast hit first. Whack. Bang. A gust of hot wind. The Turks have landed. The gas bottle has exploded. From our little field on the hillside above us rose a swirling white cloud. I dived on the children, pulling them together under me. Through half-closed eyes I watched the mushrooming cloud. Inside was the shadow of our ancient olive tree, hanging in the air, blown into parts like instructions for an Airfix model. It rained twigs and leaves and hard green olives, pattering down on the roof and the ground and my back. I waited for a trunk to break my spine or crush my skull, but got away lightly with a lancing pain in my elbow. Arfa ran out wearing only her pants, clutched her naked breasts and screamed when she saw us sprawled on the ground. The little ones started to cry.

'What happened? What happened?' she shouted.

'I've been stung by a bloody wasp,' I said. I got no sympathy. That was reserved for the children. She clasped them to her untrammelled bosom.

After reassurance and consolatory chocolate biscuits and a dab of ammonia for my throbbing elbow, we went up the path to our little field, still wide-eyed and trembling. Splintered logs lay all over the blackened grass around a smoking crater where the ancient olive tree had stood. Barba Fedon and two young lads were gathering bits of shattered wood and loading them on the donkey.

'Forgive me,' he said, smoothing down his comb-over, 'I hope it didn't frighten the little ones. The dynamite was old. I used two sticks just in case.'

'What have you done to our tree?'

He looked genuinely puzzled. 'Your tree? It's my tree.'

'It isn't. We bought it from you. Last month. Have you forgotten?'

'I sold you the field. I didn't sell you the tree. Not for that price. There's enough wood here to keep me through the winter.'

'But we wanted the tree.'

'Why didn't you say?' He looked aggrieved.

'It was a beautiful tree.'

'Eh. Your donkey will find shade under the bush. Make sure you give it enough rope.'

There was nothing more to be said. We were now the proud owners of a big hole in a little field. So much for thinking ourselves into Barba Fedon's world. We should have defied ridicule for offering good money for an old barren tree and paid whatever he said. Now whenever I walked up the hill I had to look the other way.

The children were tougher. When the dirt and soot had gone away, mostly onto their clothes, they used the crater as a foxhole, a redoubt, a ship, a dungeon, a cockpit. A week after the late summer rains they came running into the kitchen.

'Quick. Quick. The olive tree's growing again.'

'Yes, dears. Would you like a biscuit?'

But it was true. A tiny green shoot was sprouting from one end of the blackened stump.

'We have to look after it very carefully,' said Arfa.

'Will it grow up to be a proper tree?' asked Jim.

'If it isn't broken off by a child. If an animal doesn't eat it. If it can stand up to the wind. If the snow doesn't bend and break it. If it gets through the forest fires. If it's not cut for a tethering post. If it fights off canker and worms. If it survives all those things, they will make it what it will be.'

'Will we be able to sit in it again?' asked Kate.

'I don't think so. But one day other children will.'

'Where will we be?' puzzled Harry.

'Where will we be in a hundred years from now?' sang Jack and Jim to the tune of the death march. 'Your eyes drop

in and your teeth fall out. Your brains come trickling down your snout…'

'That's enough,' snapped Arfa.

'It'll be more than a hundred years,' I said. 'It could still be here in five hundred years. That little shoot is like a golden thread to the future. Think of all the things that will happen between now and then.' But I was talking to myself. They had started a wrestling match and Arfa was halfway to the house. When I caught up I realised I was in trouble.

'How could you? How could you?'

'How could I what? I was trying to give some historical dimension.'

'Teach them that song. It's horrible. The little ones will have nightmares.'

'But I didn't. They must have picked it up in the playground.'

For once it was true. I was innocent, but I still paid the price. That night I dreamed of olive trees in Golgotha, heaped with skulls, and a great white mushroom cloud sucking up our children and our children's children.

Home at last

The house was as finished as it would ever be. We went to bed one evening, weary and aching, with hands red raw from scrubbing paint and plaster and hair thick with cement and sawdust. We woke up next morning and there was nothing more to do. It was as if we had never seen the place before. We looked at it like strangers. We were glad we had taken the trouble to use old tiles, rough planed chestnut, reeds from the lake and all the other materials that we had scavenged and toiled over. We knew where everything came from, where the stones had been found, where the trees grew, who felled and sawed them. We knew every inch of it. Our skin and sweat and blood were part of it.

To celebrate, we decided to throw a party and roast a lamb on a spit. As Barba Vasilis drove his flock of fifty sheep past our house twice a day, it seemed polite to buy one from him.

'Why not Ajax? He's got a mausoleum full,' he suggested.

'I want it fresh from our own hillside.'

'Bravo. Which one do you want?' he asked, waving his stick over his protégés.

This was a good time to reinforce the morality of meat eating. Let the children choose their dinner on the hoof. If the experience made any of them vegetarians, so be it, a sound moral choice, despite the inconvenience to the rest of us. So we formed a selection committee. Arfa thought that it was ghoulish and indecent. She would have nothing to do with it, although she had no rational arguments against the process, especially as she was partial to pork crackling and rare steaks and the fatty bits of a shoulder of lamb.

The children wandered among Vasilis's flock and picked out our party food. Kate made the final choice, a sweet yearling with a patch of black wool on one side of his head like a French beret. They christened him Denis. We saw him at least twice a day, browsing in the field below, scavenging for weeds at the side of the path, mounting the olive and the mulberry for tasty new leaves, raffish in his beret. Every time the flock passed our house the children dragged their mother to the terrace and pointed out little Denis.

'Ahh, Mummy, look, isn't he sweet? Ahh, the little lamb.'

Arfa was an experienced parent and steeled herself not to run sobbing into the house with her hands over her ears but just said 'Yes, dear'. Needless to say, when the rest of the committee were out of hearing, I got into trouble despite my sensible remarks about ethical upbringing, conversations that invariably ended with 'and wipe that smirk off your face'.

The party was on Sunday. Friday was the killing day. It would give the meat a couple of days to hang. Animals killed only a few hours before the spit taste metallic and grainy. I have always thought that when the heroes of the *Iliad* sacrificed hecatombs of oxen and sheep it was a shame that that they spitted and grilled the meat while it was still warm from the sacrifice. Sensible Greeks would have hung the meat for a couple of days and only eaten the hearts and livers and other tasty bits of offal, which are best consumed fresh. Perhaps they didn't have the facilities on the plains of Troy.

On the Thursday evening, Denis trotted by the house with his little friends for the last time. It was a lovely late summer evening, golden grass glowing under the sun that he would never see setting again. The children were more subdued than usual, although they did drag their mother out to say bye-bye. '*Au revoir*, actually,' I said and got a filthy look.

'Johnny, I need you to help me kill the lamb tomorrow,' said Barba Vasilis. 'Since I had the cancer cut from my lip I can't blow properly. We'll do it in my field down below.'

He made puffing sounds by way of illustration. I knew what I would have to do. My first job would be to hold Denis's legs while Vasilis slit his throat. Then Vasilis would cut a slit in the hind leg and I would have to blow into it to inflate the skin. I had seen it done with a pump before Haralambos's wedding and even that looked hard work, worse than blowing up a double lilo.

'How are you going to kill Denis, Daddy?' asked Jack.

'Will you chop him with an axe?' asked Jim.

'Does it hurt?' asked Harry.

'Will you bring the wool back?' asked Kate.

That night we avoided meat, ate cheese fried in egg and talked about the following day. The gist of our discussion was that if you eat animals you should take responsibility for killing them, you should not palm the unpleasantness off onto other people, Denis would not have had any life at all if he was not meant to be eaten and so on. But I had a bad night's sleep. Denis popped his raffish head over the end of the bed and winked at me. I brrrhed him away, but he didn't leave me alone. He came to the side of the bed and nuzzled my arm. When I smacked him away he sighed and padded round the room. We could stomach the knife in the throat, the spurting blood, the strange metallic smell, the flies on the stomach, the black garbage bag, but it was the testicles the size of beach balls that kept me and Denis awake.

First thing in the morning I got everybody up early and, while they were still half-asleep, herded them into the camper. We passed Vasilis on the way up and I shouted out of the window that we had to go to Athens on urgent business. I drove to the other side of the island, where we played and fished on the beach all day. I felt a coward, the children had yet more evidence of grown-up double-talk, and Arfa was smug but happy that I was a sensitive soul after all. We skulked back after dark with the headlights switched off in case Barba Vasilis had not done the deed yet and was lying in wait.

He delivered Denis to us on Saturday morning, mercifully unrecognisable without his rakish black beret, wrapped in an old shirt, lolling on the back of the mule like an outlaw brought back by the sheriff. I carried him into the basement and hung him head down from a ceiling joist. I wrapped him in muslin and the flies had to make do with the little pool of blood on the floor under his nose.

Ruddy-faced Ajax lent me a spit. It was a long metal bar, pointed at one end and bent into a crank at the other. With it came two Y-shaped metal supports. I cleaned and oiled it and sharpened the point with a file. We dug a shallow trench in the field at the back of the house and stuck the Y-shaped supports in the ground at either end. We collected brushwood and sticks from the hillside. Not trusting my ability to keep the fire going on wood alone, I went to the Monopoly in Aliveri for a big sack of charcoal.

At dawn on the day of the feast we impaled our friend. I improvised a table under the olive tree out of an old door and a couple of chairs. I brought him outside and peeled off his blood-stained shroud. He was covered in a translucent white membrane, greasy to the touch. The children were fascinated by the red gash in his throat, the staring eyes and the grinning mouth. I put the point of the spit into his anus. I was gentle with him, but his resistance surprised me. With every thrust he slid along the table and his head flopped over the edge, so the children had to hold him down. I pushed the spike into the intestinal cavity and up into the rib cage, trying not to tear the flesh. With careful probing I found the thorax and pushed up into the neck.

There are two schools of thought for the head. Some push the spit through the brain so that it bursts out through the forehead. Others, who think that the brain is a delicacy, avoid damaging it by pushing the spit between the jaws so that it looks as if the animal is biting on the iron. We decided that the mouth was more elegant.

When Denis was impaled more or less in the middle of the spit, I fixed his backbone to the pole and sewed up his belly with wire. I tied his rear ankles back to the spit, fastened his front ankles to the ribs and tucked his elbows into his side. I embalmed him with oil and lemon and oregano and salt and pepper and covered him with a clean muslin shroud.

It was time to light the fire. We heaped brushwood over the shallow pit, splashed it with lamp oil and threw in a match. It flared for a few minutes, crackled and settled down to a fitful blaze. It was a hot day and we sweated to be near it.

'Po-po-po. You want to set the mountain on fire?' protested Barba Vasilis as he stomped up to us, thrashing at the dry grass with his stick. 'Go get water in case it catches.'

I ran to connect a hose to the water tank, while Vasilis beat the grass and coaxed burning branches back into the pit. This was not as easy as it sounds. In the bright sunlight the flames were invisible. When they died down I covered the white embers with charcoal.

'Are you roasting a cow?' asked Vasilis, prodding down the charcoal with his stick.

We fetched Denis from the table and mounted the spit on its supports. For a moment I wallowed in the romance of turning our own spit on our own fire in the garden of our own Greek house. Then Barba Vasilis announced that the fire was in the wrong place and facing the wrong way, I had bought the wrong sort of charcoal, the spit should have gone through the forehead, there was not enough salt and lemon, it was not tied on properly, I had used enough wire for an ox... In principle I thought highly of the out-spokenness of Greeks compared with English hypocrisy. When I was on the receiving end I found it bloody rude.

'Oh bugger off,' I said in English and by coincidence he did so in order to tend the survivors of his flock. Unfortu-nately Arfa came out of the house as the children sweetly waved him off with choruses of 'bugger off', which earned us a collective telling-off.

The hot juices and not the direct heat of the fire cook the meat and keep it moist. The trick is to turn the spit fast enough so that they don't drip onto the charcoal but con-tinually baste the meat. It was harder work than I antici-pated. I realised I should have put Denis at the end of the spit and not in the middle, so that the handle was as far away from the fire as possible. We took it in turns to squat at the handle with our faces turned away from the heat until the children couldn't stand it any longer.

Arfa fashioned a spit turner's mask for me out of a paper bag with holes for eyes and nose. My face ran with hot, salty sweat and stung my eyes. I called for a can of wine and tore a hole in my mask to drink it through. I allowed myself a swig every fifty turns, then twenty, then ten, telling myself that I was sweating out the alcohol. At the end of two hundred turns I had a splitting headache. Meanwhile, Denis shrank as if he were ageing. The tendons on his limbs stood out and the muscles turned brown and wizened. His eyeballs swelled and burst and shrivelled to black prunes in the sockets. As the flesh on his head contracted his grin grew wider. His scrotum shrank and his testicles flip-flopped as he turned.

'Hey kids, did you know that Denis is Dionysos in Greek? Greeks called him the Liberator. He liberated people from themselves by getting them drunk. You know what happened to him? The Titans got him. They were giants but they were intelligent. They liked everyone to be reasonable and rational. They didn't like all his hocus-pocus. They didn't like the way he got people out of their heads. So they killed him. They roasted him on a spit and tore him to pieces and ate him. Zeus was mad. He whacked them all with a thunderbolt. Boom. All that was left of them was smoke. And from the smoke the human race sprang up. So we mostly take after Titans but we have all got a little bit of Dionysos inside us. See?'

'Maam, Dad's drunk too much wine again,' shouted Jim.

Arfa drove down to the village for last-minute supplies. The children lost interest in the hard work of spit turning and went with her. My shoulder and elbow and wrist began to seize up. I got cramp in the legs if I squatted and a pain in the back if I stooped. I turned as fast as I could, but not fast enough. Juices escaped and dripped on the charcoal and caught fire. I beat out the flames with sprigs of brushwood that also caught fire. Flaming twigs fell into the dry grass. I stamped on the wisps of smoke and beat them with my hands. I ran for the hose and gave the ground all round a good soaking. Denis, neglected and stationary, dripped and caught fire again. I beat out the flames with a bucket and the smell of burning plastic joined that of charred meat. The skin melted away from my palms where I had burned them beating out the flames, and bloomed into blisters where the iron handle rubbed. I prayed for someone to come.

My prayers were cruelly answered by sun-touched Dionysos, sucking a crust of bread. I couldn't understand why he was looking curiously at me until I remembered the paper bag. I tore it off and beckoned desperately for him to come closer. He shuffled towards me. I pointed to the handle and made manic revolving gestures with my free hand. He gave me the patronising look that he was used to getting from other people and walked round to the other end of the fire. He stared at the revolving face of Denis, wizened, sweating fat, hollow-eyed, biting on the iron bar and grinning. Dionysos rolled his head in time with the spit. He took the crust out of his mouth, slimy and dripping spittle, and grinned back. Then he grinned the same grin at me, still rolling his head.

'You're turning it too fast,' said ruddy-faced Ajax behind me.

'Thank God,' I gasped and fell back on the grass, dizzy with heat and wine and pain.

'It takes two to roast an animal. He doesn't count,' he said, taking the spit and brrrhing at Dionysos, who obediently ambled off to the church, sucking his crust.

Arfa and the children came back and then our guests arrived with slabs of *spanakopita*, anchovies, cheeses, olives, plastic bottles of wine from their own barrels. Fighting the desire to go inside for a lie-down, I sat on the stone stairs with my back to the wall, clinging to the strip of shade cast by the eaves from the midday sun. I watched swirling whorls of colour inside my eyelids, listened to the humming in my ears and concentrated on not passing out. Now and then I opened my eyes for snapshots of our party.

Waxy-fingered Elpida took charge. She came straight from church and her best black dress was spattered with new candle grease. She brought loaves of round, flat bread left over from the service, stamped with the sign of the All Holy One. With Ajax she humped Denis onto the table covered with newspaper and attacked him with a cleaver. She ordered Arfa to fetch plates and a carving knife and fill jugs from the jerry cans and generally make herself useful. Barba Mitsos jerked his thumb at her, laughed and sat down with the men under the olive tree, where they waited for the women to bring them food.

Siren Roula alternately cuffed her children away and screamed at them to come and eat. She took a plate of food to her Dimitris, who grimaced and patted his dyspeptic stomach. He sustained himself with tumblers of wine and salt anchovies and Denis's tail, crunching the crisp yellow fat and tiny bones with the relish of forbidden fruit. Lanky Adonis the labourer smiled and drank steadily, with no apparent effect. His mother Maria brought him food and then sat apart from the rest, picking at her frugal plate and looking timorously up at the others as if one of them was about to dash it from her hands. Old Barba Fedon, his comb-over slicked with extra pommade for the occasion, picked at a piece of *spanakopita* and eyed useful bits of wire discarded from the carcase.

Showing antipodean manners, Aussie Alekos the taxi driver brought cans of lager in a crate of ice. Youthful Doctor Solomos browsed in our library inside the house. Athina and Pericles her wraith-like husband came up from the reed bed by the lake and sat with her brother Barba Vasilis, scratching the mosquito bites in her scalp with the handle of a comb. The ghosts of black-pelvis Christos and their father Panamanian Petros sat with them. Dapper Nektarios the roofer came alone, dancing along the path with a yellow flower behind each ear, his face as red as a roof tile. He clapped his hands and did a little dance around the fire. He didn't know where his wife was.

'I'm sure she set out with me this morning. But just now she wasn't in the pick-up. We called at her brother's on the way, so perhaps she's still there. Or was that yesterday?'

'When did you last see your wife, Nektarios? Tell me, how many fingers?' shouted Dimitris, sticking his middle finger rudely in the air.

'This many,' said Nektarios and thrust his open palm towards Dimitris's face in the rudest gesture of all.

Zenon the digger burned up the track on his Zün' and stood by the fire in his tank-driver's helmet ar boots, hands on his hips. He tore a bone off the pile of meat and gnawed it while he sauntered among the others, wiping his mouth with the back of his hand. Moon-faced Aristotle the hydrologist squatted beside the water tank and beamed and rhapsodised about England, where it rained all year round, Mother of God, the peaches they must have, it must be paradise. His wife brought him his plate of food and waddled round the back of the church to forage for wild greens. Spiros our carpenter came on his own, since his wife was still in Athens with their baby grandson. He sat quietly with the men under the olive tree, sucked his punk yard-brush moustache and waited for a woman to bring him something to eat.

'They should have had a carpenter from Aliveri. Spiros couldn't nail a cross for his own grave.'

'They should have had a roofer from Aliveri. Nektarios is better at mixing drinks than mortar.'

'They should have had a builder from Aliveri. Shit-houses is all Dimitris is good for.'

'They should have had a mason from Aliveri. My thing stands up longer than Barba Mitsos's walls.'

'Why do they speak badly of each other?' Arfa asked Elpida.

'Eh. Love without bitterness has no taste.'

Sassy Antigone came as the dutiful wife. Her hair was carefully set and brushed and gold dangled from her ears and neck and wrists and she wore her pale yellow honey-moon dress with high-heeled gold sandals. She kept a wad of gum in her cheek that she frenetically chewed when she thought nobody was looking. She waited on Haralambos and heaped his plate with the best of the meat and potatoes. She served her father Spiros too. The women looked at her pale face and wondered if she was pregnant yet.

Eleni came as the dutiful mother with her hair scraped back and no make-up and a long skirt and a long-sleeved shirt and ordinary sandals. She held the twins by the hand as they waddled by her side, nappies sticking out from the legs of their elasticated shorts. Their father sat under the olive, scratching his brawny forearms and flicking his handsome moustache. He and Haralambos bantered like two butting rams. Eleni brought him a plate of meat and vegetables and went back to the boys. She sat with them throughout the meal, feeding them with a spoon from a jar and wiping their cheeks after each mouthful.

When everyone had crossed themselves and started to eat, I pulled myself upright. I felt sick and sun-struck. I hoped to sneak inside without being seen. Ajax saw me and clapped his hands.

'Bravo. A speech. *Meine Damen und Herren. Es freut mich.* Speech!'

They all looked up at me, jaws chewing. I took a deep breath. But I couldn't think of a single word of Greek. It was completely gone, drowned in exhaustion and wine.

'*Eff-harry-stow,*' I managed, thank you, and Dimitris clapped. But nothing else came. Sun-touched Dionysos watched me curiously through the leaves of an oleander. Arfa slunk into the kitchen, embarrassed, and the children started to giggle.

'My friends,' I said in English. I enunciated the words slowly and deliberately and tried not to bite my tongue or the inside of my cheeks and held up my glass as if it was a strap-hanger to stop me falling over.

'*Kein Englisch*,' shouted Ajax.

'We are children of Dionysos,' I managed, in English.

'Oh don't start that again, Dad,' stage-whispered Jack.

Dionysos heard his name, shambled over and stood in front of me, his head on one side, listening intently. Out of the recesses of my brain, somewhere between the recipe for mortar and the phone number of the wood merchant in Aliveri, came memories of Greek words, which weren't my own but good enough.

'My friends. We are neighbours now. We are compatriots. We are friends. To our health and may we live many years. Thank you.'

Ajax led the applause, which was only fitting as they were his words on the fateful morning when I first saw the house. Dionysos carried on clapping after the rest until Haralambos brrrhed him away. General conversation resumed. Arfa came up and I waited for her congratulations.

'Phew,' she said, 'you'd better eat something,' and like a good Greek wife pushed a plate of Denis into my hands. He was delicious. There is no better way on earth to cook meat.

Ajax led the singing after lunch. His speciality was the love songs of Epirus, the Albanian north, full of tremolos and quarter tones. Elpida's girlish soprano gave us an Anatolian love song. Barba Fedon croaked and grumbled a *rembetika* ballad, in the way the hash-fuddled blues of

Piraeus low life should be sung. We sang pop songs, retro songs of the 1930s and in Arfa's honour everyone joined in *Never on a Sunday*, whose Greek words feature a woman with four children. In return, we gave them a raucous version of *What shall we do with a drunken sailor?*

Alekos, pie-eyed on Metaxa and lager chasers, navigated himself by touch to the boot of his taxi and brought back a loaded shotgun. He sat down with the end of the stock on his knee and fired up into the air, bringing down on himself a hail of leaves and twigs. He tried to reload but couldn't focus, so the children helped him for a second deafening salute.

When our voices cracked and people forgot the words, Ajax drove his pick-up as close as he could, stuck a cassette of wedding music into the player and turned up the volume. He and Haralambos started to dance, arms round each other's shoulders, looking down at their feet to shouts of *op-pa*. Zenon tossed his leather cap under the table, seized a napkin and joined the dancing. His right hand in the air, his left supported by Ajax holding the napkin, he cavorted with extraordinary lightness and delicacy, crouching and leaping and pirouetting and slapping his feet to more cries of *op-pa*. Others joined the fray, linking up at the other end with Haralambos. Elpida took over from Zenon at the front of the dance and led us around the yard threading between the trees.

When we collapsed in laughter and exhaustion Spiros, who had danced the last dances in the old village at his wedding, blew his nose and wiped his eyes. He staggered over to Arfa, kissed her on the cheeks and thanked her for bringing the old times back.

And so we passed the afternoon until the sun lost its strength and it was time for the evening chores. There were sheep to pen, goats to milk, grave lamps to light. With kisses and wishes of *kalo risiko* the men ambled off with flowers behind their ears, the women with empty pots and dishes. By the time bats began to flit they had all left. When the children had gone to bed, Arfa and I collapsed hand in hand on the terrace, bathed in the scent of bougainvillea and mosquito repellent, and watched shooting stars zipping past the constellations.

'Remember when you first came up to the house,' I asked, 'and we saw the view through the window? It looked like a perfect Greece. Waiting for the characters to be painted in. Well, here we are.'

'Our own little Arcadia,' said Arfa. 'I think we'll be happy here.'

The simple life

W e have been happy in Horio. The house is much the same, despite minimal upkeep. Over time the mortar in the roof reverted to its natural state. Every day a dusting of red sand drizzled down from the reed ceiling. Getting into bed was like slipping between sheets of sandpaper. If you were not careful to cover food, lunch tasted like a picnic on the beach. The only person who didn't mind was Harry, who was weaned at Klimaki and had a taste for gritty food. We woke up one morning like Bedouin in a sand-storm and decided to replace it, using more cement this time.

An earthquake left a crack in a wall. Arfa and I were asleep when it struck. An express train roaring through the bedroom woke us up. The bed shook, pans fell off the shelves, melons rolled round the floor. Arfa's earthquake drill was to put her pillow over her face. I watched the beams above our heads and prayed they would fall diagonally. We should have done what the rest of the village did: run into the square in front of the church. Apparently the range of nightware and bedtime hairdos was a spectacle not to be missed.

The mule paths up to the Old Place have been bulldozed into dirt roads and the old stone walls used for hardcore. The sky is strung with telephone and power lines. Old Yannis now calls his coffee-ouzo-everything-emporium a mini-market. We have a new taverna, which we call the easytav because of its bright orange plastic furniture.

Jack is now a film director, Jim a surgeon, Kate an artist, Harry a legal headhunter. Seven grandchildren relive the experiences of their parents and add their own. I patched up the Mirror dinghy for them, so red sails adorn Klimaki beach again.

Arfa is a renowned human rights lawyer. For thirty years I have been privileged to listen to a breakfast lecture on the lawyerly topic of the day. Once I came to Horio alone on the pretext of pruning the mulberry. I was eating yoghurt and honey in the early-morning sunshine and enjoying the guilty pleasure of missing my customary tutorial. I flicked on the transistor for the BBC World Service. Who should I hear putting us right on Article Five of the European Convention on Human Rights? In my haste to turn her off I knocked the tranny on the floor, where it broke into pieces. We haven't had a wireless in the house since.

It was never our intention to drop out and grow olives or rear sheep. The rustic life can get pretty boring and there's just as much hard work and worry in Arcadia as anywhere else. Homes are for leaving as much as for going back to. But Horio has always been a place to hold in our hearts, not because of the pile of stones we did up but because of the generous people who became our friends.

Some of them have taken the low road to the cemetery and then to the bone house. The door is unlocked. The air is musty like a charity shop. Dust swims in the beam of light from the open door. They say household dust is mostly human skin, but in here it's bone. On the shelf are Iphigenaia who rhapsodised over the fireplace, Barba Petros the cigarette pioneer, whom I saw die, and Barba Christos, whom I saw dug up.

Nektarios was rushed to hospital with vomiting and yellow eyes, where they gave him a year to live unless he gave up the booze. He went back to work, but his hands shook so much with sobriety that he lost his grip and fell off the school roof. Haralambos's heart gave out among the bathroom fitments. His father-in-law Spiros the carpenter lives on in the four-inch gap under our front door, gaps in the windows and cracks in the floor, lovely in summer with plenty of ventilation but a devil in winter. He obviously did not make his own perfectly rectilinear bone box.

Elpida and Mitsos are next to each other, as they were for seventy years except for the couple of months between their deaths. Mitsos lives on in our cess pit. It has never given us any trouble, though I shudder to think what it looks like inside. Aristotle the water diviner, Aussie Alekos, Fedon with the comb-over, Konstantinos the priest, Maria the dirge singer, Vassilis the stylish shepherd – all stare from the other side through their fading photographs.

The children and grandchildren of our old friends have become truly European. One of Ajax and Eleni's twins is an aeronautical engineer, the other a software designer in California. Mitsos and Elpida's granddaughters studied in Sweden. One is a biochemist, the other a cardiologist.

Dyspeptic Dimitri went into intensive goat rearing to keep his granddaughter at Essex University.

*I*n the early 1990s I suffered the delusion of being stalked by Kevin Keegan, the famous footballer. I stroll along a mule track in the mountains or down to the village and out of the corner of my eye catch a glimpse of a curly perm popping up over a wall or peeping through a bush. I turn to look and it disappears. I stop. I watch. I listen. Nobody. The first time it happens I blame it on a trick of the light. The second time on a breeze ruffling the leaves. It gets worse. I see two Keegan mullets at a time, then three.

They were my first Albanians. In 1991 the Communist regime in Albania collapsed, swiftly followed by the economy. Tens of thousands of people crossed into Greece looking for work. Ethnic Greeks were given visas. Ethnic Albanians walked over the mountains. Within three years about a quarter of a million were living illegally on the mainland and in the islands. This is only a rough estimate, as Greek ability to manage a coherent immigration policy was then, as now, lamentable.

The Keegan coiffure, a periwig of curls at the front and a mullet at the back, was as fashionable in Albania as it was among English footballers and fans in the 1970s. Urban sophisticates of Tirana disparagingly called it the Kosovo Haircut. It lingered on in the ditches of Evia until the owners twigged that they might as well put a placard round their necks: I am an illegal immigrant. Even with a short back and sides it was possible to pick them out. They looked stunted and ill-nourished, as if they had been incarcerated in the peculiar little concrete mushrooms that dot their native landscape, which metaphorically they had. A few months of a wholesome diet worked wonders.

With no papers they hid from strangers. They lived in ruins and sheep pens and scavenged for food and work. A favourite place was the rubbish dump on a cliff overlooking a ravine. Nobody braved the stench and rats and seagulls unless they had to and there were deliveries of refuse to pick over for scraps of food or clothing. At night, cooking fires glittered among hillocks of decomposing garbage. The police rounded them up as well as that dysfunctional force was able. Those they managed to catch were fingerprinted and robbed of their pitiful earnings before being driven back up north to the border. They went home to see their families and in a few days walked back over the mountains.

Our house was broken into. They took single mattresses, blankets, big pans, ladles, spoons, bowls, a bread knife, the gas hob and a bottle of gas. They left the rest. It was difficult to be angry. We would gladly have given them these things. In Athens, Albanian gangs stripped houses and shipped their loot north. Our Albanians just wanted to keep warm and make soup. As soon as a work permit system was put in place, the break-ins stopped.

The authorities were hampered by the willingness of Greeks to employ the Albanians at rock-bottom wages. They were cheap to feed on bread and water and soup. Nevertheless, they were generally reviled, *kakoi anthrophoi,* bad people, dirty and unreliable and dishonest. If a tool was lost or a chicken went missing, Albanians took the blame.

"Johnny, they're bad people. They aren't Christians even if they say they are. Make sure you lock everything up. And don't leave your keys in the car..." warned Vitalis.

"What about your Albanian, Vitalis?"

"Sami's a good man. Aren't you, Sami?"

Sami was sitting with us at the easytav tucking into a kilo of panzetta, a staple of the Mediterranean diet, grilled strips of juicy pork belly. Vitalis grew tomatoes and melons on the drained bed of Lake Dystos, fertile soil and water near the surface. Sami did the heavy lifting. He ignored us, used to the vilification of his race and the patronising of his boss.

To have a personal Albanian to do the dirty work was as essential an accessory as clickety worry beads and a gold cross nestling in the chest hair. They were borrowed and lent by the day like donkeys and tractors. Women cleaned houses, looked after children, nursed the demented and the dying. Men worked in the gardens and the fields and the workshops. My Albanian was honest and hard working, your Albanian slacked when you were not looking, his Albanian was a thieving rascal. The unattached sat outside the café waiting to be hired for a day's work.

Sami lived in the humming and clicking of the new Telecom sub-exchange outside the village. He could now appear in public with whatever hairstyle he liked. Although Albanians were not yet given residence or work permits, they were no longer rounded up and deported. Over the following years Sami became the first Albanian to buy a plot of land, build a house, marry a local girl, send children to the village school, own a car, set up his own building business. Any spare money he spent on buying land, little plots here and there, on which he planted olive trees. After twenty-five years he became the first Albanian to be buried in the village cemetery, as far from the rest as possible, since he was not Orthodox. After three years his bones were dug up, as is customary, but not put into the bone house. Perhaps they were deported to Albania. Most of the living Albanians have now gone back too because there is no work.

We also borrowed some cut-rate Albanians: Mikis, Panos and Takis. These were *noms de travail*. Their real names were Viktor, after Victor Mature who was popular in Albania before the clampdown on everything western; Memet, brave of his parents in the self-proclaimed World's First Atheist State; and Traktor, whose father had ambitions on his collective farm. When we rebuilt our house the art of stone walls and schist slab roofs had been lost by all except old men, who no longer had the strength to heft the material. In Albania building technology had not moved on and their builders were much in demand by proprietors like us and owners of sheep pens.

They lived in fear of a police raid. I went down to the village to buy bread and run errands for them. We joked that every Greek has an Albanian and every Albanian an Englishman. Money was the main problem. They soon learned not to keep it about them in case they were arrested. Yannis our cafetier became their banker. He looked after their money and went to the Post Office to send it back home. They did a good job on our terrace and I invited them to dinner. I thought of treating them to shepherd's pie. When Traktor translated the invitation, Viktor and Memet looked embarrassed and uncertain.

"What's the problem?" I asked.

"They don't know what food you eat. They have heard English food is very bad."

"Don't worry. I'll get meat from the taverna. No English food, I promise."

I bought roast chickens and lamb chops. The trio came at sunset, freshly shaven, hair slicked down and perfumed, best clothes. I served up the food and expected them to dive in. Instead, they protested they were already full and I had to force every morsel on them. They would only drink wine with a toast, in unison. At the end they they left food on the plates and dishes, wine in the bottles and glasses, and refused to take anything back with them. It wasn't only their technology and their skills that were old-fashioned but their manners.

Finally, over glasses of Glenhaggis single malt, Traktor spoke for them all.

"Mister Johnny, please explain to us. We do not understand. At home we are poor. We have no money for meat. No money for clothes. No money for cars. Our houses are old like this. Every Albanian dreams of the life in England. Why do you live like a poor man in these ruins?"

"The simple life" was all I could think of, the stock answer I gave to Greeks. I hated the question because it made me wonder the same thing.

We continued to leave the keys in the car, despite the warnings. I wished anybody luck with our fifteen-year-old VW Jetta with UK plates and right-hand drive. Or rather it was two written-off Jettas, the front of one welded to the back of the other by the father of a friend who had a fish and chip shop in Derby and rebuilt cars on the side. It endured the snows of winter, the downpours of spring and the baking sun of summer. It spent the winters in the chicken yard at the back of Yannis's café covered in a tarpaulin, which did not not deter nesting creatures, from chickens to mice to spiders. Rust had done for the window winders. To facilitate opening and closing them I took off the inside door panels, so you could lift the windows up and down by hand and wire them in position on various protrusions of the mechanism. The bodywork was rusted and scratched and dented. Chrome peeled, rubber perished, hubcaps absconded. Tattered wipers flailed at a windscreen that became more chipped and blue-mottled with the years. Passengers in the back could admire the road whizzing along under their feet until I refloored it with bits of chipboard. As a precaution, children were told to sit well back in their seats.

The most inconvenient reminder of its various collisions was when I ran into a bollard and bent the wishbone, part of the mechanism that connects the steering column with the wheels. My mechanic, George, straightened it as best he could, but left it with an inability to turn right in more than a gentle curve. The driver was advised to overshoot a right turn in favour of making a series of left turns, and never to park in a place that required right-hand-down-a-bit to get in and out. Fortunately there are no hairpin bends on the way to the beach or to Aliveri and we were careful not to venture further, to the airport for example. An added disincentive for hitting the high road was that it had been in the country five years and the time limit on imported cars was six months. My passport was stamped to this effect, but since I had lost that, along with the registration papers, and got a new one, the vehicle was undocumented. A thief taking our illegal-right-hand-drive-no-right-turn-venti-lated-rust-bucket off our hands would be doing us a favour.

After our first disastrous shepherd's pie and crumble dinner party, it was some time before we dared to invite neighbours again. Greeks are keen to embrace many aspects of American and European culture. When we moved to Athens in the 1970s, Christmas was celebrated with pork and Saint Basil brought presents on January 1. By the 1980s, Santa Claus had taken over along with Christmas trees, turkey, reindeer, artificial snow and other seasonal clichés. We have been to weddings where the bride and tuxedoed groom cut a three-tier wedding cake and danced the first dance, all new traditions gleaned from American films. But the element of foreign culture that is resolutely resisted is food.

A young friend from Horio studying in London witnessed with horror our honey glaze on a roast turkey. To this day he has never let us forget it. Word went round the village. For years relative strangers sidled up to us and asked quietly if it was true that foreigners put sugar on meat. Every dish bears its dogma of ingredients and woe betide the cook if she apostasises. Pepper on tomatoes, fruit with meat, lemon juice on a Greek salad, any herb except dill with lettuce are greeted with the brusque anathema *then bainei*, 'it doesn't go'. Heresies like rare-cooked meat, curry, fish with pasta are shunned. To minimise the risk of being served such abominations, our invitations to come to us are subtly and politely turned to invitations to go to them. To which we make only token resistance.

One way we can reciprocate is when our neighbours come to London. They arrive on shopping trips or for hospital consultations. Our first service is to give them a list of Greek restaurants. Some years ago we were introduced to a family who lived in Skourta, a small village in the Parnitha mountains north of Athens. Mikis and Voula had three young sons and her parents living with them. At the first fall of snow Grandpa went to bed in the 'cellar', a separate barrel-vaulted building mostly underground where wine and olive oil, hams and sausages and a stove were kept, and staggered out in spring, pale but well nourished. They kept sheep and goats, not the hobby flocks of Horio, but over a thousand of each. Yannis had sous-shepherds and kept an eye on them all from a white horse he rode bareback. The EU decided that his flock was too small and gave him grants to get rid of the animals and grow things. They spent the money on a Toyota pick-up and a massive two-storey house with marble bathrooms, flock wallpaper and gilt furniture. They kept their flock and continued to live in the little stone house that her great-grandparents built. The big house was for special occasions like the baptism feast of their youngest son, when Mikis and his brothers rattled the chandeliers with shotguns fired from the balcony.

The reason we were introduced was that their second son, Yannakis, had something wrong with his foot and couldn't follow the sheep or, more importantly, play football. He came to London for an operation followed by six weeks of physiotherapy. The medical treatment was paid for by the Greek health service, but where would he and his parents and his grandmother live? In our sitting room, was the answer.

For two months we lived the Horio life in London. Voula and her mother took over the cooking. They plucked up courage to buy bread and potatoes locally and the rest they brought over from Skourta in massive suitcases. Rustic sausages dangled over our faux-Georgian fireplace. Sheep dangled nose down in the cellar. Fifteen-kilo tins of feta dribbled cheesy brine over the laundry-room tiles. Tomatoes, peppers and aubergines filled the fridge. Every ten days or so Mikis flew back for more provisions, including plastic jerry cans of retsina and sheep's milk. We had a spit on the lawn, an airing cupboard full of yoghurt, buckets of fizzing beans and chickpeas. Only one British staple took Voula's fancy. She rhapsodised over ketchup, which she emptied into stews and soups in preference to fresh tomatoes. She stocked up for a year and sent it back in the empty suitcases. As for putting it on chips and sausages, *then bainei*.

Mikis was in his element cantering up the mountain on a white horse, roasting a sheep on a sapling spit over a fire of twigs, loosing off a shotgun at scuttering quail. He floundered in a South London suburb, ill at ease and awkward. I took him for a drive in the country. As we pottered along B roads marvelling at England's green and pleasant land, or rather yellow and pleasant as rapeseed was in bloom, we came across a rare patch of green dotted with sheep. Mikis's face lit up for the first time since he arrived. He leaped over the gate and strode up the hill, keen and lithe and in his element again. He brrhed at the sheep in Greek, which they understood, and examined them closely. His interest attracted their farmer, who charged up on a quad bike. Hoping he didn't tote a shotgun and think we were rustlers, I explained and introduced them to each other. Houses on fire doesn't begin to describe how they got on, despite the barriers of sign language and my interpretation. It severely tested my ovine vocabulary as they discussed the difference in price between hoggets and theaves and the merits of different kinds of pour-on as a prophylactic against scrapie and the intricacies of EU subsidies. Both surely came away with a distorted idea of sheep rearing in each other's country, but Mikis was happy for the rest of his stay.

Since joining in 1975 Greece had done well out of the European Union. Grants for agriculture and infrastructure transformed the country and the personal finances of politicians and bureaucrats responsible for allocating them. The little fishing village of Limanaki was corralled by a massive breakwater and a wharf for a score of offshore fishing boats. Development opened up the coast to foreign tourists, especially Germans – and why not, their taxes paid for it. Windmills nag at our environmental consciences with their ugliness and thrumming. Just outside Horio we admired a state-of-the-Australian-art winery with shiny refrigerated fermentation tanks that put Kyria Dimitra's brick vat out of business.

The real bonanza years started when Greece joined the euro and money was plentiful and cheap at German interest rates. Modest houses in Horio became suburban villas with lawns and satellite dishes and air conditioners in the windows. The countryside was pocked with white concrete and blue swimming pools. One place even had a helipad. Then came the debt crisis of 2009 and the continuing catastrophe of bailouts, elections, referenda and increasing austerity.

Last summer I went into Sofia's bakery for a loaf and our daily wine ration. The modern winery is now a litter-strewn, broken-windowed ruin, bankrupted by poor management and a failing bank. Sofia did not resurrect her mother's brick vat, but sells her cousin's wine that he makes in a concrete shed next to his house. It comes in handy two-litre bottles and is the same price as water. Like all great estates, he has a photo of his winery on the label. We call it Château Garage. Sofia was upset.

"Alekos just graduated from the Polytechnic. In the top quartile."

"Congratulations." I meant it. The Athens Polytechnic, the National Technical University, is the most prestigious Greek university.

"Bah. Engineering and business studies. What does he do with that? All the money we spent on his education. Now what? Nine months wasting his time in the army and back here making bread."

"I'm sure he'll get a good job. He speaks good English."

"We don't have contacts. In any case, the government isn't hiring."

"I meant companies."

"For Greek companies you need contacts. Foreign companies you need experience. He has no future. What can he do?"

I was too considerate to give her the obvious one-word answer. It would upset her more. She knew it anyway. Emigrate.

Another reason for not saying the word is that I couldn't remember what it was in Greek. You would think that after forty years in Greece I would be fluent. Some hope. Not long ago I was standing in the line for a cash machine in Aliveri. To avoid panic withdrawals and capital flight, there is a limit of €60 a day, £45, on how much you can take out of a Greek account. We are in Greece, so the daily queues are social events. I joined in the chat.

"I've been standing in urine for twenty minutes... fortunately I have a foreign table map... I need to pay Achilles for painting our beetroots."

Ah, the subtle differences between *oúro* (urine) and *ourá* (queue); *trapézi* (table) and *trápeza* (bank); *chártis* (map) and *kárta* (card); *padzária* (beetroot) and *padzoúria* (shutters). But foreigners are funny and I am happy to contribute to the entertainment.

~~~~~

So I sit outside the café with other white-haired old codgers and make a coffee last for an hour, until the sun goes down and I can have an ouzo with an easy conscience while Arfa is up at the house doing interesting things with beans. I plan my next road trip with my old travel buddy, Harley Davidson. Harley is a twenty-year-old Yamaha 50cc step-through. In motorcycle years that would make him about my age. We have made several trips together round the island and I have almost enough material for a book. My working title is *Zeno and the Art of Motorcycle Maintenance.* My friend Nick prefers *Harley and Me,* also a rip-off but snappier. I have a hankering to bike up to Mount Athos, the ancient monastic community and spiritual home of Orthodoxy, where women are banned and you have wine for breakfast.

There is still so much to see. And Horio is still our home to come back to.

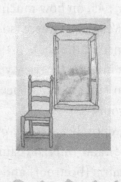

~~~~~